Psychology for Dancers

Psychology for Dancers: Theory and Practice to Fulfil Your Potential examines how psychological theory can be related to dance practice. Aimed at the dancer who wants to maximize their potential but has no grounding in psychology, the book begins with an examination of basic psychological concepts, approaches and methods, before applying theory to dance.

The book explores why dance is so important in many people's lives: as a form of fitness, a profession, or visual entertainment. Each chapter then examines a different aspect of psychology related to dance in an applied context. Self-perception is examined as dancers are under great scrutiny; a grounded sense of self will ensure a positive perception of self-worth and body image, and suggestions are made as to how a healthy and motivational climate can be created. The book also places an emphasis on how cognitive skills are as important as technical skills, including the ability to learn and recall steps and choreography as efficiently as possible. Social factors are related to the dance context, with a discussion of effective leadership and communication skills and the importance of group cohesion. Finally, there is a review of the impact of emotions on dance practice and how best to manage these emotions.

Each chapter reviews important psychological theories, offering practical suggestions on how they can be applied to dance practice. *Psychology for Dancers* is an invaluable resource for students, professionals, and teachers of dance.

Cathy Schofield has been a lecturer in sport and exercise psychology for over 15 years. She has also been dancing for 45 years, including ballet, tap modern/jazz, salsa, street, jive, lindy hop, Zumba and FitSteps. She still appears in local shows as well as enjoying dancing in social contexts, most specifically funk, jazz and northern soul.

Lucy Start began her dance training aged 3 and after dancing professionally in various stage productions turned to teaching 10 years ago. She holds a Diploma in Dance teaching with the British Ballet Organisation and Diploma in Teaching in the Lifelong Learning Sector from Trinity College, London. She has taught many styles of dance in the private sector from Classical Ballet, jazz, tap, to musical theatre and contemporary She also writes, develops and delivers dance qualification courses for primary, secondary and Further Education institutions. She has developed CPD modules for Primary teachers to aid in their delivery of dance in accordance with the National Curriculum, mentored PGCE students and has delivered a seminar to teachers at 'Move It' London on behalf of Trinity College in dance teacher practice.

Psychology for Dancers

Theory and Practice to Fulfil
Your Potential

Cathy Schofield and Lucy Start

LONDON AND NEW YORK

First published 2019
by Routledge
2 Park Square, Milton Park, Abingdon, Oxon OX14 4RN

and by Routledge
711 Third Avenue, New York, NY 10017

Routledge is an imprint of the Taylor & Francis Group, an informa business

© 2019 Cathy Schofield and Lucy Start

The right of Cathy Schofield and Lucy Start to be identified as authors of this work has been asserted by him in accordance with sections 77 and 78 of the Copyright, Designs and Patents Act 1988.

All rights reserved. No part of this book may be reprinted or reproduced or utilised in any form or by any electronic, mechanical, or other means, now known or hereafter invented, including photocopying and recording, or in any information storage or retrieval system, without permission in writing from the publishers.

Trademark notice: Product or corporate names may be trademarks or registered trademarks, and are used only for identification and explanation without intent to infringe.

British Library Cataloguing in Publication Data
A catalogue record for this book is available from the British Library

Library of Congress Cataloging in Publication Data
Names: Schofield, Cathy author. | Start, Lucy, author.
Title: Psychology for dancers : theory and practice to fulfill your potential / Cathy Schofield and Lucy Start.
Description: New York : Routledge, 2018. | Includes bibliographical references and index.
Identifiers: LCCN 2018004492 (print) | LCCN 2018012708 (ebook) |
ISBN 9781315111469 (Master e-book) | ISBN 9781138085176 (Hardback : alk. paper) |
ISBN 9781138085183 (Paperback. : alk. paper) | ISBN 9781315111469 (Ebook)
Subjects: LCSH: Dance—Psychological aspects.
Classification: LCC GV1588.5 (ebook) | LCC GV1588.5 .S34 2018 (print) |
DDC 792.8—dc23
LC record available at https://lccn.loc.gov/2018004492

ISBN: 978-1-138-08517-6 (hbk)
ISBN: 978-1-138-08518-3 (pbk)
ISBN: 978-1-315-11146-9 (ebk)

Typeset in Sabon
by Florence Production Ltd, Stoodleigh, Devon

 Printed in the United Kingdom by Henry Ling Limited

Contents

List of illustrations ix
Acknowledgements xi

1 Introduction   1

Introduction 1
    Why is this book necessary? 1
Introduction to psychology 4
    Perspectives in psychology 4
    Research methods in psychology 11
    Methods of investigation 13
    Psychological concepts 17
Why do humans dance? 19
    Evolutionary explanations 19
    Contemporary explanations 22
    Structure of the book 23
    Key concepts glossary 25
    References 25
    Further reading 27

2 Self-perception   29

Context 29
Theory 30
    Self-concept 30
    Self-worth 32
    Body image 35
    Two-Component Model of impression management 39
    Impact of negative self-concept 43
Practice 46
    Feedback 46
    Being aware of your self-concept 49
    Dealing with perfection 50
    Realistic expectation 51
    Dealing with advice 53
    Key concepts glossary 55
    References 55
    Further reading 57

3 Motivation — 59

Context 59
Theory 60
   The Hierarchical Model 60
   Achievement Goal Theory 66
   Hierarchy of Needs 70
   Burnout 74
Practice 75
   Motivation to join the group 75
   Motivation in training and rehearsal 77
   Motivation to perform 79
   Motivation in performance 80
   Identifying needs 82
   Key concepts glossary 87
   References 88
   Further reading 89

4 Skill acquisition — 91

Context 91
Theory 92
   Information Processing Model 92
   Attention 92
   Encoding 96
   Memory storage 98
   Memory recall 100
   Stages of skill acquisition 100
   Imagery 102
   Self-talk 107
Practice 111
   Imagery 111
   Skill acquisition 114
   Remembering choreography 117
   Performance enhancement 122
   Key concepts glossary 124
   References 125
   Further reading 127

5 Social factors — 129

Context 129
Theory 130
   Leadership 130
   Groups 134
   Interactions 138
   Conflict 143
Practice 146
   Communication 146
   Leadership qualities 152
   Cohesion 155

CONTENTS

    Key concepts glossary 159
    References 160
    Further reading 161

6 Managing emotions   163

Context 163
Theory 164
    Preparation for action 164
    Cognitive appraisal 170
    Types of anxiety 171
    Impact of anxiety on performance 173
    Other emotions 176
Practice 179
    Preparation for an event 179
    Somatic anxiety relief 182
    Cognitive anxiety relief 184
    Group approaches 188
    Key concepts glossary 189
    References 190
    Further reading 191

Index   193

Illustrations

Figures

1.1 Interaction of psychological perspectives
1.2 Brain structure
1.3 Functions of brain structures
1.4 The mind-computer analogy
1.5 Cognitive processes
1.6 The research process
1.7 Overview of methodologies
1.8 Scaled response of feelings towards dance
1.9 Dimensions of feelings towards dance
1.10 Interaction of dimensions of feelings towards dance
2.1 Components of self-concept
2.2 Hypothetical self-concept of Jon
2.3 Hypothetical self-concept of Jen
2.4 Self-concept and congruency
2.5 Sources of self-efficacy
2.6 Tripartite Influence Model
2.7 Impression motivation
2.8 Multidimensional model of perfectionism
3.1 The Hierarchical Model
3.2 Impact of regulation on behaviour and effort
3.3 Levels of motivational autonomy
3.4 Task and ego orientation
3.5 Interaction between orientation, climate and involvement
3.6 Hierarchy of Needs
4.1 Information Processing Model
4.2 Dimensions of attentional and interpersonal style
4.3 Types of selective attention
4.4 Divided attention
4.5 Representation of memory stores
4.6 Capacity of the working memory
4.7 Representation of imagery within the brain
4.8 Functions of imagery
4.9 Multisensory imagery

4.10 Dimensions of self-talk
4.11 Interaction of motivation and valence dimensions
5.1 Multidimensional Model of Leadership
5.2 Conceptual Model of Group Cohesion
5.3 Impact of types of dependency
5.4 Teacher behaviours
5.5 Types of conflict
5.6 Competence-Based Model of Interpersonal Conflict
5.7 Outcomes from the Competence-Based Model of Conflict
5.8 Dual Concern Model
6.1 Overview of arousal and performance factors
6.2 Impact of arousal on performance
6.3 Impact of arousal based on the experiences of the performer
6.4 Impact of arousal based on the complexity of the skill
6.5 Arousal response
6.6 Arousal experience
6.7 Bidirectional relationship between cognitive and somatic anxiety
6.8 Differences in optimal functioning between cognitive and somatic anxiety
6.9 Catastrophe Theory
6.10 Relationship between anxiety and event
6.11 Impact of arousal on attention
6.12 Reversal Theory

Tables

2.1 Factors affected by perfectionism type
3.1 Characteristics of climates
4.1 Examples of effective and ineffective attentional styles

Acknowledgements

Thank you to Katie Bell for her valued contribution to the production of this book.

CHAPTER 1

Introduction

> **Learning outcomes**
>
> By the end of this chapter readers should be able to:
>
> - recognise that there are a range of perspectives within psychology
> - define key research methods
> - describe some key concepts within psychology
> - explain why dance is a universal behaviour
> - propose why dance is still important in contemporary Western society

Why is this book necessary?

Using psychology to enhance dance

As an undergraduate you have committed yourself to at least three years of study, probably on the back of many years at dance school. From these experiences you will have noticed that there is a vast amount of competition for places in dance schools and companies. With so many proficient dancers to compete with, how can you stand out from the pack? The answer is, in the same way as many athletes get the millisecond edge on their opponents – not just through having the skill to perform, but knowing how to maximise this talent.

Dance psychology will give you the edge by allowing you to be in touch with who you are and help you to develop a healthy sense of self. Dance psychology will show you how to optimise the drive to get through the hard times in order to reap the benefits later. Dance psychology will teach you how to maximise training and rehearsal time, to enhance performance. Dance psychology will show you how to bring the company together and develop positive forms of communication within the group. Dance psychology will show you how to manage your emotions on and off stage, giving you the confidence to manage stressful situations.

Using the principles of sport and exercise psychology to supplement the evidence base, this book aims to show you how you can increase your

© Shutterstock

understanding of how your body and mind function, as well as offering you techniques that can be integrated into your practice as a student, teacher or professional dancer.

Dance for society

Dance, in its various forms, has many functions within society. It is a social activity and weekend entertainment for the youth of each generation. It is the Saturday morning escapism for young girls at their weekend dance classes, and it is an uplifting form of entertainment to audiences through shows and productions across the land.

One of dance's newest and most vital roles is that of increasing physical activity levels among the general population. With the current level of obesity increasing nationally, it is vital that more people engage in physical activity in order to remain fit and healthy. Recent UK data suggests that two-thirds of men, and only half of women, meet the government's weekly recommendations for physical activity levels (Townsend, Wickramasinghe, Williams, Bhatnagar, & Rayner, 2015), figures that correlate with the number of overweight UK adults (HSCIC, 2016). As girls have shown an interest in more creative and expressive activities, such as dance (Bailey, Wellard, & Dismore, 2005), recreational dance classes may be a way of engaging sedentary females in much-needed physical activity to improve their physical and mental health.

The benefits of engaging in dance are vast, and go beyond the typical Saturday morning ballet classes. Research has repeatedly shown dance's potent effects are diverse with respect to who may benefit, and how. Positive health and well-being benefits have been observed in school, community and recreational dance classes. Here are a few examples of how dance has been used across generations with varied outcomes.

- Increased social competence in pre-school children (Lobo & Winsler, 2006).
- Increased lung and aerobic capacity, and increased flexibility in teenagers (Quin, Frazer, & Redding, 2007).
- Enhancing adolescent girls' perceptions of their physical self-worth, attractiveness, competence and strength (Daley & Buchanan, 1999).
- Increased social, emotional and physical benefits in adults (Quiroga Murcia, Kreutz, Clift, & Bongard, 2010).
- Increased feelings of being young and part of a community again in older adults (Cooper & Thomas, 2002).
- Increased balance and walking ability in older adults (Verghese, 2006).
- Increased functional capacity and quality of life for chronic heart failure patients (Belardinelli, Lacalaprice, Ventrella, Volpe, & Faccenda, 2008).
- Enhanced mental and social functions for dementia patients (Palo-Bengtsson, Winblad, & Ekman, 1998).

Having an understanding of how dance can increase health, fitness and well-being may inspire a new generation of dance teachers to engage local communities in projects and classes to address these problems – and that could be you.

INTRODUCTION TO PSYCHOLOGY

As a dance student, it is unlikely that you will have a background in psychology, and indeed it is not the role of this book to teach you psychology, rather this book's function is to show you how you can use psychological theory to enhance your practice. But in order to get the most out of the psychological aspects of the book, it will be beneficial if you have a basic grounding in psychological perspectives, methods and concepts.

The term *psychology* is the combination of two other words; *psyche* being the Greek word for mind, and *logia* meaning to study, therefore psychology is the scientific study of the mind and subsequent behaviour. Psychology can be described as a *social science* as it examines the behaviour of humans at an *intrapersonal* and *interpersonal* level. Unlike the natural sciences, social science needs to be more circumspect when offering explanations for behaviour as humans do not react in the same reliable way as chemicals and forces do within the natural sciences. For this reason, there are several schools of thought that aim to explain human behaviour from their different *perspectives*. Having more than one explanation for behaviour can lead to confusion when new to the study of psychology – surely only one theory can be right? The answer is not that some of the theories are incorrect, but a more accurate explanation is that the combination of the theories offers a more complete picture of how and why we behave in certain ways.

There are many such perspectives, but this chapter will examine the biological, social and cognitive perspectives in more detail (Figure 1.1).

Perspectives in psychology

Biological psychology

Biological psychologists claim that biology lies at the heart of our thoughts, feelings and actions (Corr, 2006). As a branch of biology, biological psychology can be traced back to ancient Greece where it was believed that the brain was

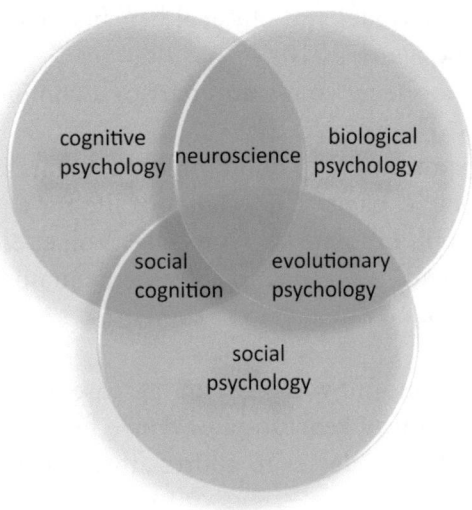

Figure 1.1
Interaction of psychological perspectives

responsible for human reasoning (Wickens & Wickens, 2009). As scientific methods and technology evolved and became more sophisticated, so the biological explanations for behaviour have become more detailed. The basic structure of the brain was first understood from simple observations, and then in the early 1800s greater depth of understanding about the mechanisms of the brain was established from ground-breaking laboratory experiments. Discoveries at a cellular level were made throughout the late nineteenth century, and the twentieth century brought with it technology, such as fMRI scanners, which has allowed us to see the brain in action (Wickens & Wickens, 2009).

There are many explanations in biological psychology as to how our biology influences our thoughts, feelings and actions, three of which will be focused upon here.

Evolution and genetics

In the same way that animals have evolved certain physical characteristics to ensure their survival, such as the giraffe's elongated neck allowing it to reach the higher branches, then humans have evolved to behave in certain ways to ensure their survival. The guiding principle of *evolution* being that if a behaviour offers a survival advantage, then it will be passed on to our offspring through genetic inheritance. If the behaviour has no survival properties, then that behaviour should die out.

Evolutionary psychology helps explain how behaviours that might seem very current are in fact linked to quite primitive drives to survive. Unfortunately, our genes have not necessarily evolved at the same rate as society, and therefore some behaviours may appear quite at odds with our survival instinct. For example, being a chocoholic may increase the chance of becoming obese and lead to vulnerability to diseases such as diabetes, therefore this seems like a counterproductive drive to survive. The explanation is that we are hard-wired to seek out sources of energy as a means of survival, therefore our drive to eat chocolate does not allow for the fact that many of us live in a period and in places of abundance.

It is genetic inheritance that makes evolution possible. Biological psychologists argue that individuals may be biologically predisposed to certain behaviours based on the genes inherited from their parents. Genes may influence aspects of cognition and personality, as well as predisposing someone to certain physical and psychological abilities and disorders. Genetic explanations may make us vulnerable to a behaviour, but these may be altered by environmental factors (McGue & Bouchard, 1998).

Brain structure and functions

Alternative biological explanations relate to the structure of the brain, where different areas of the brain are tasked with different functions. The brain may be divided into three main sections: forebrain, midbrain and hindbrain (Figure 1.2).

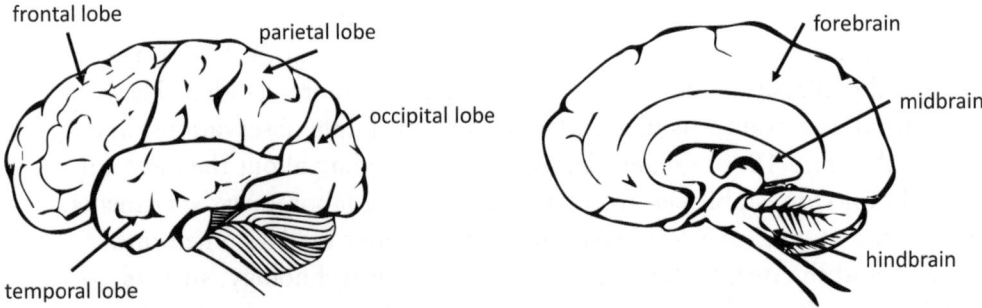

Figure 1.2
Brain structure

The forebrain includes the outer shell, referred to as the *cerebral cortex*, which is split into two hemispheres from front to back, which is further broken down into different lobes. Each lobe has very specific functions.

Figure 1.3 shows the distributed nature of brain activity. If your dance teacher says 'hop', your temporal lobe will process the auditory information, retrieve a memory of what a hop is, the hypothalamus will then organise the frontal lobe to make the movement. The message will be sent through the midbrain to the pons in the hindbrain, which will inform the various muscles throughout the body to hop, while the cerebellum ensures that the movement is well coordinated and balanced.

It is not just activity that can be traced throughout the brain, emotional responses can also be observed throughout. You may be nervous before a performance as your occipital lobe processes visual information about the busy atmosphere in the dressing room, while the temporal lobe processes the sounds of audience chatter and the opening bars of the music. The hypothalamus combines these sensations with information from the frontal lobe where these stimuli are interpreted as worry. In the midbrain, the reticular activating system triggers the arousal response, and in the hindbrain, the medulla corresponds with changes to the body such as increased respiration and heart rate.

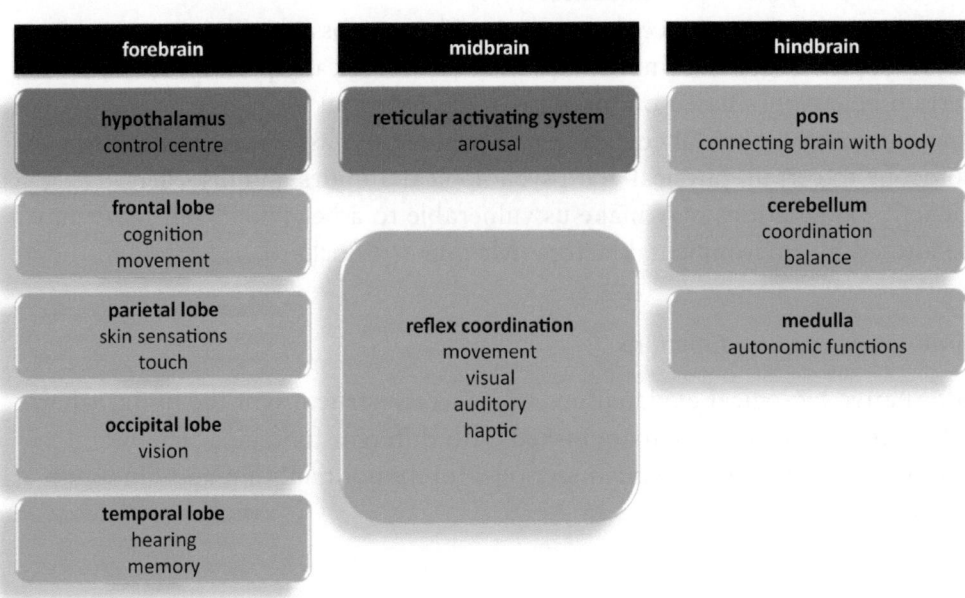

Figure 1.3
Functions of brain structures

INTRODUCTION

Biochemical transmission

Having identified that there are many regions of the brain, we next need to consider how these areas communicate with each other and the body. There are two means of communication: the central nervous system and the neuroendocrine system.

The *central nervous system* comprises the brain and spinal cord, connected together by cells called neurons, which communicate through a process known as neurotransmission. *Neurotransmission* is an electrochemical process, where messages are sent through cells via an electrical current. Because cells do not touch each other, messages are then sent between cells by the release of a chemical. When the receiving cell absorbs the chemical, it triggers an electrical current through this cell, and so the process continues. The chemicals that communicate between the cells are called *neurotransmitters*, of which there are many, each having different functions (Corr, 2006). When the same type of message is sent frequently enough, the repeated triggering of the neurons creates a neural pathway, which makes this form of communication faster.

At a functional level, the central nervous system receives information from the sensory receptors around the body, such as touch, sound and sight. This information is sent to the brain for interpretation. The brain then sends messages back to muscles to perform an appropriate response.

The second form of communication is through the *neuroendocrine system*, which sends messages around the body by the secretion of *hormones* from glands. Hormones are another form of chemical messenger, and are transported to target receivers around the body through the bloodstream. Glands are distributed throughout the body, each having associated hormones and their specific functions. As the means of communication is through the bloodstream, hormonal communication is much slower than neurotransmission (Corr, 2006).

The functions and time frame of hormonal communication are varied. At one end of the scale they operate slowly, informing our growth and development throughout the lifespan. Hormones also regulate our energy levels through our metabolism and maintain optimum levels of functioning through homeostasis. At a more reactive level they help us respond to emergency situations by activating the fight-or-flight response (Corr, 2006).

Methods of investigation

As these explanations of behaviour relate to biological processes the methods used to investigate these theories are techniques and equipment familiar to biologists. One of the problems of using such technology is that it is often quite invasive, so researching biological explanations of behaviour while dancing is quite impractical and may affect the performance.

Cognitive psychology

Cognitive psychology emerged in the 1950s as a means of understanding how we store knowledge, process information and problem solve (Gentner, 2010). Where biological psychology focuses on the *organism* of the brain and central nervous system, cognitive psychology concentrates on the *functions* of the mind.

This perspective is concerned with how we process and respond to information around us.

Cognitive psychology emerged at about the same time as computers were being developed. This new breed of psychologist equated the information processing qualities of the mind to that of the computer. Starting with the analogy of the brain being the hardware, then the mind becomes the software. In the same way that computers receive information from the environment through a range of mechanisms, so does the human mind (Figure 1.4).

Computers receive *input* from a variety of interfaces, such as the mouse and keyboard, as well as information sources via external drives and the internet. The mind can also receive information from a variety of sources, externally from the senses, or internally by downloading previously stored information from our memory.

The processes that mediate input and output are also comparable. Computers store information in organised hierarchies in a similar way to the various memory storage units of the mind. The main difference being that computers' recall processes are far more reliable than humans' ability to retrieve information, which is fallible, and memories are open to corruption.

Human *output* is our ability to communicate with others in a range of ways, an ability that computers also possess, but computers lack the interpretive abilities of humans who can sense mood or use additional sensory cues from the message sender. Humans can also move and affect the environment, abilities that computers are increasingly being programmed to do.

Cognitive psychologists do not believe that computers and the mind are the same, but the analogy allowed the early theorists to conceptualise cognitive processes and start to investigate them in a systematic manner.

Information processing

From this early analogy, cognitive psychologists were able to construct a model of information processing, understanding that this was a complex procedure made up of many smaller processes.

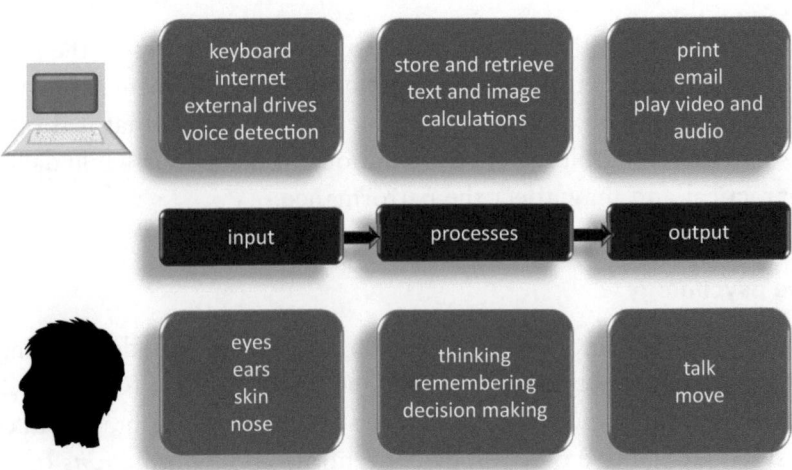

Figure 1.4 The mind-computer analogy

According to Neisser (1967), cognition is the processing of sensory input through six stages, as shown in Figure 1.5. First, the physical sensations of sound or light waves need to be *transformed* into cognitive code so the mind can interpret the incoming information. The information is then *reduced* to the important features of the sensory input. This is why you cannot recall a speech word-for-word, or recall every feature of an image. This information is then integrated with information that you already have stored through a process of *elaboration* as a means of *storing* the memory. A memory is only of use if we can recall it, so there needs to be a process of *recovery* of the information at an appropriate time, and so that the information can be *used*.

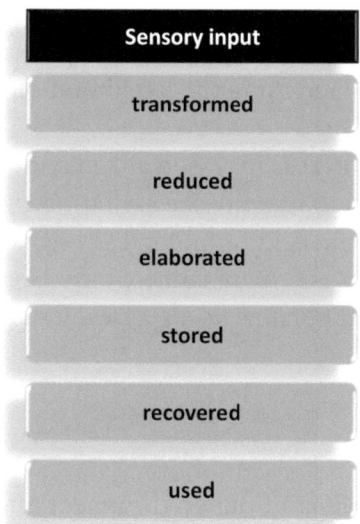

Figure 1.5
Cognitive processes

Methods of investigation

As we cannot see inside the mind, all that can be done to investigate it is to infer what internal mental processes are occurring by the observation of behaviour. In order to do this, cognitive psychologists designed ingenious ways to manipulate internal mental functions and then measure the behavioural outcomes. As technology has developed, they too have created more sophisticated ways to examine our mental functions. As there is evidently an overlap between the brain and cognitive functions, there has been a blending of cognitive and biological psychology, through the study of *neuroscience*.

Social psychology

Where the previous perspectives have dealt with internal factors that affect human behaviour, social psychology looks to external causes. *Social psychology* is the study of how humans' thoughts, feelings and actions are influenced by others. There are three important areas of investigation in social psychology: group behaviour, attitude formation and social cognition (Ross, Lepper, & Ward, 2010).

Group behaviour

The most logical place to look at social interaction is through observing group behaviour. For humans, it is important that we feel that we belong to a group, be it a family group, a friendship group or a group that relates to each other based on a shared activity. Research in this area has focused on how, when in a group, we focus on our similarities to each other, and how we emphasise the differences between our group and other groups. The different types of in-group and out-group views have been seen as a source of prejudice and discrimination within society.

How we act within groups is also important. Research examining group dynamics and cohesion has shown that behaviour within our group can impact on our mental state and performance. The construction of the group may affect our feelings and behaviour, where some group leaders inspire and engage us, whereas we may feel others are bullying or manipulative. Inspirational leaders may become role models, increasing the likelihood of us adopting their behaviours.

Because humans are social beings, social behaviours have been examined by *evolutionary psychologists* to identify the evolutionary roots of different behaviours, crossing into the field of biological psychology. Behaviours, such as non-verbal communication and mate choice, have been studied in their current context to help understand humans as a species, looking for universal patterns of behaviour.

Attitude formation

We are very much the product of our environment and from birth we absorb information from others. Dependent upon who the important people are in our lives, and our view of them, we may adopt or reject their views on the world. Once attitudes are formed, they have a strong influence over our behaviour and can be very difficult to change.

Social cognition

When in a group situation, individuals may interpret the same interaction in different ways, one person may hear and interpret a comment at the literal level, where another may interpret the same words as irony or sarcasm. This is because, although they have received the same sensory information, the way that we think about what we see and hear (cognition) affects how we feel about the interaction (social). These interpretations may be based on attitudes, where we use cognitive shortcuts to deal with social situations efficiently. One of these cognitive shortcuts is stereotyping, where we make judgements of others, based on limited information.

Social cognition also explains the views we hold of ourselves, as well as our views on others. Based on how we perceive others, what they look like and how they act, we make value judgements about ourselves. This can impact upon our mental well-being if we perceive ourselves to be lacking by comparison.

INTRODUCTION

Methods of investigation

Because the focus of this perspective is on group behaviour, it is difficult to test by using the controlled experimental techniques favoured by the biological and cognitive psychologists. The best quality data is collected when the situation is natural and it is not obvious to the participants that they are being examined. This in itself can be ethically problematic if it is not carefully managed, and the resultant behaviour may still not inform us about their internal processes, such as thoughts and feelings.

A consideration of performance anxiety through the psychological perspectives

Cognitive psychology
Explanation: According to cognitive psychologists, performance anxiety may link to the recall of previous similar experiences, which affects how you process current information.

Example: Standing in the wings, you *remember* the last time you were on stage. You *remember* the panic and your inability to *recall* even the most basic steps. You *recall* the humiliation in front of the audience, and as you step out onto the stage you become fixated by the audience, unable to break your *concentration* upon them.

Social psychology
Explanation: Social psychologists may explain performance anxiety through the impact that others may have on you. Significant others may not be pressuring you, but you may feel pressured to perform well so as not to let them down. You may also assess your own performance by comparison to that of others.

Example: The *pressure* to perform well is great as you think the audience will be *judging* you, people you know will *see you fail*. If you fail this time you will *let down* the director, especially when she *compares* your performance to others.

Biological psychology
Explanation: Biologically speaking, the experience of anxiety is a response to a perceived threat – a survival mechanism.

Example: As the performance has been interpreted as a threat, the *fight or flight* mechanism is engaged. This alters the physiological state, preparing you to deal efficiently with the perceived threat, but this biological response interferes with your ability to perform.

Research methods in psychology

Ethics

Before we start to delve into the various ways psychologists go about the business of research, it is important that we focus on who will be helping them to investigate their theories. As the participants' welfare is paramount, this must be at the forefront of researchers' minds when designing studies. In order to ensure that the correct procedures are applied, and to minimise the chance of causing stress and discomfort, it is important to consult the British Psychological Society (BPS) guidelines on using humans participants in psychological research (BPS, 2010). The BPS have highlighted these factors as important when undertaking research.

Respect for autonomy and dignity

Participants are assured of the following:

- *Informed consent* Having shown an interest in taking part in a research study, it is important that potential participants are fully informed as the

purpose of the study and the procedures involved. This ensures that participants are giving their informed consent to take part, but are also offered the chance to decline involvement.
- *Right to withdraw* Although they may have agreed to take part in a study, the participant must be informed of their right to withdraw at any point throughout, without consequence.
- *Privacy* Having agreed to take part, the researchers must respect the privacy of the participants, ensuring that confidentiality and anonymity are adhered to.

Scientific value

Research studies should be designed and conducted in such a way as to add to the body of knowledge in a meaningful way. They must ensure that any findings reported are full and accurate, and not misleading in any way.

Social responsibility

Research must ensure the welfare of humans, being respectful of all participants, regardless of background.

Maximising benefit and minimising harm

Throughout the process the safety and well-being of the participants are key. Steps should be taken to ensure that there are no physical risks from the procedures. No psychological harm should be experienced, including anxiety, humiliation or anger. Particular care must be paid to research processes when working with vulnerable members of society.

There must be no deception with respect to the purpose or procedure of the research study as deception may contravene the participants' ability to give their informed consent, and may be a source of stress.

Scientific method

In essence, we are all scientists; every day we may question why something happens, or offer explanations for the behaviour of others, but when we want to contribute to the broader body of knowledge, then tried and tested methods must be used.

As a social science, psychological research should be based on the *scientific method*, through systematic and controlled methods of investigation. The social element of the discipline relates to the examination of human behaviour. As humans are not as consistent in their responses as phenomena in the natural sciences, we therefore never prove a hypothesis, we just contribute evidence to support the theory.

The process used to add new knowledge to the existing knowledge base can be seen in Figure 1.6.

- *Idea* Research often starts with someone having an idea. This may be based on something they observe or wondering how an existing theory may work in a different context. '*Why do children struggle with the double chaffa?*'

INTRODUCTION

Figure 1.6
The research process

- *Theory* A theory is developed from the idea into something more coherent to explain the phenomena. This may include causes, mediators, moderators and effects. *'Could it be that they cannot process the conflicting information of arm and leg movements?'*
- *Hypothesis* From the theory, testable statements are produced which will indicate if the predicting factors cause the effect, or whether there are relationships between factors. *'There will be a significant improvement in coordination of arm and leg movements as children grow older.'*
- *Test* At this point the theory is still an idea until it has been tested. Therefore, relevant research methods need to be applied to identify whether the hypotheses stand up to testing. *'I will undertake a study with children of five different age groups to establish whether their performance improves with age.'*
- *Reflect* Based on the findings of the testing the researcher may accept or reject the hypothesis. Reflection at this stage suggests the next course of action. Acceptance of the hypothesis may lead to reflection on how the theory may apply to society. The rejection of the hypothesis may lead to reflection on the methodology used to test it, and whether this needs reviewing and retesting. *'There was a significant improvement in coordination of arm and leg movements based on the age of the children, so it would be interesting to establish at what point their behaviour reflects that of an adult.'*

Methods of investigation

There are many methods that can be used when researching psychological phenomena, but there are no right or wrong methods, it is a case of choosing the most appropriate method for the topic of investigation. Figure 1.7 summarises a range of frequently used methods, applied to an example with associated points of evaluation. As you work your way through the different

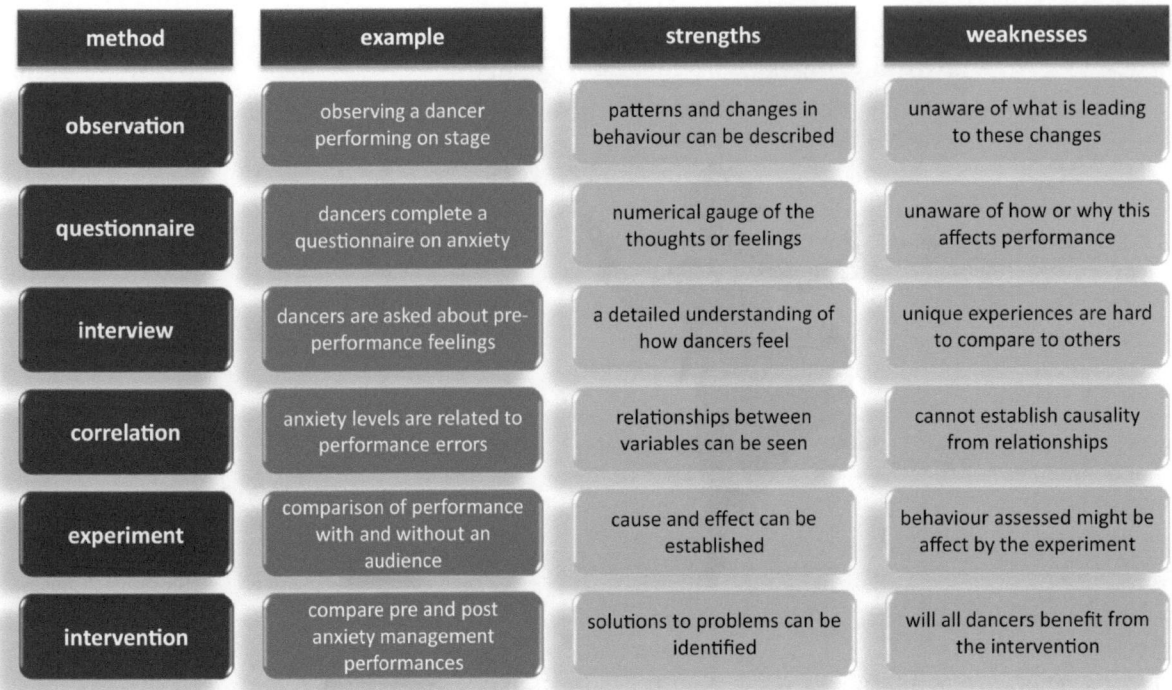

Figure 1.7 Overview of methodologies

chapters, it might be helpful for you to refer back to this section as you encounter new research studies. In addition, each chapter includes *Research in Focus* sections where research studies are outlined in more detail so you can get a feel for how the findings discussed in each chapter are achieved.

Observations

As the focus of psychology is that of behaviour, then observing a chosen behaviour is a good place to start. Observations can be undertaken in controlled settings to ensure that no other factors are affecting performance, but this may feel strange to the dancers participating, and may affect performance quality. Alternatively, observations undertaken in real-life settings are more likely to represent normal behaviour, but may be difficult to undertake without being noticed.

Many different types of data can be collected from observational methods. Quantitative data can be collected, through counting different aspects of behaviours. For example, this may be counting the number of chaffa steps someone new to bhangra can do in a set time, or timing how long dancers can balance on each leg. Alternatively, the approach may be more qualitative, recording quality of dance moves or types of interaction between dancers and teacher.

In the example in Figure 1.7, a dancer is being observed performing on stage. The researcher may note that there are more performance errors than would be expected with this level of dancer, and also note that his facial expression indicates anxiety.

Although observations are an excellent technique for describing behaviours, it is not possible to make statements about what is occurring internally, either

INTRODUCTION

cognitively or biologically. This makes observations useful as a starting place for research as they highlight potential problems from which theories may be developed. In this case, the researcher may theorise that anxiety affects performance quality, but this is only a theory until it has been tested.

Questionnaires

As a means of establishing what dancers are thinking or feeling, questionnaires can be a useful tool. If correctly constructed and standardised, questionnaires can be used to study a huge range of mental states and constructs.

Questionnaires are made up of a list of questions which have been carefully worded to test very specific constructs. The respondents are required to tick a box on the scale that corresponds to either their current or usual feeling, resulting in a score for each of the behaviours under investigation. They are useful to look for trends within and between groups, as well as looking at how individuals develop over time. Problems with such means of data collection are that respondents might alter their answers to present themselves in a particular way, rather than how they actually are. In some cases, the answers may be incorrect due to problems with recall rather than purposeful deception.

In the case shown in Figure 1.7, dancers have completed a questionnaire that has been designed to measure two different types of anxiety: somatic and cognitive. From this, the researcher can establish what type of anxiety dancers may be more prone to. But how does knowing this help in any way? Therefore, other methods are worthy of consideration.

Interviews

Interviews are an extension of questionnaires, where they are trying to extract information about the participants' internal processes through forms of questioning. But whereas questionnaires offer a set of predefined questions with scaled answers, interviews allow the interviewee to respond in their own words, offering explanations for feelings they may have.

The data collected from interviews is therefore rich and detailed and offers a more holistic view of the experiences and the individual, but because this type of data is qualitative, it is time-consuming to analyse and it is difficult to make comparisons between interviewees.

In the example in Figure 1.7, the interviewer can try to get to the bottom of the anxiety experienced. They can ask questions about when it occurs, and can probe further into how the dancer feels when experiencing anxiety. From such a method the researcher can build a more complete picture of the experience, but must always bear in mind that we do not all experience phenomena in the same way.

Correlations

Correlation is a statistical method for establishing whether there are relationships between thoughts, feelings, attitudes or behaviours. Any numerical data can be used to undertake a correlation. In this case the researcher has taken data from the observation of performance errors and correlated them with the data from the questionnaire. From this they can calculate whether there is a stronger relationship with somatic anxiety and performance errors than cognitive anxiety and performance errors. Although it is valuable to test hypotheses using statistical methods, it must be remembered that the findings from correlations only ever highlight relationships. They can never show that one variables causes a change in another.

Experiments

Experiments are controlled processes where variables are compared in such a way that the resultant quantitative data allows the researcher to establish cause and effect. Experiments are constructed to include two different types of variable: the independent and dependent. The *independent variables* (IV) are the conditions that are being manipulated, whereas the *dependent variables* (DV) are outcomes being measured.

Experiments can use one group of participants to see what impact different situations may have on them. This can be seen in the example where dancers perform in front of an audience and perform again without an audience (IV). The number of errors made during each performance is then calculated and compared (DV). This will help the researcher understand whether audiences cause the effect of anxiety. The comparison can also be between groups of individuals, such as a comparison between experts and novice dancers (IV), and the number of turns they can do before they lose balance (DV).

Although experiments do offer causal explanations for behaviours, it must be noted that the controls put in place to ensure the rigour of the process may affect the participants' behaviour. This is most problematic when participants are performing in situations that are foreign to them, or when asked to perform in ways that do not reflect their normal repertoire, or are being assessed using unusual techniques. Therefore, the more natural the setting to those participating, the more natural the behaviour observed, but the more prone to external influences due to the reduced levels of control.

Intervention studies

An extension of the experiment is to develop an intervention as a means of solving a problem. An experimental method is then applied to assess the effectiveness of the solution in a controlled manner. A comparison is between groups (IV), where one group try the anxiety management technique (experimental group) and the other group do not (control group). The technique may be deemed effective if the experimental group experience significantly less anxiety than the control group (DV).

Alternatively, one group may be used, as in this example. Dancers' initial performance errors were assessed to create a baseline reading. They then took part in an anxiety management training workshop. They were then assessed again and their post-intervention performance errors were compared to the baseline readings, where a significant reduction in errors would suggest that the intervention was successful.

INTRODUCTION

Psychological concepts

Learning a new topic is sometimes like learning a new language, where it all sounds like gobbledegook until someone gives you the translations. What follows are some key psychological concepts that occur throughout the book. Understanding these concepts will help you understand the material being presented here, and will help in your understanding of articles that you may subsequently seek out. A useful glossary of these key concepts is provided at the end of the chapter.

Attitudes

Attitudes are learned and relatively stable tendencies to respond to people, events or concepts in an evaluative way. They are comprised of three components:

- *Cognitive component*, which is what you *know* about the target.
- *Affective component*, which is what you *feel* about the target.
- *Behavioural component*, which is how you *respond* to the target.

> **Attitude to strength and conditioning training**
>
> **Cognitive**
> I *know* that these sessions will help improve my core strength and technique.
>
> **Affective**
> I *hate* going to the gym because it requires effort and I ache afterwards.
>
> **Behavioural**
> I do *go* to these sessions because I know it is the only way to progress.

Bear in mind that our feelings and emotions may not necessarily predict our behaviour. Just because we may have a strong dislike for something does not necessarily mean that we will not do it. Equally we may have a great affection for something, but it does not mean we will engage with it.

Sources of behaviour

Psychology aims to explain different behaviours, but behaviours may come from different sources:

- *Traits* are enduring personal qualities or the characteristics of a person, often linked to personality.

- *States* are not enduring in the way that traits are, but are brief, temporary mental states, which are externally caused.
- *Drives* are internal states that arise when a physical or psychological need has not been met.
- *Fight-or-flight response* is an internal response triggered when faced with a threat, which prepares the body for fighting or fleeing.

Understanding what the cause of the behaviour is may help us manage the situation or individual. If a dancer has an aggressive outburst and this is explained as a personality trait, then anger management may be helpful as this will be their typical response to situations. Alternatively the outburst may be due to a specific situation, and is a state-based response. The outburst may be because their aim to secure a lead role has been thwarted, which is an interference to their drive to perform, so their motivation needs to be channelled towards the next goal. The outburst may be due to stage fright as part of the fight-or-flight response, therefore, techniques can be used to manage this stress.

Dimensions

Psychologists often measure mental states or behaviours on a scale or *dimension* where labels are given to each end of the scale, but there are many points in between. As shown in Figure 1.8, we may start with a scale where the dancer plots the intensity of his feelings towards dance, but this is represented as a dimension as can be seen in Figure 1.9.

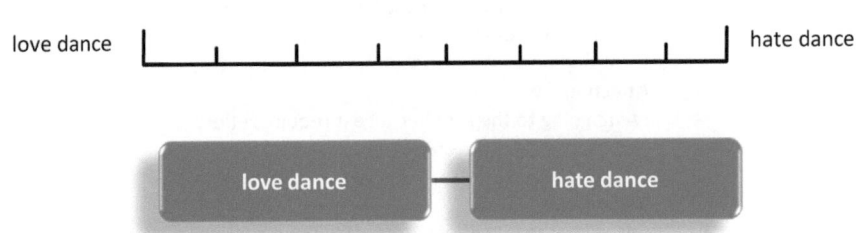

Figure 1.8 Scaled response of feelings towards dance

Figure 1.9 Dimensions of feelings towards dance

If we have more than one dimension, they may interact as shown in Figure 1.10, where hopefully by the end of this book the top-left quadrant best expresses how you feel!

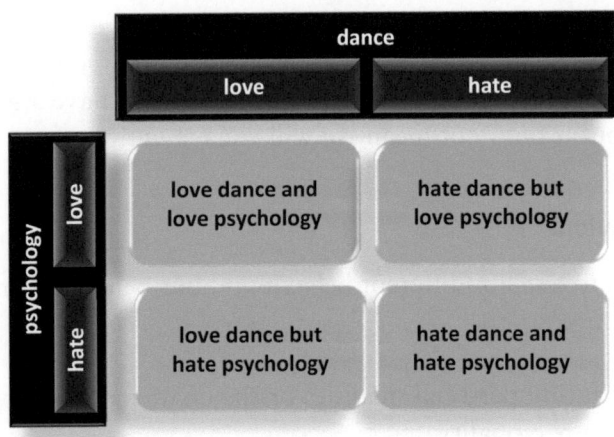

Figure 1.10 Interaction of dimensions of feelings towards dance

INTRODUCTION

Just because two dimensions may interact, it does not mean that you will be high in both, or low in both. In essence, your feelings about psychology and dance are completely independent of each other. When we have independent scales, we refer to them as being *orthogonal*.

WHY DO HUMANS DANCE?

Dance is experienced universally across time and cultures, therefore, it must play an important role in our existence. The following section offers some explanations as to why it is such an enduring phenomenon, and then considers the role it plays in contemporary Western culture.

Evolutionary explanations

Dance has proven to be universal, as the behaviour is evident in all cultures. Not only is dance evident in all cultures, but research with babies shows that there is an innate drive to move in time to rhythm and anticipate beats (Winkler, Háden, Ladinig, Sziller, & Honing, 2009). This reflex indicates that the need to dance is inborn, and not a product of learning from the environment (Richter & Ostovar, 2016). The universality of the need to dance indicates that there is an evolutionary explanation for the behaviour, suggesting that it aids survival in some way, but there are several reasons why this is counterintuitive. For humans to survive they need to conserve energy and ensure that they remain hidden from predators. Dancing expends a vast amount of energy, and when done to a beat, is noisy. This suggests that by dancing, humans would be burning energy unnecessarily and making their whereabouts known to predators (Miller, 2000), therefore, there must be other, more essential advantages to dance.

Sexual attraction

The most obvious survival advantage that dance could provide is to increase the chance of attracting a mate. Male mating dances can be seen in cultures across the world, such as the African courtship dances of the Acholi in Uganda, the Medlpa from New Guinea, and the Norwegian halling dance (Hugill, Fink, & Neave, 2010). Research has shown that there are correlations between how attractive women perceive a man to be based on the man's ability to dance. Dance ability is an indicator of strength, with bigger moves a sign of vigour (Neave et al., 2011), an important sign to females of the male's ability to protect her and their offspring. It may be that a man's ability to dance for prolonged periods is an indicator of the stamina he may have when hunting, and dances performed in a group formation may reflect the organised and cooperative nature hunting (Miller, 2000).

With respect to women dancing, research has shown that at times of high fertility, women's dance behaviour changes to appear more attractive to men (Fink, Weege, Neave, Pham, & Shackelford, 2015), and that men relate dance ability to femininity and attractiveness (Röder et al., 2016).

It is possibly the link between dance and sex that has led some countries to ban dance, especially between men and women, in the belief that it is immoral and may encourage lustful behaviour. This is only one explanation of the function of dance, and does not include other forms and contexts of dance such as its personal and social functions.

Social bonding

Dancing rarely occurs alone, it is generally the product of group activity, which suggests some social advantage from the activity. Synchronicity in steps and movement has been shown to increase positive feelings towards group members, increasing trust, cohesion and willingness to help (Tarr, Launay, Cohen, & Dunbar, 2015). Seeing such a cooperative community may suggest to those outside of the group that this community has an organised approach to group protection, thus warding off potential attacks (Richter & Ostovar, 2016).

Dance can also help form new social bonds, as can be seen in marriage rituals. The groom's dance shows the bride's family his strength and agility, qualities that demonstrate his ability to provide for his new family. The bride's dance shows her grace, a quality that would be passed on to their offspring (Richter & Ostovar, 2016).

Aggression

War dances have been seen across the world over time. Some war dances are used to prepare warriors for action, and request success from gods and spirits. This can be seen in the day-long dances by many Native American tribes, whereas African tribes, such as Ndembu, use dance to show status among warriors (Hanna, 1987). Some war dances can be seen as rituals to ward off attack, such as aspects of the Maori Haka, made famous by the New Zealand All Blacks rugby team (Clément, 2017). In some cases, such as Brazilian Capoeira, dance has merged with martial arts, blurring the boundaries between the two behaviours.

Dance has also been used as a means of reducing incidents of aggression and physical violence. The Ngoni have use dance as a form of emotional displacement, where the negative pent-up energy is used through dance and not violence (Hanna, 1987). Using dance as ritualised behaviour can remove the need to fight, as was seen in New York breakdance battles between rival gangs. More recently, the power of dance is being harnessed by therapists in dance interventions as a means of reducing violence (Koshland, Wilson, & Wittaker, 2004).

Comfort and emotional well-being

There is evidently something about rhythm and repetitive motion that humans find calming, through the secretion of hormones, such as endorphins, to induce sleep and reduce pain in babies (Johnston, Stremler, Stevens, & Horton, 1997). The positive feelings experienced on their release can improve our well-being and increase our self-confidence (Christensen, Cela-Conde, & Gomila, 2017).

The social elements of dance, and feelings of mastery as we accomplish new moves, may also be important features in our mental health. A review by Mala, Karkou, and Meekums (2012) found that different forms of dance therapy, from folk to jazz dance, reduced depressive symptoms in studies from across the world. In addition, the synchronicity and exertion of dance have shown to act as pain relievers through the release of endorphins (Tarr et al., 2015).

Communication

Dance is a form of non-verbal communication, it communicates bonds between family and community, and expresses emotions. Research has shown that we communicate our mood states through the velocity and complexity of dance moves as natural expressions to positive emotions (Saarikallio, Luck, Burger, Thompson, & Toiviainen, 2013), and audiences are capable of interpreting the emotional states from observing dance performances (Camurri, Lagerlöf, & Volpe, 2003).

Dance is also used to communicate at more spiritual levels. Shamans use dance to communicate with the spirit world by entering into trance-like states (Keeney, 2005), experiences that can be mimicked when dancing to current techno, trance and house music. Dance is also used to pass on stories between generations. Kathak dancing in India is used to narrate historical incidents, similarly, the Hula dancers of Hawaii pass on myth and legend as there was no written form of communication (Beaman, 2018).

Contemporary explanations

Although we have evolved culturally, dance is still a very important feature of modern Western society. Although technology increasingly features in our lives, it has not displaced dance, indeed, it could be argued that has dance has benefitted from the technological advancement through entertainment, social engagement and fitness.

Entertainment

Dance is an increasingly popular form of entertainment, democratised by television. Prior to the twenty-first century only the richest members of society could afford to pay to watch the ballet, the poorer folk watching the bawdier can-can dancers in the music halls. Today we all have access to a plethora of dance-related media, its popularity reflected in the success of shows like *Got to Dance*, *Dancing with the Stars* and *Strictly Come Dancing*.

Social engagement

The links explored earlier between dance and mating are evident across time. Dating back to the Middle Ages, folk dances have been expressions of fertility, such as the kissing dance. Throughout history, as society became more demure about courtship, tea dances were an opportunity for men and women to dance together in a socially acceptable manner. Throughout time young couples were most likely to meet at social events that involve dancing. Social dance styles have evolved to reflect societies' views on promiscuity, and dance styles evolve as the younger generation finds its own way of expressing itself; from dance hall to disco to clubbing.

Fitness

In a time of internationally increasing obesity it is interesting to note how dance is offering solutions, especially to sedentary females who may be inactive because sport was believed to be the only physical activity option. There has been an increase in dance-related fitness classes, some highly success franchises, such as Zumba, or related to television shows such as the *Strictly Come Dancing* spin-off FitSteps. These classes are encouraging predominantly female engagement with dance for recreation and fitness. For those unwilling to dance in public, there are a huge range of dance fitness videos available, from nightclub-related DVDs from Ministry of Sound through to a range of celebrities putting their own spin on dance fitness. Dancing has never been so popular as a means of getting fit.

For many reasons dance is an important part of our lives and our culture, and therefore worthy of further investigation.

Structure of the book

This book has been structured so that readers may focus on any one topic of interest without having read the previous chapters, although at times you may want to refer back to this introductory chapter to refresh your memory about some of the new concepts. Each chapter has been designed in the same way to help you navigate the new topic. Each chapter has associated *Learning Outcomes* which highlight what you should be able to know and do by the end of each chapter.

Each chapter is then divided into four sections. The *Context* identifies why the topic is of importance to the study of dance, be it related to personal development of professional practice or your roles as a student.

The *Theory* section describes the psychological explanations that are relevant to each topic area. Theories, as we have already discussed, are only as good as the evidence used to support them. As dance psychology is relatively new and under-researched, research linked to physical activity, exercise and sport has been included to support the theories referred to. To enhance your understanding of how psychologists go about the business of researching aspects of dance psychology, each chapter includes several research studies covered in greater detail – referred to as **Research in Focus.**

The *Practice* section of each chapter is the application of the theories covered. This section outlines a range of ways that understanding the theory can help improve practice. Suggestions are made for ways that you can improve your self-confidence in areas of your practice, there are techniques to manage emotions and methods for developing mental skills. The suggestions also cover aspects related to the teaching of dance, which, if not relevant now, may inform your practice if you are aiming to become a dance teacher.

To help reinforce the learning of new concepts there is a glossary of *key concepts* at the end of each chapter. This is further extended by suggestions for *Further Reading* to develop depth of understanding in topics that may have been of particular interest.

There is a logic to the order of the chapters. Commencing with the sense of self, differentiating the *us* from *others*. This leads into our motivation to dance, without which you would probably not be reading this book. Once we have the drive, we next need to acquire and develop the skills. Dancers rarely perform alone and even solo performances are the product of a group effort, so the social aspects are considered next. The final focus is on the management of the different emotions that we may experience at different points in our professional practice.

Chapter 2 'Self-perception' focuses on the dancer as an individual. If we are to be successful in dance at any level, we must have an understanding of who we are, and have a positive outlook about ourselves, our abilities and how we look. This chapter considers issues of self-reflection and judgement, highlighting problems of perfectionism. The Practice section offers some techniques to help develop a positive sense of self.

Chapter 3 'Motivation' highlights how we need to maintain a drive to perform and progress. In a career that can be quite all-consuming, in terms of time and energy, it is important that we understand what motivates us, but also the role that others play in affecting dancers' motivation levels. Problems of burnout are also considered, where motivation needs to be reined in for the sake of our physical and mental well-being. The Practice section offers ways that motivation might be maintained or increased in a range of different dance-related contexts.

Chapter 4 'Skill Acquisition' uncovers the complexities of the mind by examining theories that show how the mind works when acquiring new skills or trying to learn new information. The Practice section offers a range of techniques that allow you to maximise time in and out of the training room.

Chapter 5 'Social Factors' identifies the range of social facets involved in the profession of dance. It examines how our interactions with others can have positive and negative effects on our performance. The Practice section offers ways to increase group cohesion and maximise the outcomes of our interpersonal communication.

Chapter 6 'Managing Emotions' identifies what emotions are, at a biological and cognitive level, and examines what impacts emotions may have on our ability to perform. The Practice section offers a range of techniques that can be used to manage anxiety and anger in different contexts.

> **Key concepts glossary**
>
> **Biological psychology** An approach to the study of behaviour through the consideration of biological factors
>
> **Cognitive psychology** An approach to the study of behaviour through the consideration of the processes and functions of the mind.
>
> **Correlations** A method of investigation where variables are assessed to establish whether there is a relationship between them.
>
> **Ethics** Guidelines of acceptable behaviours to be adhered to when undertaking research.
>
> **Experiments** A method of investigation where variables are manipulated and controlled to show cause and effect.
>
> **Hypothesis** A statement of prediction to be tested through scientific methods.
>
> **Interviews** A method of investigation where participants are questioned to produce explanations of thoughts or feelings on a given topic.
>
> **Observations** A method of investigation where participants' behaviour is examined to explain phenomena.
>
> **Questionnaires** A method of investigation where participants are asked to respond to a set of questions using predetermined options.
>
> **Social psychology** An approach to the study of behaviour through the consideration of social factors.
>
> **Theory** An explanation for a specified behaviour that has been tested and found to be valid.

References

Bailey, R., Wellard, I., & Dismore, H. (2005). *Girls' participation in physical activities and sports: Benefits, patterns, influences and ways forward.* Geneva: World Health Organization.

Beaman, P. L. (2018). *World dance cultures: From ritual to spectacle.* London: Routledge.

Belardinelli, R., Lacalaprice, F., Ventrella, C., Volpe, L., & Faccenda, E. (2008). Waltz dancing in patients with chronic heart failure. *New Form of Exercise Training, 1*(2), 107–114. doi:10.1161/circheartfailure.108.765727

BPS. (2010). *Code of human research ethics.* Leicester: The British Psychological Society.

Camurri, A., Lagerlöf, I., & Volpe, G. (2003). Recognizing emotion from dance movement: Comparison of spectator recognition and automated techniques. *International Journal of Human-Computer Studies, 59*(1), 213–225. doi:10.1016/S1071-5819(03)00050-8.

Christensen, J. F., Cela-Conde, C. J., & Gomila, A. (2017). Not all about sex: Neural and biobehavioral functions of human dance. *Annals of the New York Academy of Sciences, 1400*(1), 8–32. doi:10.1111/nyas.13420.

Clément, V. (2017). Dancing bodies and Indigenous ontology: What does the haka reveal about the Māori relationship with the Earth? *Transactions of the Institute of British Geographers, 42*(2), 317–328. doi:10.1111/tran.12157.

Cooper, L., & Thomas, H. (2002). Growing old gracefully: Social dance in the third age. *Ageing and Society, 22*(6), 689–708. doi:10.1017/S0144686X02008929.

Corr, P. J. (2006). *Understanding biological psychology*. Malden, MA: Blackwell.

Daley, A. J., & Buchanan, J. (1999). Aerobic dance and physical self-perceptions in female adolescents: Some implications for physical education. *Research Quarterly for Exercise and Sport, 70*(2), 196–200. doi:10.1080/02701367.1999.10608037.

Fink, B., Weege, B., Neave, N., Pham, M. N., & Shackelford, T. K. (2015). Integrating body movement into attractiveness research. *Frontiers in Psychology, 6*(220). doi:10.3389/fpsyg.2015.00220.

Gentner, D. (2010). Psychology in cognitive science: 1978–2038. *Topics in Cognitive Science, 2*(3), 328–344. doi:10.1111/j.1756-8765.2010.01103.x.

Hanna, J. L. (1987). *To dance is human : A theory of nonverbal communication*. Chicago: University of Chicago Press.

HSCIC. (2016). *Statistics on obesity, physical activity and diet*. London: Health and Social Care Information Centre.

Hugill, N., Fink, B., & Neave, N. (2010). The role of human body movements in mate selection. *Evolutionary Psychology, 8*(1), 66–89.

Johnston, C. C., Stremler, R., L. , Stevens, B. J., & Horton, L. J. (1997). Effectiveness of oral sucrose and simulated rocking on pain response in preterm neonates. *PAIN, 72*(1), 193–199. doi:10.1016/S0304-3959(97)00033-X.

Keeney, B. (2005). *Bushman shaman: Awakening the spirit through ecstatic dance*. Rochester, VT: Destiny Books.

Koshland, L., Wilson, J., & Wittaker, B. (2004). PEACE through dance/movement: Evaluating a violence prevention program. *American Journal of Dance Therapy, 26*(2), 69–90. doi:10.1007/s10465-004-0786-z.

Lobo, Y. B., & Winsler, A. (2006). The effects of a creative dance and movement program on the social competence of head start preschoolers. *Social Development, 15*(3).

Mala, A., Karkou, V., & Meekums, B. (2012). Dance/movement therapy (D/MT) for depression: A scoping review. *The Arts in Psychotherapy, 39*(4), 287–295. doi:10.1016/j.aip.2012.04.002.

McGue, M., & Bouchard, T. J. (1998). Genetic and environmental influences on human behavioural differences. *Annual Reviews, 21*, 1–24.

Miller, G. F. (2000). Evolution of human music through sexual selection. In N. L. Wallin, B. Merker, & S. Brown (Eds.), *The origins of music*. Cambridge, MA: MIT Press.

Neave, N., McCarty, K., Freynik, J., Caplan, N., Hönekopp, J., & Fink, B. (2011). Male dance moves that catch a woman's eye. *Biology Letters, 7*(2), 221–224. doi:10.1098/rsbl.2010.0619.

Neisser, U. (1967). *Cognitive psychology*. Englewood Cliffs, NJ: Prentice Hall.

Palo-Bengtsson, L., Winblad, B., & Ekman, S.-L. (1998). Social dancing: A way to support intellectual, emotional and motor functions in persons with dementia. *Journal of Psychiatric and Mental Health Nursing, 5*, 545–554.

Quin, E., Frazer, L., & Redding, E. (2007). The health benefits of creative dance: improving children's physical and psychological wellbeing. *Education and Health, 25*(2), 31–33.

Quiroga Murcia, C., Kreutz, G., Clift, S., & Bongard, S. (2010). Shall we dance? An exploration of the perceived benefits of dancing on well-being. *Arts & Health, 2*(2), 149–163. doi:10.1080/17533010903488582.

Richter, J., & Ostovar, R. (2016). "It don't mean a thing if it ain't got that swing": an alternative concept for understanding the evolution of dance and music in human beings. *Frontiers in Human Neuroscience, 10*(485). doi:10.3389/fnhum.2016.00485.

Röder, S., Carbon, C.-C., Shackelford, T. K., Pisanski, K., Weege, B., & Fink, B. (2016). Men's visual attention to and perceptions of women's dance movements. *Personality and Individual Differences, 101*(Supplement C), 1–3. doi:10.1016/j.paid.2016.05.025.

Ross, L., Lepper, M., & Ward, A. (2010). History of social psychology: insights, challenges, and contributions to theory and application. In S. T. Fiske, D. T. Gilbert, G. Lindzey, & A. E. Jongsma (Eds.), *Handbook of social psychology* (5th ed.). Hoboken, NJ: Wiley.

Saarikallio, S., Luck, G., Burger, B., Thompson, M., & Toiviainen, P. (2013). Dance moves reflect current affective state illustrative of approach–avoidance motivation. *Psychology of Aesthetics, Creativity, and the Arts, 7*(3), 296–305. doi:10.1037/a0032589

Tarr, B., Launay, J., Cohen, E., & Dunbar, R. (2015). Synchrony and exertion during dance independently raise pain threshold and encourage social bonding. *Biology Letters, 11*(10), 20150767. doi:10.1098/rsbl.2015.0767.

Townsend, N., Wickramasinghe, K., Williams, J., Bhatnagar, P., & Rayner, M. (2015). *Physical activity statistics 2015*. London: British Heart Foundation.

Verghese, J. (2006). Cognitive and mobility profile of older social dancers. *Journal of the American Geriatrics Society, 54*(8), 1241–1244. doi:10.1111/j.1532-5415.2006.00808.x.

Wickens, A. P., & Wickens, A. P. (2009). *Introduction to biopsychology*. Harlow: Pearson Education Limited.

Winkler, I., Háden, G. P., Ladinig, O., Sziller, I., & Honing, H. (2009). Newborn infants detect the beat in music. *Proceedings of the National Academy of Sciences of the United States of America, 106*(7), 2468–2471. doi:10.1073/pnas.0809035106.

Further reading

British Psychological Society (2010). *Code of human research ethics*. Leicester: BPS.

Coolican, H. (2014). *Research methods and statistics in psychology*. London: Psychology Press.

Glassman, W. E., & Hadad, M. (2013). *Approaches to psychology*. Maidenhead: McGraw-Hill Education.

CHAPTER 2

Self-perception

> **Learning outcomes**
>
> By the end of this chapter readers should be able to:
>
> - recognise the importance of a dancer's sense of self
> - define key terms related to the self
> - describe different theories of self-worth and impression management
> - explain how a negative self-concept may impact on dance performance
> - propose how to encourage a sense of self while acknowledging the contributions of others

CONTEXT

Being a professional dancer is unlike many other careers. You will have committed years of dedication to learning your craft. Competition for places at dance school or for parts in shows adding to the trials and tribulations. Finally achieving a role which may require you to be out on the road, or at least working highly unsociable hours, means that the job often dominates your life. With this in mind it is important to have a sense of self, and to be able to recognise that there are other roles in your life – recognition of this will help you maintain perspective throughout the difficult times.

Not only is it important to have a meaningful sense of self at a psychological level through your self-concept, it is also important to have a realistic sense of your body through body image. In dance the physical self is the medium, and it puts you and your body under great scrutiny, so it is important to make objective assessments about how you look physically, as well as how you move. Having made this assessment, it is important to acknowledge your strengths and limitations. Failure to acknowledge what is realistically required in terms of technique may lead to problems of perfectionism, whereas a distorted body image may lead to social physique anxiety. Adopting a positive self-image may increase self-confidence and potential performance quality too.

THEORY

Self-concept

Definition of self

Self-concept can be defined as 'all the elements that make up a person's view of himself' (Statt, 1998, p. 119) and indeed there are various ways that we may define and describe ourselves. William James believed there were three components to the self (Brown, 1998), but before we look at these in detail, write a list of ten aspects that you feel define your self-concept, starting each with the words 'I am'.

> self-concept
> I am tall
> I am a house owner
> I am a principle dancer
> I am outgoing
> I am a vegetarian
> I am too eager to please

Now let's see how they compare to James' ideas as shown in Figure 2.1. The *material self* he considered to be made up of two subcomponents. The *bodily self* refers to our actual body, such as 'tall'. The *extended self* is things that we see as belonging to us such as 'house owner', as we often define ourselves by our possessions. The next component is the *social self* which refers to the roles and relationships we make, such as 'principal dancer'. The final component, the *spiritual self*, refers to the psychological components, which are often evaluative. This would include attitudes, abilities and personality traits, such as 'outgoing', 'vegetarian' or 'too eager to please'.

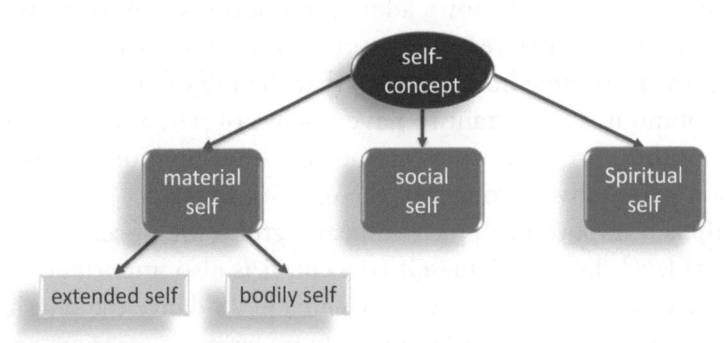

Figure 2.1
Components of self-concept

Self-complexity

Some argue that there is not one self, but the self is an amalgamation of many components. McConnell and Strain (2007) suggest that the self may be a construct of different *aspects*, such as:

- role – our role at that moment
- relationship – how we are related to others
- affective – related to our feelings

SELF-PERCEPTION

- true self – how you know yourself to be
- situational – how you manage different situations
- temporal – how you are at different points in the past, present and future
- goal – what you aim to be

And within any expressed aspect we will have different *attributes*. As can be seen in Jon's hypothetical self (Figure 2.2), he includes the aspect of *friend* to which the attributes of honesty and trust are associated.

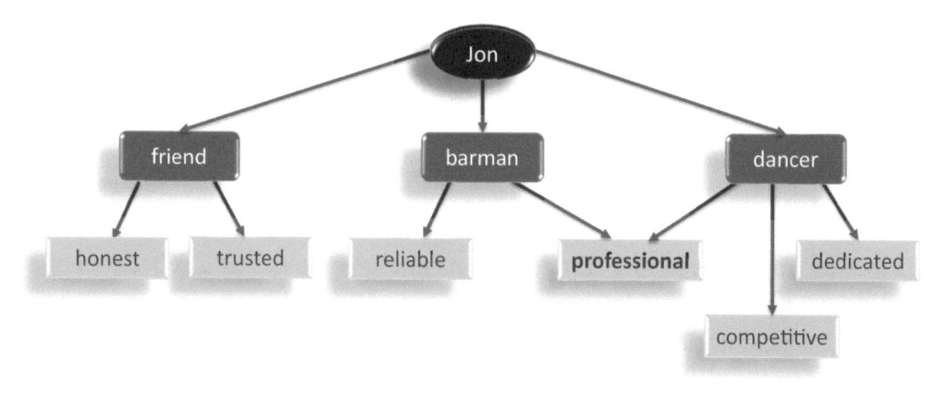

Figure 2.2 Hypothetical self-concept of Jon

These aspects and attributes can have various effects on our mental health and well-being. First, we can see that some attributes have an *overspill* between different aspects (as shown in bold). For Jon, there is an overspill of *professionalism* shown in his roles as a dancer and as a barman, whereas Jen (Figure 2.3) has shown several overspills (caring, loyalty and dedication). If we suffer a dent to an attribute, the impact that this has on our well-being may be affected by how much we perceive it to be part of our self-concept. Therefore, a director challenging Jon's professionalism may create more distress than challenging his reliability, as professionalism is related to two aspects of his self-concept. Such a criticism may lead him to worry about his professionalism in his bar work as well as a dancer.

The more aspects and attributes that an individual perceives themselves to have, the more self-complexity they have, as can be seen in Jen's case (Figure 2.3). There is less impact on her well-being if an overspill attribute is challenged, for example, her *dedication*. Even though dedication relates to her role as a dancer and a student, it is one of many aspects to her self-concept. While this may be disappointing to her, she can rely on her other relationships (mother, wife and friend) to reduce any negative impact.

There are mixed arguments for the benefits of greater or lesser self-complexity. On the one hand, if there is less self-complexity, we are more

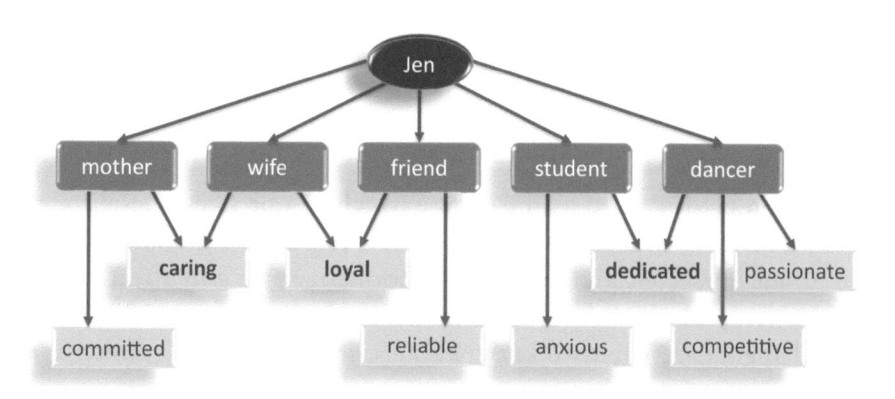

Figure 2.3 Hypothetical self-concept of Jen

negatively affected by any critique of an aspect, as it features more strongly in our self-concept, whereas those with a more complex self-concept may place less emphasis on the aspect being criticised. Alternatively, the more aspects we may have, the more problems there may be with respect to control, so Jen may find her role as a dancer conflicts with her role as a mother. If she cannot control this, it may impact on her well-being.

Criticism of our attributes will only have a negative impact if it is inconsistent with our own self-evaluation (McConnell & Strain, 2007). This would mean that Jen would not be affected by a lecturer calling her a 'stress head' as she already perceives anxiety to be a feature of her student role, whereas if the lecturer accused her of 'lacking dedication', this would impact negatively as this challenges her self-concept.

Self-regulation

Our view of ourselves is not static, and, as such, the changing self-concept regulates our behaviour (McConnell & Strain, 2007). By making assessments of our current self, compared to what we want to achieve (our goal self), we discover where the differences are, referred to as *incongruence*. When the incongruence is small and the goal is achievable, it motivates action to reach the desired goal (Figure 2.4a). Unfortunately, where the incongruence is deemed too great, this may be demotivating as it seems unachievable, leading to no effort to reach our goal self, impacting on our value of self-worth (Figure 2.4b).

Other perceptions of congruency of self-concept may affect our well-being. If we compare our current self-concept to how we feel we *ought* to be, then incongruence may lead to feelings of guilt or anxiety that we are not as we should be (Figure 2.4c). Alternatively, incongruence with our *ideal self*, how we wished we were, may lead to depression due to disappointment (Figure 2.4d).

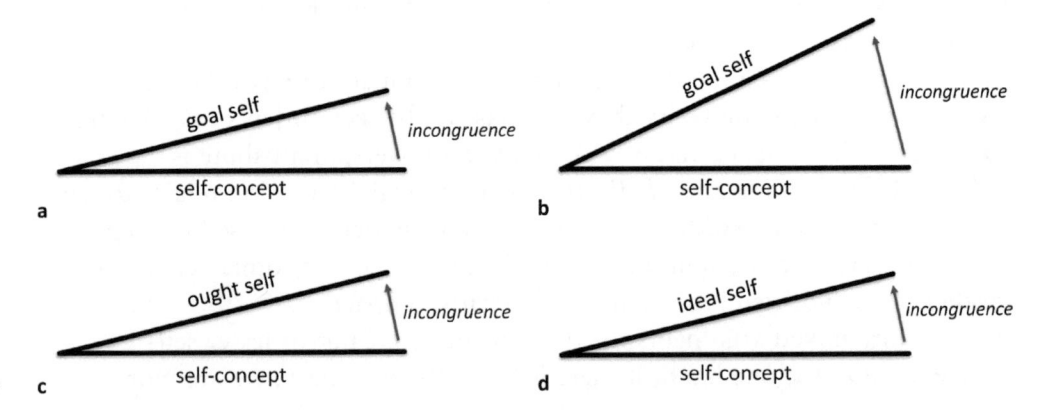

Figure 2.4
Self-concept and congruency

Self-worth

Self-esteem

Self-esteem can be described as the degree to which one likes oneself or the worth that one gives oneself (Statt, 1998). Self-esteem is a global attitude that we hold about ourselves, and as such has both cognitive and affective components (Rosenberg, Schooler, Schoenbach, & Rosenberg, 1995). The cognitive elements are what we know about ourselves, and the affective is how we feel about this knowledge, which may be positive or negative and expressed with varying levels of intensity. Our level of global self-esteem has been closely related to well-being, higher self-esteem leading to higher levels of self-acceptance and respect (Rosenberg et al., 1995).

Self-esteem may be seen as a trait component, suggesting an enduring disposition potentially resulting from childhood experiences of mastery feedback. More state-based explanations relate to how we evaluate ourselves with respect to the expectations of others or society, allowing for fluctuations in our self-esteem (Brown, 1998). Self-esteem is important as higher levels are related to a range of outcomes relating to positive mental health and enhanced life potentials.

Self-efficacy

Self-efficacy can be considered as the confidence we derive from specific forms of self-esteem, and therefore relates to behavioural outcomes rather than general well-being (Rosenberg et al., 1995). Bandura (1994) describes self-efficacy as an individual's belief about their ability to produce designated levels of performance. It is our ability to compartmentalise aspects of our lives and acknowledge that we are not going to be excellent at all things. Self-efficacy is important due to its impact on our thoughts, feelings and behaviour. Self-efficacy has been linked to positive forms of motivation (as will be discussed in Chapter 3), rising to meet challenges, resilience in the face of adversity, the ability to correctly identify performance deficits, and lower levels of anxiety (as will be considered in Chapter 6).

Self-efficacy has four sources as can be seen in Figure 2.5 (Bandura, 1994). First, we gain a feeling of achievement through *mastery experiences*, which we experience by engaging with a challenge and realising a level of success by being able to consistently reproduce the skill. The second source is through *vicarious experiences*, which is watching those whom you perceive as similar to yourself being successful at the skill. This increases the belief that you too can succeed. The third source of self-efficacy is from *social persuasion*, verbal advice, reassurance and encouragement from others that help override the inner voice of doubt. This can lead to sustained effort and increased performance. The final source is through the promotion of *positive emotions* and the understanding of the impact that mood has on personal performance.
In Chapter 6 we will consider how emotion may predict the direction of the performance.

Figure 2.5
Sources of self-efficacy

Source: Photo courtesy of Emily King and Trinity Laban Conservatoire of Music and Dance

Body image

Dance body image

Body image can be defined as 'a person's perceptions, thoughts and feeling about his or her body' (Grogan, 2017, p. 3), which includes how we see ourselves, the evaluations we make about our bodies and how we experience our body. Dance can create different views about our body image, dependent on dance *type* and *level*.

Dance type

Different dance genres put different emphases on body composition, suggesting that there are ideal body types and shapes for different forms of dance. This is epitomised by the *ballet body* which is portrayed as an extreme idealised thinness, where genetic factors (height and body proportions) have traditionally been as important in the choice of dancers for dance school as their technical ability (Oliver, 2008). This idealised slenderness is not only seen in traditional forms of dance, Heiland, Murray, and Edley (2008) found that media pressure has led to similarly poor body image issues for commercial jazz dancers. However, in more free form, creative types of dance, such as modern (Langdon & Petracca, 2010) and street (Swami & Tovée, 2009), dancers have shown a lower drive for thinness and a more positive appreciation of their body. One argument for this may be the degree of body exposure, where ballet and commercial jazz dancers traditionally wear tight clothing, whereas street dancers favour less exposing, baggy attire. This argument has been challenged by Tiggemann, Coutts, and Clark (2014) who have found that belly dancers have a positive body image, suggesting that it is the attitude towards the body that is important, rather than the clothes that expose it.

Dance level

With respect to the *level* of dance, there are oppositional effects with respect to body satisfaction. Novices show positive mental states when engaging in dance classes, as a result of the mastery of the new skills being acquired, and due to the body empowerment that may result from fitness and physiological changes (Langdon & Petracca, 2010). As our skills develop, we might experience a plateau in skill acquisition, this may lead to a change in our perception of our body. At this level of engagement there are higher levels of scrutiny on the body through physical body exposure, reducing body satisfaction (Langdon & Petracca, 2010). There are several theories that can explain these dance-related differences in body satisfaction: Social Comparison Theory and The Tripartite Influence Model.

Social Comparison Theory

Festinger (1954) argues that we are driven to evaluate our abilities, and one way that we do this is by our comparison to others, most especially our peers, referred to as *Social Comparison Theory*. We are also driven to make

> **Research in focus**
>
> **Dancers' Body Esteem, Fitness Esteem, and Self-esteem in Three Contexts**
>
> **Aim** The purpose of dance is to express yourself through your body movements whilst an audience watches, therefore there is an emphasis on how you look and move. As there is such scrutiny over their form, dancers have shown a high levels of body consciousness. Although this area has been previously researched, what has not been considered is whether dancers' body esteem is context-dependent.
>
> **Method** A total of 62 college dance students were questioned: 59 female and 3 male.
> A survey was used to collect data about:
> - Dance genre (ballet or modern)
> - Body Esteem Scale (rating figure, waist, legs, buttocks, hips, and weight)
> - Fitness esteem (rated their energy level, agility, and physical condition)
> - Single Item Self-Esteem Scale
>
> Dancers were asked to rate these types of esteem in three different contexts:
> - dance class
> - dance performance
> - at a party
>
> **Results**
> - *Dance genre:* modern dancers had higher esteem than ballet dancers
> - *Context*: highest esteem was in performance, lowest was in training
> - *Esteem:* body esteem was lowest and fitness esteem was highest
>
> **Conclusions** Esteem was lowest with respect to the external factor of how the body looks. This was experienced most within training as this context allows for the greatest level of body comparison. Dancers feel best about themselves on when on stage.
>
> (Van Zelst, Clabaugh & Morling, 2004)

comparisons on the basis of what is deemed important or attractive, which in dance might not be purely your technical ability but an idealised body shape as determined by the dance culture that you inhabit. Although such comparisons may be motivating as we may regulate our behaviour to emulate those with the skills or stature, this is not universally the case. A perpetual upwards comparison may leave a dancer feeling disappointed that she has not achieved the level of the class star, but what she may fail to see is how much progress she has made, and improvements relative to those less able in the class (Van Zelst, Clabaugh, & Morling, 2004). Where images are idealised and not necessarily achievable, such comparisons can lead to higher levels of body image dissatisfaction, an issue which is more likely to occur throughout adolescence (Krayer, Ingledew, & Iphofen, 2008).

The Tripartite Influence Model

The *Tripartite Influence Model* expands on the Social Comparison Theory (Figure 2.6). Developed by van den Berg, Thompson, Obremski-Brandon, and

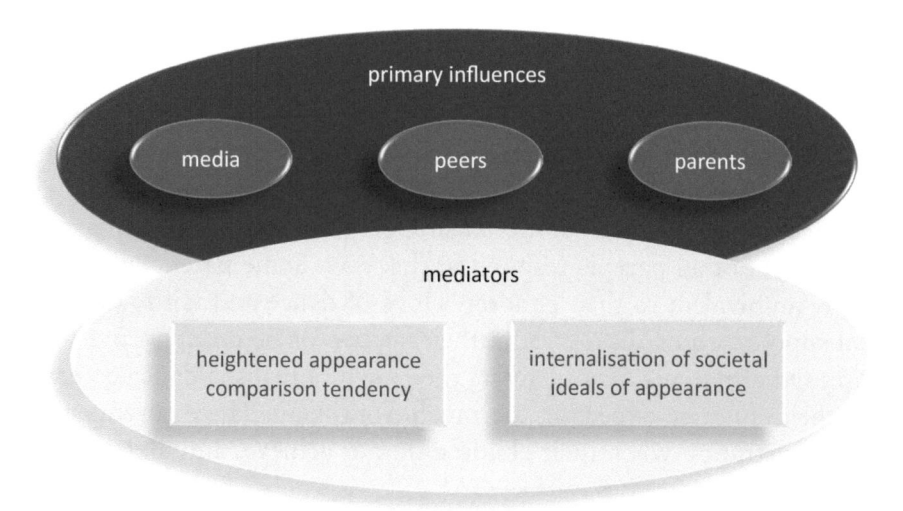

Figure 2.6
Tripartite Influence Model

Coovert (2002), the model suggests that there are three *primary influences* on our body image: the media, our peers and our parents.

Media influence

The media represents ideals of lifestyle, looks and behaviour, through films, television, magazines and the internet, but often these ideals do not reflect real life. The incongruence experienced by the ideals portrayed through the media have become a problem in society at large, but are also a problem within the dance community. This is not a new phenomenon, over two decades ago Abraham (1996) noted that the dance media of the time presented idealised thin and athletic role models, and with the more recent advent of photo-editing software, the problem has been exacerbated.

Peer influence

Our peers set the social norms of attitudes and behaviour. With respect to body image, the social norms set by peers may be the expression of concern about appearance, or discussing the impact of different diets, or talking about other behaviours that might lead to weight loss (van den Berg et al., 2002). If such conversations are normal within the group, this may then normalise the behaviours associated with the conversations. The influence of peers has shown to be especially influential with respect to negative health behaviours (van den Berg et al., 2002), and may lead to disordered eating and other behaviours that will negatively impact on dance performance. In the context of dance this may be problematic as there is not only friendship between dancers, but potential competition for recognition and selection for roles. This might increase the chances of dancers adopting negative health behaviours to remain competitive.

Parental influence

Those who play significant roles in dancers' lives can have an impact over how we feel about ourselves. Van den Berg et al. (2002) developed the Tripartite

Influence Model as a general explanation as to which factors affect our body image. Parents may have a strong influence over the dancer's progress at a practical and emotional level. Those dancers who have supportive parents, especially in childhood and adolescence, may benefit from the practical aspects of being supported financially, being driven to classes, rehearsals and performances, as well as the emotional support of encouragement. Unfortunately, not all parents respond in this way. Some parents may be completely ambivalent to their children's love of dance and fail to offer practical support, show disinterest at their success or be unsupportive at points of failure. Other parents may be living their own unrealised dance career through their children, expecting too much from them. These parents may show anger and frustration when their children do not achieve, and may not be satisfied with their successes.

When applying the Tripartite Influence Model to dance specifically, it may be appropriate to add *dance teachers* to this influence as the impact that they may have as an older role model may be similar, and as strong, as the parental influence. There are many historical accounts of the punishing regimes of the ballet mistress who encourages starvation to achieve the ideal physique (Ravaldi et al., 2006). Currently there is an increasing awareness of the potential mental and physiological outcomes from restricted eating and over-exercising, with dance teachers being taught the signs of potential problems on courses and through dedicated dance conferences.

Mediators are factors that affect the likelihood of the primary influences impacting on thoughts, feelings and behaviour. The factors which will mediate the impact of the media, peers and parents were proposed to be whether the individual has a heightened tendency to compare appearances and whether they internalised societal ideals of appearance (van den Berg et al., 2002).

Internalised societal ideals of appearance

Alongside the drive for ideal body, personified within Western media, a similar drive is observed in the world of dance. Here a culture is emerging where slim and slender is the norm. If a dancer is immersed in such a world, they do not have the opportunity to observe normal body size and shape, therefore they are more likely to internalise these values (Langdon & Petracca, 2010).

Heightened appearance comparison tendency

Linked to Social Comparison Theory, this mediator will impact on the thoughts, feelings and behaviours if the individual is likely to make comparisons of themselves to others. With respect to media, research has shown that females who compared themselves to media images were more likely to experience body image dissatisfaction, depression and low self-esteem, a pattern that was not observed in men (van den Berg et al., 2007). At a group level, even when working as a corps or troupe, there maybe competition within the group to be noticed and selected, which may encourage appearance comparisons.

In addition, there is the perpetual visual field within the typical dance studio where one is confronted with their own physique alongside that of the class reflected in the mirrors. Unavoidable exposure to the reflected self through

> **Research in focus**
>
> **Body Image and Mirror Use in the Ballet Class**
>
> **Aim** The studio mirrors are part of dance culture and a tool to aid learning, but research has shown that the perpetual reflection of your body can lead to self-consciousness and negative body image. The purpose of this research was to explore the impact of mirrored reflections on body image.
>
> **Method** A total of 22 females at two beginner ballet classes.
> Independent variable:
> - class taught with mirrors
> - class taught without mirrors
>
> Dependent variables:
> - Multidimensional Body-Self Relations Questionnaire (MBSRQ)
> - Radell Qualitative Questionnaire (RQQ)
>
> Dancers completed the MBSRQ, then attended 14 weekly ballet classes. They then repeated the MBSRQ and completed the RQQ.
>
> **Results**
> - *Low performing dancer:* mirrors reduced their body concerns
> - *High performing dancer:* mirrors increased their body concerns
> - *Mirror class*: the majority of dancers preferred mirrors as it helped them grasp the concepts
> - *No mirror class:* half the dancers preferred having no mirrors as it helped them understand the concepts
>
> **Conclusions** Mirrors can be distracting to proficient dancers as they may tend to use them to compare themselves to others. For beginners the mirrors are more likely to be used to concentrate on technique and skill development, and not for social comparison. Consideration of use of mirrors should be made dependent on skill level.
>
> (Radell, 2012)

studio mirrors has been shown to increase body image dissatisfaction and weight concerns in high level dancers, although not in low ability dancers (Radell, 2012). The difference in body image concerns seen in the different level of dancer may be explained by the importance put upon the ideal physique as dance becomes more important. Any negative impact the training room has on body image must be seen in terms of social context, as the body esteem experienced by dancers in a performance context was more positive than when in training (Van Zelst et al., 2004).

The Two-Component Model of impression management

Impression management is defined as 'the process by which individuals attempt to control the impressions others form of them' (Leary & Kowalski, 1990, p. 34). The Two-Component Model of impression management considers what

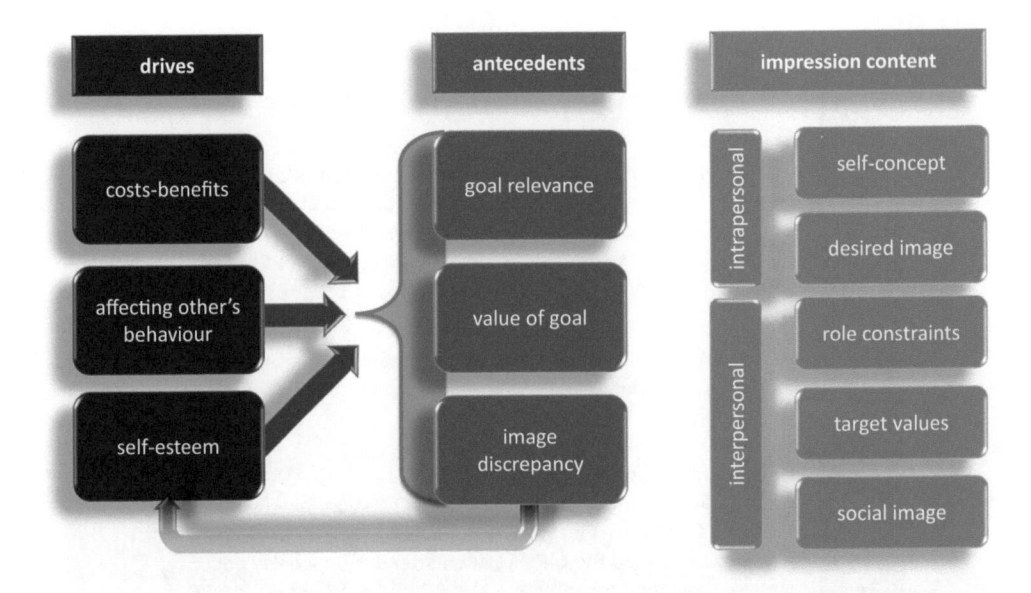

Figure 2.7
Impression motivation

may motivate us to manage the impression that we have on others (drives), and then suggests how we go about constructing such an image (Figure 2.7).

Drives

The reasons that we may feel driven to manage the impression that others may have of us are threefold. First, we are driven to maximise the rewards we get in life, and minimise the punishments. Therefore, through a *costs-benefits* analysis we calculate how to maximise our social or material outcomes. By affecting others' views of us we may also *affect their behaviour* towards us, and increase the positive behaviours (rewards and praise), while reducing the negative behaviours (criticism and rejection). Through these experiences we construct our identity, part of which is our *self-esteem*, the value that we place on ourselves (Leary & Kowalski, 1990).

Antecedents

Goal relevance

The more we are observed by those who can have an impact on us, the more likely we are to adapt our self-presentation as the behaviour has a *relevant goal*. The more important the observers are to the fulfilment of the goal, the more motivated we will be to manage the impressions they have about us. Therefore, dependent upon your motivation to dance, you may be more likely to manage the impression you have on judges, assessors or casting directors.

Value of goal

Likewise, the importance of the goal is associated with impression management, the more *value the goal* has, the more we will manage our impression to increase the likelihood of the positive outcome through goal achievement.

This is especially relevant in times of limited opportunities – the fewer the opportunities, the stronger the drive becomes. This will explain why we may be more likely to manage the impression we make to a casting director due to limited roles availability, than to an assessor who will grade the performance based on its qualities.

Image discrepancy

Further increasing the likelihood that we may manage the impression that others may have of us is when we feel there is discrepancy between the current and the desired image. The discrepancy may be due to a poor performance or an embarrassing incident. Interestingly impression management appears to be important, even when current observers have not witnessed the negative event. This suggests that it is not just the views that others hold of us that are important, but that these impact on our self-esteem, therefore we need to feel competent to ourselves, as well as others (Leary & Kowalski, 1990).

Impression content

There are many facets of the self that one may wish to construct: abilities, beliefs, attitudes, interests, moods, status or roles, where *intrapersonal* and *interpersonal* factors play a role in impression construction (Leary & Kowalski, 1990).

Intrapersonal content

When presenting ourselves to others, we tend not to construct a false portrayal, so what we do present represents a true reflection of our self-concept. Here we promote our best, or situationally relevant features, limiting ourselves to the image that we are capable of creating. We need to be able to demonstrate true features of ourselves to reduce the likelihood of deceit, as being realised as a charlatan will be counterproductive to the impression construction. False presentation is only likely to occur when the relationship is fleeting and superficial, reducing the chances of exposure to the truth. The second intrapersonal factor is to construct a *desired image*, focusing on what we wish others to see of us while minimising exposure of any undesirable features.

Interpersonal content

At an interpersonal level, the role one adopts needs to meet the expectations that others may have of us. If our behaviour does not meet these expectations, doubt may be cast as to our suitability for that role. *Role constraints* indicate how we should present ourselves based on our role. Therefore, a dance teacher needs to show knowledge and technique, while a choreographer needs to show creative vision and leadership. This may also be linked to preconceptions of dance genres, where the ballerina may be expected to show poise and class in a way that might not be expected of a street dancer. As there is an interaction between the self and the observer, there is the tendency to portray the values

© Shutterstock

that you assume the observer to hold as a means of increasing attractiveness and liking, described as *target values*. We are not constrained by solely the current *social image* that others may hold of us, but may be laying the foundations for future views.

Impact of negative self-concept

Self-handicapping

Self-handicapping can be described as the behaviours adopted that act to protect an individual's social or self-esteem by actively excusing future performances or suggesting why success may be constrained (Carron, Burke, & Prapavessis, 2004). This includes the creation of situations where poor performance is excused and success is exaggerated through the highlighting of negative external factors, creating a win-win outcome.

Self-handicapping may be evident in two ways: behavioural and claimed. *Behavioural* self-handicapping is the conscious choice of an action that will reduce performance, such as drinking or drug taking, where any failure to perform can be blamed on the chosen action. In some cases we may select a goal beyond that is beyond our ability so there is no expectation of success, therefore no loss of self-esteem. Another form of behavioural handicapping is self-injury, an extreme method of impression management. *Claimed* self-handicapping are verbal references to events that suggest impeded performance, such as saying that you are sick, injured or anxious without there being any obvious signs of this to the observer (Martin Ginis & Leary, 2004).

Those who are likely to self-handicap are less likely to put effort into training, as this can also be used as an excuse for failure. Those who are low in the self-handicapping trait are more likely to work hard at training as they do not need an excuse for poor performance because they do not consider poor performance to be an option. Self-handicapping is therefore a way to manage the impression you make to others, by protecting your self-esteem which might be damaged by any performance deficit (Carron et al., 2004). Self-handicapping will also reduce progress as the dancer is not being honest about what may be limiting their skill acquisition or performance quality. The energy being put into making excuses should be channelled into mastering the skill that is lacking.

Social physique anxiety

Social physique anxiety can be defined as 'concerns with others' evaluations of one's physique rather than bodily concerns that involve one's ability to perform certain physical task' (Hart, Leary, & Rejeski, 1989, p. 96). As the purpose of dance is to present movement of the body to an audience for scrutiny, social physique anxiety is an issue for some dancers. This may be compounded by the scrutiny of others and self-scrutiny through studio mirrors (Hausenblas, Brewer, & van Raalte, 2004). Often considered a trait issue, it is predominant in females and has been linked to disordered eating, therefore making this an area of concern.

The amount of scrutiny that the dancer feels is placed on them may explain why the levels of social physique anxiety experienced by individual dancers is greater than that of partnered dancers (Oliver, 2008) or group performers (Gay, Monsma, & Torres-McGehee, 2011). When dancing alone, you are aware that all eyes are on you, whereas when dancing as a group there are more dancers for the audience to focus on, reducing the level of anxiety.

Perfectionism

Perfectionism is a multidimensional personality trait, and has been defined as 'striving for flawlessness and setting exceedingly high standards for performance, accompanied by tendencies for overly critical evaluations' (Stoeber, 2011, p. 128). Perfectionism, in a situational context, can be good for generating high quality performance which enhances our self-worth, but as a trait it can sometimes be counterproductive due to a lack of ability to control these thoughts (Eusanio, Thomson, & Jaque, 2014).

Perfectionism is considered multidimensional as there are two interacting dimensions; perfectionistic striving and perfectionistic concerns (Stoeber, 2011). *Perfectionist striving* is an approach-based motivation, where the dancer is aiming to achieve perfection. This type of perfectionism increases the likelihood of performance standards being met as achievable goals are set, and strategies devised to achieve these goals, whereas *perfectionistic concern* relates to an emotional, avoidance-based state. The dancer will be preoccupied with potential errors and the consequences of any such mistakes. This creates feelings of anxiety which may negatively affect performance quality (as will be discussed in more detail in Chapter 6). Perfectionistic striving is a cognitive function as the dancer will be thinking about how to make the performance right, whereas perfectionistic concern is an affective view as the dancer will be worried about how to avoid making mistakes. Those who are perfectionists will usually experience a mix of both perfectionist concerns and strivings. The impact this has on performance and well-being is dependent on the degree to which each form of perfectionism is experienced. The interaction of these dimensions is shown in Figure 2.8. Where a dancer strives to achieve, and has low perfectionist concerns, this may be viewed as healthy perfectionism, whereas high perfectionist strivings combined with high perfectionist concerns may be seen as negative.

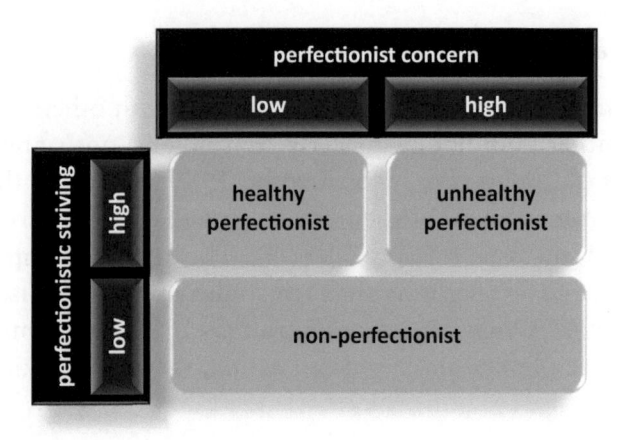

Figure 2.8
Multidimensional model of perfectionism

In Table 2.1 it can be seen that there are vitally different impacts dependent upon how perfectionism is expressed. This does not suggest that you are either one type or the other. Essentially the chances are that you will have varying degrees of both types, but it has become evident that the perfectionist concerns suppresses the perfectionist striving, reducing the positive outcomes of the striver (Stoeber, 2011).

Dancers tend to have higher levels of perfectionism than the general population, potentially due to the highly competitive nature of the profession (Eusanio et al., 2014). This may have an impact on our self-concept, mediated at times of failure by shame. Shame is a potent emotion creating feelings of inadequacy, inferiority and worthlessness, impacting negatively on self-esteem.

Table 2.1 Factors affected by perfectionism type

Factor	Perfectionistic striving	Perfectionistic concern
Affect	Positively related to positive mood. Higher positive affect when successful	Positively related to negative mood. Higher negative affect when failing
Anxiety	Positively related to self-confidence. Negatively related to somatic and cognitive anxiety	Positively related to somatic and cognitive anxiety. Poor at coping
Social physique anxiety*	Lower social physique anxiety	Higher social physique anxiety. Higher physical and psychological exhaustion
Body image*	Less body-related concerns	Higher body-related concerns
Motivation	Positively related to achieve success. Negatively related to avoidance of failure	Negatively related to achieve success. Positively related to avoidance of failure
Training	Increased performance	No effect
Performance	Increased performance	No effect

Source: Based on Stoeber (2011); *Cumming and Duda (2012).

PRACTICE

Feedback

Verbal

Getting feedback is a vital component in the acquisition and development of skills, without which it would be difficult to know if we were progressing in the right direction, but it is important that the feedback we get is constructive and accurate. It is also important that teachers know how to maximise the manner in which feedback is given by understanding its impact on our sense of self. Being mindful of individual differences and personal issues that may be concerning individual dancers when giving feedback can increase its effectiveness.

The point of feedback is that once the technique and choreography have been learnt, the feedback can be withdrawn so performance becomes independent – you would not expect your teacher to be shouting instructions from the wings, mid-performance!

Corrections

Verbal feedback ensures that the dancers are getting accurate information regarding their performance rather than relying on their own interpretation of their performance, or comparisons to others (Radell, 2012). Ensure that there is parity of constructive feedback to all group members. This will ensure that each dancer has something to work on, however small, and they feel that their performance has not been ignored. Feedback from a role model will not only inform their technical ability but also develops their feelings of self-efficacy.

Praise

As well as technical instruction, it is important to feel that progression is being made to increase self-efficacy. Even if there has not been a demonstrable improvement in the task set, praise can be given for other factors. For example, where there is a lack of improvement in technique, praise could be given for determination, application or characterisation.

Individual difference

It is important to remember that we are all different in how we perceive situations and how we relate to others. Consideration of these differences can be important when giving and receiving feedback.

Receiving feedback

Different teachers or choreographers may respond to the same performance in different ways for different reasons. It may be that their personality makes them more abrupt or less tolerant than others. When receiving feedback, consider who the sender is and do not take it personally when feedback is offered in a negative manner.

Alternatively, feedback may be abrupt due to time constraints. The nearer to the first night, the more fraught the director may be to get things right. They may be abrupt in their direction because there is limited time to review the issue, or they may be abrupt due to pressures from other elements of technical rehearsals not going to plan. In such circumstances try not to take the manner of feedback personally.

Offering feedback

As a teacher, it will become evident that dancers progress at different rates due to their inherent ability or due to other situational factors. Knowing that it takes a certain dancer longer to pick up the initial choreography indicates that there is no point pushing her on this as it will only serve to increase anxiety levels. Sometimes dancers may be affected by situations and life events outside of the studio, so allowing for the impact that this has on performance, and offering more supportive feedback, will minimise the negative impact that this may have in the studio.

We all experience an off-day from time to time, where previously acquired skills are suddenly unachievable. This may be due to external distractions or physiological issues, so constant critiques of the downturn in performance are unlikely to be helpful, and only serve to embarrass the dancer in front of their peers. Instead, try a supportive response, making light of the temporary change if appropriate.

Visual

One of the defining aspects of the studio is the wall of mirrors. The mirror is there to aid the dancer's understanding of their technique by giving real-time feedback, but this can be counter-productive for a range of reasons.

First, for the ultimate performance the dancer needs to be able to perform the piece without visual feedback at some point. The feedback that they need to be relying on is proprioception, which is the dancer's ability to feel where their limbs are without having to see them.

Second, the mirrors allow too much scrutiny of one's body, increasing the chance of self-criticism and body dissatisfaction.

Third, while being able to look at ourselves in the mirror, we also have the opportunity to look at others. This unavoidable reflection may heighten the chance of social comparison and affect our judgements of our ability and our body. If we make negative comparisons between ourselves and our peers, this may affect our self-esteem.

Directed activity

To maximise the use of mirrors in class, and reduce negative perceptions that dancers may have at being confronted with the class refection, teachers should ensure that clear instruction is given. By directing the dancers' attention to their arm placement or leg extension the dancers' concentration will be drawn to that area and distracted from negative comparisons and evaluations.

Technique development

Use the mirror sparingly early in the learning phase of a new skill. This will give the dancers the ability to compare their image to the teacher's. Once they have the basics of the skill, cover the mirror or rotate the class away from the mirrors so the dancer learns to feel the movement, which is their ultimate aim.

Once they have basics of the manoeuvre, they may then face the mirror to enhance facets of the action, but maintain limited access to this (IADMS, 2012).

Choreography

As we all learn at different rates, it may take dancers different times to learn a set piece. It can be quite stressful if a dancer feels that she is not learning at the same rate as others, and the mirror might increase the awareness of this. To reduce this and to increase the dancer's focus on themselves, do not use mirrors through the early stages of learning a piece. Once there is an element of coherence within the troupe, and you are ready to refine the piece, then use the mirrors to help the dancers come together as one.

Body image

If you feel that there may be concerns about how the dancers feel about their body, especially if you are working with a competitive group of adolescents or a leisure class, it may be useful to reduce the opportunity for scrutiny of the body. This can be achieved through turning away from mirrors, or encourage loose fitting clothes. Having baggy t-shirts printed with the dance school logo can overcome any stigma and increase group cohesion as we will see in Chapter 5.

Being aware of your self-concept

Compartmentalisation

It is easy to judge your life and abilities by how you feel in the moment, and never is this more so than at a time of failure or disappointment. It is therefore important to be able to view yourself in a more objective manner by compartmentalisation. This is the ability to separate elements of your life into different aspects, and assess each aspect independent of other aspects.

Your role as a dancer

Dance can be all-consuming due to the commitment required while training, and the impact on your personal life if appearing in a stage show. Due to the amount of time dance may take up, it is natural to define yourself as a dancer, but this may be at the expense of many other aspects of your life. In order to compartmentalise, first, you need to acknowledge what other roles you have in your life, and then ensure that there are times dedicated to engaging in these roles.

If your life is overly consumed by your identity as a dancer, you may need to employ strategies to help move between your life roles.

Training

Try to create a ritual at the end of a day in training where putting your shoes away in a locker or bag signifies the end of dancing for the day. The commute home can be used to mentally digest the events of the day and plan for the next day. If the plans for tomorrow continue to buzz around your mind when you get home, write them down as a way of parking them safely, where they can be picked up again in the morning.

Stage

If you are engaged in a show, especially if you are out on the road, it is even more important to separate out your *dancing day* from the rest of your life, as you may well be living and travelling with the rest of the cast. Time compartmentalisation may be required where you identify time zones dedicated to the other roles in your life, such as socialising (even if it is through social media or other electronic correspondence), and trying to engage in the non-dance-related activities that you would do at home. Compartmentalise time spent with the cast outside of training and performances by banning dance talk at certain times.

Skills and mastery

It is not possible to be excellent at everything so it is important that realistic assessments are made about different aspects of your dance skills. Some dancers pick up and retain choreography effortlessly, while others have amazing turning skills. Indeed, some of these abilities may even be genetic, giving the dancer a natural flair for something, whereas others are skills that may have been adopted early and are well learnt.

Self-efficacy requires that you acknowledge each element of dance performance and not judge your ability as a dancer by your poorest technical ability. A strategic way to achieve this is through *performance profiling* which will be examined in more detail in Chapter 3.

Dealing with perfection

Perfection

There is no such thing as perfection, be that the perfect body or the perfect performance, so it is important to make this clear.

A healthy body image comprises of having a positive view of your body regardless of its actual shape and size; acceptance of body weight, shape and any imperfections; and showing respect for your body by engaging in healthy behaviours and rejection of the media ideal (Grogan, 2017).

Body type

Essentially there is no perfect body type for any form of dance. Although more classical forms of dance have promoted idealised body shapes, even these have evolved over time. If dancers with skills avoid their preferred dance genre because they feel they do not have the right body type, then dance will not evolve into a more equitable profession.

To some degree there is little we can do about our bodies – they are genetically set to be a shape, size and proportion. The only element that remains changeable to some degree is our weight, but too much focus on this can lead to a range of physiological and psychological problems that will impede your dance practice. Dieting and over-exercise can weaken your body, which is the most vital tool of your trade, so do not compromise its effectiveness. A balanced diet and training routine will help you achieve the skills you desire and your body will adapt to reflect this. Therefore, focus on your individual skills, deciding what you need to improve on, and ensure any specific training is based on fitness not aesthetics.

Avoid comparing your body to others, but focus on what you need to work on as an individual. Bear in mind that having an ideal body shape or size does not guarantee any level of technical skill or stage presence.

Dance performance

What is perfection, and who decides whether something is perfect? Acknowledging that there is no such thing as perfection is a step towards a positive mindset with respect to your own dance ability and skills.

Performance errors

To overcome *perfectionist concerns* first ask yourself, *'If you make a performance error, what is the worst thing that can happen?'*

First, it is worth considering, who would even notice? Obviously you would, and possibly (but not necessarily) fellow performers might. It is less likely that the audience would. And even if they did, this would be one tiny moment, in one dance, in one show. So again, ask yourself, *'What is the worst that can happen as a result of one error?'*

Remember your role

Too much emphasis can be placed on the technical aspects of dancing when an audience have come to experience a spectacle. There are very few members of the audience who will know what technical perfection is, so consider what your role is within the production and ensure that those needs are being met, be it characterisation, synchronisation or storytelling.

Dance ability

In the same way as the Paralympics has inspired disabled people from around the world to embrace the possibilities, the same is happening within dance. Around the globe dance companies are pushing the boundaries of dance, from Indian amputees performing highly technical Bharatanatyam dances in wheelchairs, and ballet companies for Down's Syndrome dancers, through to integrated companies involving physical and mentally disabled dancers alongside non-disabled dancers.

Not only do these companies challenge the idealised body image, they also challenge society's perceptions as to what dance is and who can be involved – challenging the notion of perfection.

Realistic expectation

Acknowledging the self

Although no one is perfect, to some degree, the understanding of our imperfections can be motivating and help push us harder, but what we are aiming for needs to be realistic and achievable so it does not become self-destructive. Where these ideals come from may vary. It may be the result of exposure to the media, pressure from others, or an internalisation of these factors affecting your self-concept. Reviewing where these ideals originate from, and what impact they may have on you as a dancer is important for body and dance satisfaction.

Ideal self

Obviously we can always do more to improve, but first consider what is your concept of *ideal*, and where it comes from. If you are sure that your ideal self is realistic and achievable, then incremental steps towards achievement must be taken, otherwise a subsequent lack of success may be demotivating.

If the ideal self is related to body size, reflect where your notion of ideal originates. If it is media-based, go back to the magazines that are setting the standard for you, and look at the photographs throughout an entire issue and think about the variety of body sizes and shapes portrayed, and consider these questions:

- Do they reflect the people you see around you?
- Is there a possibility that the photos have been edited?
- Would working towards this body shape be achievable?
- How would it improve your performance?

Remember that a body shape or size does not predict dance ability, instead try to focus on dance-related elements that you would like to achieve, and take steps towards skill development, rather than focusing on the ideal body.

Ought self

If you feel you are not as you *ought* to be, then consider who is setting the agenda for how you ought to be. It suggests that you are dissatisfied with yourself due to the needs and standards of others, and not for yourself.

If you feel the standard of how you ought to be is coming from others, consider the motives and expertise of those putting the pressure on:

- If it is a family member – are they qualified to make such recommendations?
- If it is a dance peer – why are they not focusing on their own performance instead of trying to manage yours?
- If it is a teacher – are they giving sufficient information about what the outcomes of these changes will be with respect to your dance practice?
- If in doubt, consult other sources for a balanced view of the situation.

Ultimately, having taken advice, review your progress. If you do not feel this is the right change for you, reconsider whether it is interfering with your practice or satisfaction.

SELF-PERCEPTION

Dealing with advice

Role models

We are not born knowing everything and in many aspects of life we benefit from hearing about the experiences of others. Those who can offer some of the best advice are those within the profession, such as teachers, directors, and mentors.

When to listen

Dance teachers are a font of knowledge due to their training and professional experiences. Much can be learnt by listening to their tales, both their successes and failures, but remember that you are your own person and consider if and how this may apply to you and your career.

Part of their wealth of experiences is an understanding of potential. This will make them best placed to evaluate your performance, rather than your own subjective interpretation of how you are progressing. Embrace perfectionist strivings, but acknowledge that other professionals may have a better understanding as to the realistic rate to show development.

Manage the perfectionist concerns by taking the advice given by the professionals. Not only their constructive feedback for technical progression, but also praise for skills and efforts applied. There is no point in them offering supportive praise if it is not accepted.

When to ignore

Be inspired by the life, performance and advice of others – but do not be bound by it. You are an individual with your unique talents and desires. Every dancer's life is different, so be true to yourself. Listen and make judgements as to what is relevant to you and your situation. Just because it worked for them does not mean that it is transferable to you, times change and their experiences may be too dated to be of value.

Significant others

Those who are important in your life will tend to want the best for you, but they should not be living their lives through you. Bear in mind that the qualifications of friends, family and peers are limited to knowing you as they do, and probably not any knowledge of the career path that you wish to follow.

When to listen

When friends and family are offering support and advice on non-dance-related aspects, such as time management or finance, this may be of benefit. They may also see physical or psychological changes in you over time and can suggest that you are working too hard. Reflect on their comments as they can stand back from the situation where you cannot, and consult others for corroboration. Weight loss or personality change might be a symptom of other problems which may need intervention.

When to ignore

Consider the qualifications and agendas of family, friends and peers when offering technical or career advice as they may not be best placed to offer it. Although they may want the best for you, this does not mean that they understand the profession, and their advice may conflict with that being offered by those directly related to your career path.

Equally challenge comments or advice regarding not being the ideal body size for your chosen genre. The focus should be on skill development, and too much emphasis on body size and shape may lead to physical and psychological problems.

Self

As a unique individual, you need to consider who you are, where you are going, and how best to get there. Do not forget you are also dynamic in your wants and needs, so it is fine to change direction. Indeed, it may not be possible to pursue your favoured career from the outset, but taking opportunities that are less than ideal may allow you to acquire experience and meet the people who may help you into preferred career.

When to listen

At the end of the day, it is your body, and your career, so you must be true to yourself. If the advice you've taken is taking away the enjoyment, this will ultimately lead to demotivation, where you find yourself going through the motions. A disconnection with the dance may become evident in your performance.

Equally, if you find the advice you have taken, especially with respect to diet and training schedules, is impacting on your physical health, stamina and energy levels, then again it is vital to listen to your body. Everyone's body responds differently, so what may suit one dancer may be counterproductive to another.

> **When to ignore**
>
> When you realise that you are being led along a certain path motivated by external factors, then it is time to reconsider the purpose of your actions. Dance requires such commitment that it must be done for the pleasure and not the desire to please others. These feelings should trigger a review of your career path.

> **Key concepts glossary**
>
> **Body image** The thoughts and feelings an individual has over the way that their body looks.
>
> **Impression management** How an individual presents themselves to others in order to be seen in a specific way.
>
> **Perfectionism** A drive to achieve perfection in our pursuits.
>
> **Self-concept** The view we have of all the aspects that make us who we are.
>
> **Self-efficacy** The confidence we have in our abilities in specific tasks.
>
> **Self-esteem** The value or worth that one places upon oneself.
>
> **Self-handicapping** Behaviours adopted to excuse poor performance as a means of protecting our self-esteem.
>
> **Self-regulation** The adoption of different behaviours to help retain self-esteem.
>
> **Social physique anxiety** An emotional response to worries about how others may view our body.

References

Abraham, S. (1996). Characteristics of eating disorders among young ballet dancers. *Psychopathology, 29,* 223–229.

Bandura, A. (1994). Self-efficacy. In V. S. Ramachaudran (Ed.), *Encyclopedia of human behavior* (Vol. 4, pp. 71–81). New York: Academic Press.

Brown, J. D. (1998). *The self.* Boston: McGraw-Hill.

Carron, A. V., Burke, S. V., & Prapavessis, H. (2004). Self-presentation and group influence. *Journal of Applied Sport Psychology, 16*(1), 41–58. doi:10.1080/10413200490260044.

Cumming, J., & Duda, J. L. (2012). Profiles of perfectionism, body-related concerns, and indicators of psychological health in vocational dance students: An investigation of the 2 × 2 model of perfectionism. *Psychology of Sport and Exercise, 13*(6), 729–738. doi:10.1016/j.psychsport.2012.05.004.

Eusanio, J., Thomson, P., & Jaque, S. V. (2014). Perfectionism, shame, and self-concept in dancers: A mediation analysis. *Journal of Dance Medicine & Science, 18*(3), 106–114. doi:10.12678/1089-313X.18.3.106.

Festinger, L. (1954). A theory of social comparison processes. *Human Relations, 7*(2), 117–140. doi:doi:10.1177/001872675400700202.

Gay, J. L., Monsma, E. V., & Torres-McGehee, T. M. (2011). Developmental and contextual risks of social physique anxiety among female athletes. *Research Quarterly for Exercise and Sport, 82*(2), 168–177. doi:10.1080/02701367.2011.10599744.

Grogan, S. (2017). *Body image: Understanding body dissatisfaction in men, women and children.* London: Routledge.

Hart, E. A., Leary, M. R., & Rejeski, W. J. (1989). The measurement of social physique anxiety. *Journal of Sport and Exercise Psychology, 11*(1), 94–104. doi:10.1123/jsep.11.1.94.

Hausenblas, H. A., Brewer, B. W., & van Raalte, J. L. (2004). Self-presentation and exercise. *Journal of Applied Sport Psychology, 16*(1), 3–18. doi:10.1080/10413200490260026.

Heiland, T. L., Murray, D. S., & Edley, P. P. (2008). Body image of dancers in Los Angeles: The cult of slenderness and media influence among dance students. *Research in Dance Education, 9*(3), 257–275. doi:10.1080/14647890802386932.

IADMS. (2012). Handout 4: Considerations for mirror use in teaching dance. *International Association for Dance Medicine & Science Bulletin for Teachers, 4*(1), 15.

Krayer, A., Ingledew, D. K., & Iphofen, R. (2008). Social comparison and body image in adolescence: A grounded theory approach. *Health Education Research, 23*(5), 892–903. doi:10.1093/her/cym076.

Langdon, S. W., & Petracca, G. (2010). Tiny dancer: Body image and dancer identity in female modern dancers. *Body Image, 7*(4), 360–363. doi:10.1016/j.bodyim.2010.06.005.

Leary, M. R., & Kowalski, R. M. (1990). Impression management: A literature review and two-component model. *Psychological Bulletin, 107*, 34–47.

Martin Ginis, K. A., & Leary, M. R. (2004). Self-presentational processes in health-damaging behavior. *Journal of Applied Sport Psychology, 16*(1), 59–74. doi:10.1080/10413200490260053.

McConnell, A. R., & Strain, L. M. (2007). Content and structure of the self-concept. In C. Sedikides, & S. Spencer (Eds.), *The self in social psychology*. New York: Psychology Press.

Oliver, W. (2008). Body image in the dance class. *Journal of Physical Education, Recreation & Dance, 79*(5), 18–41. doi:10.1080/07303084.2008.10598178.

Radell, S. A. (2012). Body image and mirror use in the ballet class. *International Association for Dance Medicine & Science Bulletin for Teachers, 4*(1), 10–13.

Ravaldi, C., Vannacci, A., Bolognesi, E., Mancini, S., Faravelli, C., & Ricca, V. (2006). Gender role, eating disorder symptoms, and body image concern in ballet dancers. *Journal of Psychosomatic Research, 61*(4), 529–535. doi:10.1016/j.jpsychores.2006.04.016.

Rosenberg, M., Schooler, C., Schoenbach, C., & Rosenberg, F. (1995). Global self-esteem and specific self-esteem: Different concepts, different outcomes *American Sociological Review, 60*(1), 141–156.

Statt, D. A. (1998). *The concise dictionary of psychology.* London: Routledge.

Stoeber, J. (2011). The dual nature of perfectionism in sports: Relationships with emotion, motivation, and performance. *International Review of Sport and Exercise Psychology, 4*(2), 128–145. doi:10.1080/1750984X.2011.604789.

Swami, V., & Tovée, M. J. (2009). A comparison of actual-ideal weight discrepancy, body appreciation, and media influence between street-dancers and non-dancers. *Body Image, 6*(4), 304–307. doi:10.1016/j.bodyim.2009.07.006.

Tiggemann, M., Coutts, E., & Clark, L. (2014). Belly dance as an embodying activity?: A test of the embodiment model of positive body image. *Sex Roles, 71*(5), 197–207. doi:10.1007/s11199-014-0408-2.

Van den Berg, P., Paxton, S. J., Keery, H., Wall, M., Guo, J., & Neumark-Sztainer, D. (2007). Body dissatisfaction and body comparison with media images in males and females. *Body Image, 4*(3), 257–268. doi:10.1016/j.bodyim.2007.04.003.

Van den Berg, P., Thompson, J. K., Obremski-Brandon, K., & Coovert, M. (2002). The Tripartite Influence model of body image and eating disturbance: A covariance structure modeling investigation testing the mediational role of appearance comparison. *Journal of Psychosomatic Research, 53*(5), 1007–1020. doi:10.1016/S0022-3999(02)00499-3.

Van Zelst, L., Clabaugh, A., & Morling, B. (2004). Dancers' body esteem, fitness esteem, and self-esteem in three contexts. *Journal of Dance Education, 4*(2), 48–57. doi:10.1080/15290824.2004.10387256.

Further reading

Grogan, S. (2017). *Body image: Understanding body dissatisfaction in men, women and children.* London Routledge.

Leary, M. R., & Kowalski, R. M. (1990). Impression management: A literature review and two-component model. *Psychological Bulletin, 107*, 34–47.

Mainwaring, L. M., & Krasnow, D. H. (2010). Teaching the dance class: Strategies to enhance skill acquisition, mastery and positive self-image. *Journal of Dance Education, 10*(1), 14–21.

Sabiston, C. M., Pila, E., Pinsonnault-Bilodeau, G., & Cox, A. E. (2014). Social physique anxiety experiences in physical activity: A comprehensive synthesis of research studies focused on measurement, theory, and predictors and outcomes. *International Review of Sport and Exercise Psychology, 7*(1), 158–183.

CHAPTER 3

Motivation

> **Learning outcomes**
>
> By the end of this chapter readers should be able to:
>
> - recognise why motivation is important to dancers
> - define key terms related to motivation
> - describe different theories of motivation
> - explain how different forms of motivation may impact upon dance performance
> - propose ways to encourage positive forms of motivation within dance practice

CONTEXT

Motivation is an internal state that drives behaviour to achieve your needs and goals. Need is an important factor in motivation as it suggests a deficiency – if you need something this suggests that you currently don't possess it. In order to achieve this need, action will have to be taken, therefore we are driven to change or sustain a behaviour. So far this sounds as though the drive is an internal factor, but motivation is far more complex than this. Your motivation is often affected by social factors too, this may include your family, peers, dance teacher or director. It is this complex interaction of thoughts and experiences that impact on our motivation.

Motivation is required at all levels of engagement with dance. It is required to embark on, adhere to, apply effort to and persist in an activity. To initiate an engagement with dance, there needs to be an element of motivation to embark on the new activity at the outset. To arrive at a new class, and to start an activity you may never have done before requires drive. To stick at the activity while having to learn the basics requires sustained levels of motivation, especially if there is little immediate success. Even if the activity is only continued at a recreational level, there needs to be the drive to adhere to it when there are so many pressures on our time.

If we decide to take dancing to the next level, there will be the need to adhere to training routines in order to pass exams. If we take a step further towards a professional career, it will take great effort and persistence to drive the career forward, often competing against others for roles, and maintaining motivation after rejections. Motivation will need to be maintained when the odds are stacked against you, and you have no control over the outcomes. Even when you have made it to the West End, possibly performing in eight shows per week, you must still be motivated to perform each night to the best of your ability to give the audience what they have paid for.

To get to the top requires hard work, which is a product of motivation. Reality television shows, such as *Britain's Got Talent* and *Got to Dance*, have helped create an instant celebrity culture, giving the impression that anyone can become famous overnight just by entering. There are no real shortcuts. Even the street dance troupe Diversity had been working at their trade for two years before winning *Britain's Got Talent* in 2009, so what looks like an overnight success comes from years of practice with high and low points. Motivation is key; motivation to train hard and motivation to perform to your potential.

So where does motivation come from? As individuals we will all have our drives to engage in different activities, but this can be enhanced, or indeed reduced, by our interactions with others – most especially our teachers. Teachers who adopt a motivational climate that matches your personal needs can help enhance performance and even well-being in recreational dance situations (Goulimaris, Mavridis, Genti, & Rokka, 2014).

THEORY

The Hierarchical Model

The Hierarchical Model is a theory that has been developed by different researchers over time creating a complex, but more inclusive explanation of motivation. Each aspect of this model shown in Figure 3.1 will be considered.

Motivational hierarchy

Motivation is not a singular drive; it is dependent on many factors. To help consider these factors Vallerand (2001) argues that there are three levels of

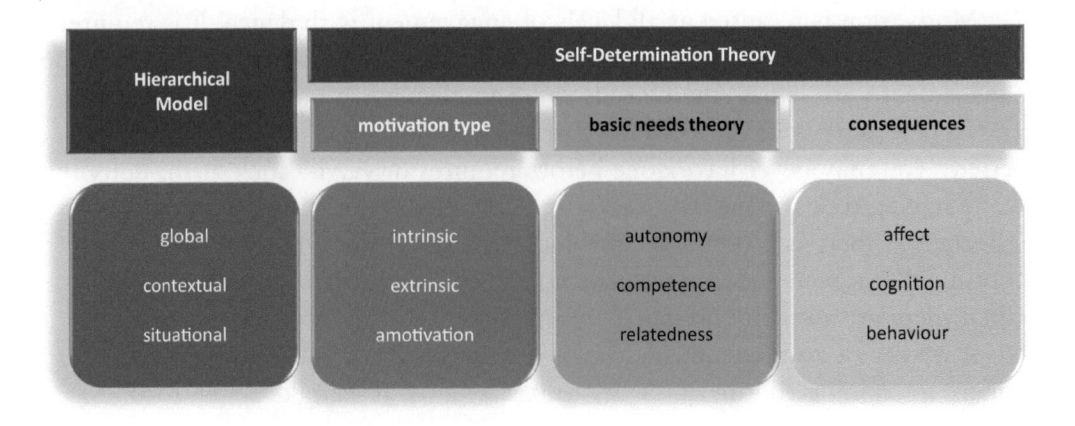

Hierarchical Model	Self-Determination Theory		
	motivation type	basic needs theory	consequences
global	intrinsic	autonomy	affect
contextual	extrinsic	competence	cognition
situational	amotivation	relatedness	behaviour

Figure 3.1
The Hierarchical Model

motivation. There is your *global* level, which refers to your typical level of motivation. This drive is quite stable and therefore may be seen as a trait or disposition. This does not suggest that someone who has a high global drive will approach all facets of their life with the same motivational drive, this will depend on the context. The *contextual* level suggests that you will be motivated differently towards your dancing than you might be to your academic work, and differently again with respect to your weekend job. Even within these contexts we may not necessarily be constant in our motivation. This state-related motivation is referred to as *situational*, and helps us understand the daily inconsistencies in our behaviour.

Motivation type

Intrinsic motivation

Intrinsic motivation is the drive to undertake an activity based on our interest, enjoyment and confidence. Due to the deep engagement and satisfaction we derive from an intrinsically motivated activity we are more likely to produce an improved performance, persist for longer and adhere to programmes (Thogersen-Ntoumani, Shephard, Ntoumanis, Wagenmakers, & Shaw, 2016), which has positive impacts on self-esteem and well-being (Ryan & Deci, 2000).

Vallerand (2001) suggests that intrinsic motivation is not a simple love of the activity, but that this may be broken down into three more discrete internal drives. The first type of intrinsic motivation is the drive *to know*. This is the drive to learn and explore; it is intellectual and curiosity-driven. This would include the academic study of dance, its historical, social and cultural contexts, as well as the understanding of the physical body and the techniques of the genre. At a performance level there is the motivation *to accomplish*, which is the drive to improve and master your technique. Finally, there is the drive *to stimulation*. This is the sensory element combined with pleasure, which may be enhanced by the opportunity to learn new choreography or work collaboratively. This is the enjoyment through to peak performance where flow may be experienced.

Cognitive Evaluation Theory

Unfortunately there are factors which may reduce our intrinsic motivation therefore *Cognitive Evaluation Theory* seeks to explain what factors help or hinder intrinsic motivation (Ryan, Williams, Patrick, & Deci, 2009). The types of conditions that thwart intrinsic motivation are negative social forces, or situational factors such as deadlines, or challenges that are beyond the competency level of the performer. These forces diminish the enjoyment of the activity and therefore reduce the intrinsic motivation to engage (Ryan et al., 2009). This is not to say that we will always enjoy every aspect of our dance-related activities, training can be gruelling and choreography may have to be learnt within deadlines, but the important factor is that there is still the drive for the performance element.

Extrinsic motivation

If we are not intrinsically motivated to undertake an activity, and yet are still motivated to take part, that form of motivation may be considered *extrinsic*. This is the performance of a behaviour where the drive is not for the enjoyment of the activity, but to satisfy an external need or achieve a separate outcome (Ryan & Deci, 2000). There are inherent problems with externally motivated behaviour. The less intrinsic motivation you may have for the activity, the less interested you will be, therefore less effort may be expended in its pursuit, leading to a poorer performance (Ryan & Deci, 2000). As it is the external outcome that is the aim, rather than pleasure derived from the activity, there is the increased likelihood of cheating (Ozdemir Oz, Lane, & Michou, 2016). Extrinsic motivation can be broken down into four levels of behavioural regulation as can be seen in Figure 3.2.

- *External regulation* may occur when we are motivated to achieve something that is disconnected from the enjoyment of dance, which may include rewards, punishment or compliance. If we engage in dance purely for the rewards, such as being employed on a long-term contract in a show you do not enjoy, then doing the job solely for the money may result in alienation from the performance (Ryan & Deci, 2000). This does not mean that dancers should not be paid for performances, or win trophies if in competitions, but these rewards must be related to levels of competence, and engagement must be for the love of the activity (Deci & Ryan, 2008).
- *Introjected regulation* is the drive to take part because of the pressure put on you by others, such as guilt from controlling teachers or demands made by pushy parents (Ryan et al., 2009). This may also be the pressure you put on yourself to outperform others, and an inability to meet these external forces results in negative emotional experiences. These may include frustration, leading to anger or anxiety, alternatively there may be feelings of guilt or shame at underperformance.

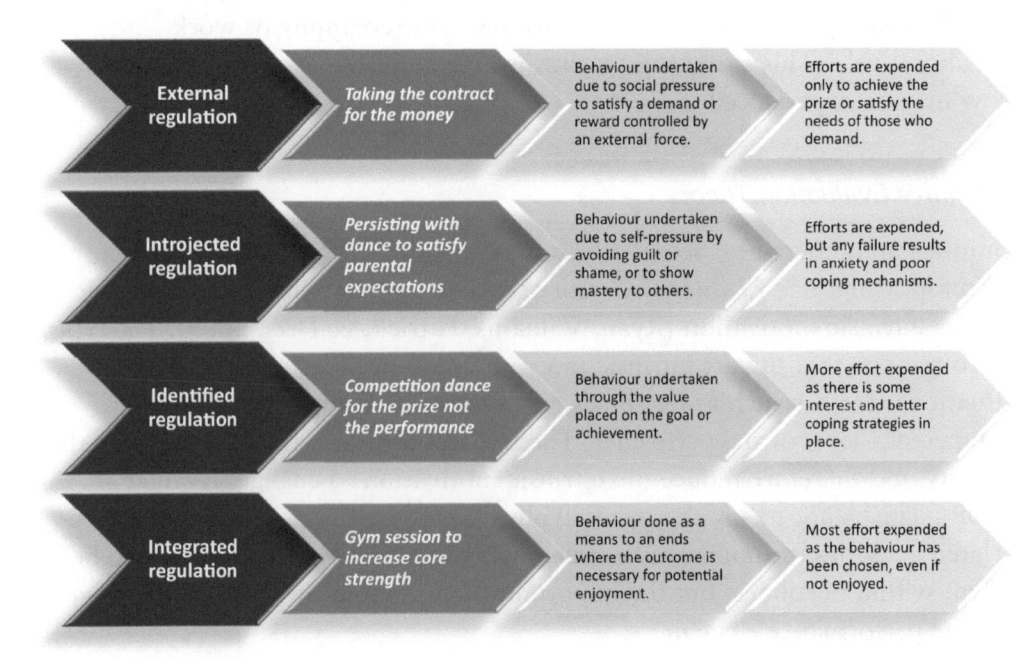

Regulation	Example	Behaviour	Effort
External regulation	Taking the contract for the money	Behaviour undertaken due to social pressure to satisfy a demand or reward controlled by an external force.	Efforts are expended only to achieve the prize or satisfy the needs of those who demand.
Introjected regulation	Persisting with dance to satisfy parental expectations	Behaviour undertaken due to self-pressure by avoiding guilt or shame, or to show mastery to others.	Efforts are expended, but any failure results in anxiety and poor coping mechanisms.
Identified regulation	Competition dance for the prize not the performance	Behaviour undertaken through the value placed on the goal or achievement.	More effort expended as there is some interest and better coping strategies in place.
Integrated regulation	Gym session to increase core strength	Behaviour done as a means to an ends where the outcome is necessary for potential enjoyment.	Most effort expended as the behaviour has been chosen, even if not enjoyed.

Figure 3.2 Impact of regulation on behaviour and effort

- *Identified regulation* may occur when it is not the performance per se that is important, but the ability to say you achieved the level, therefore the focus is on the product of performance (exam certificate) rather than the process (dance performance).
- Even if we love dancing there will be some factors that can be considered extrinsically motivated, such as enduring a daily gruelling barre session or strength and conditioning exercises because we know they will improve our core strength, which in turn will enhance our performance. This is defined as *integrated regulation* as it is a freely chosen behaviour that may support the process of dance. Self-regulation is the degree to which we absorb social values and integrate them as our own, and the more we internalise them as our own values, the more we are likely to expend effort and cope better with poor performance. This can be seen as regulation moves from external regulation (doing the strength and conditioning class as part of your employment contract) to integrated regulation (engaging in the strength and conditioning class because we know it will be good for our practice).

Amotivation

Both intrinsic and extrinsic motivation leads to engagements with an activity – but for different ends, this is not the case if we are *amotivated* (Vallerand, 2001). When amotivated, there is an unwillingness to undertake the behaviour, therefore this is a state we may wish to avoid or prevent. This may lead to three different forms of reduced engagement:

- not to undertake the behaviour
- to do so but not feel any personal value in the contribution made
- to do so but feel incompetent. (Ryan & Deci, 2000)

This would lead to dancers giving up, or only going through the motions.

Basic Needs Theory

The social environment is very important for motivation as what others say and do affects our self-perceptions and self-efficacy. Therefore, in order to enhance the chance of dancers being intrinsically motivated, there are social conditions that must be met that relate to autonomy, relatedness, and competence (Ryan & Deci, 2000).

Autonomy

Autonomy is the individual's belief that their behaviour is self-determined and not controlled by others – the act of choosing to do something. Indeed, one of the reasons that dancers have cited choosing a career in dance is because of the autonomy it allows them (Aujla & Farrer, 2015). Therefore, the more internalised the regulation of behaviour, as shown in Figure 3.3, the higher the degree of autonomy we may feel we have (Ryan & Deci, 2000). Although autonomy hints at working alone, autonomy is important when working in

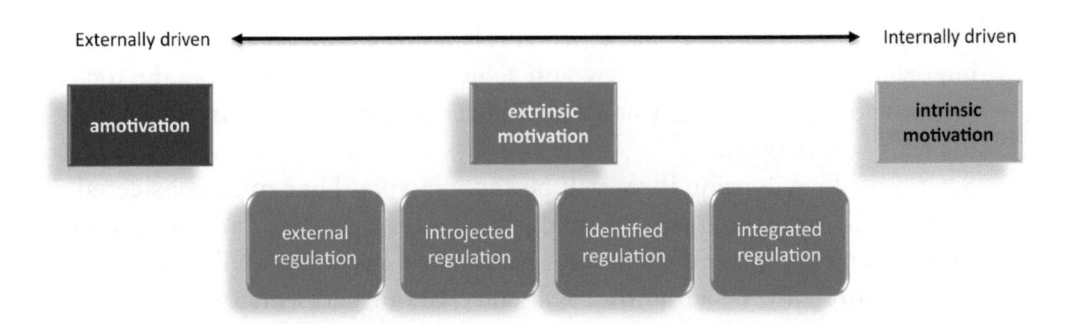

Figure 3.3 Levels of motivational autonomy

groups, as when working together we still need to feel we have control over our choices.

Working in an autonomy-supportive climate leads to higher levels of satisfaction and engagement in the task (Ryan et al., 2009), and ultimately a better performance quality (Gillet, Vallerand, Amoura, & Baldes, 2010). When personal control has been lost, so has the initiative to undertake the activity, therefore, extrinsic motivation replaces our curiosity and enjoyment, a state that can become emotionally and physically exhausting (Adie, Duda, & Ntoumanis, 2008).

Relatedness

Relatedness occurs when we feel that the social climate is supportive, encouraging and informational, rather than controlling (Deci & Ryan, 2008). It is not only the teacher who contributes to a supportive climate, but the group members can also play a role, enhancing the feelings of connectedness through recognition and respect shown to each other (Ryan et al., 2009). Of the three basic needs, relatedness has been shown to be the strongest predictor of positive affect in dance classes (Quested, Duda, Ntoumanis, & Maxwell, 2013).

Competence

When undertaking an activity, we need to feel we have a level of competence, which we assess through social and environmental feedback and comparisons (Ryan & Deci, 2000). This may be experienced through your teacher's authentic recognition of your progress, or group members complimenting your skills. Competence can be encouraged through positive and constructive feedback when learning in a supportive environment (Vallerand, 2001), increasing the likelihood of internalisation of knowledge and skill, leading to intrinsic motivation (Ryan & Deci, 2000).

Feelings of competence are vital when there is an emphasis on performance quality, where negative feelings of competence predicted negative affect in both rehearsal and performances, as these situations will be under scrutiny by colleagues, family and the public (Quested et al., 2013).

Consequences

The outcomes of basic needs being met are that we will have a positive attitude towards our performance. At an affective level there will be positive emotions

© Shutterstock

felt about what we are engaged in as we are intrinsically motivated. The intrinsic motivation increases our desire to learn more and process corrections. The cognitive and affective components lead to more dedication and application, resulting in a positive work ethic and increased performance quality.

Achievement Goal Theory

Achievement goals

As dancers, there is a need to show continued development within your art, but there are several ways that this striving to achieve may be demonstrated, which will have different effects on performance and learning. These differences are initiated by our concept of ability, which forms the basis of *Achievement Goal Theory*. From a developmental perspective, until our teenage years, ability is seen as *undifferentiated*, where we do not understand the difference between effort and ability as factors that lead to success (White, 2007). Thereafter we may see ability as *differentiated* where we understand that we may demonstrate ability without putting in the effort (Nicholls, 1984). From this point on we tend to use strategies that align with our chosen perception of ability. These *achievement beliefs* will inform our *achievement goals*, which will in turn affect the behaviours we choose to achieve such goals (Roberts, Treasure, & Conroy, 2007). As these beliefs are developed early in life, they have a lasting effect on our orientation to performance of tasks; through either *task orientation* or *ego orientation* as dispositions (Figure 3.4). These dispositions then predict our future involvement with tasks, leading to *task involved* and *ego involved* states (Roberts, 2001).

Task orientation

Those who are *task oriented* continue to consider ability as undifferentiated, in that they apply effort to maximise their ability, and the success of this action

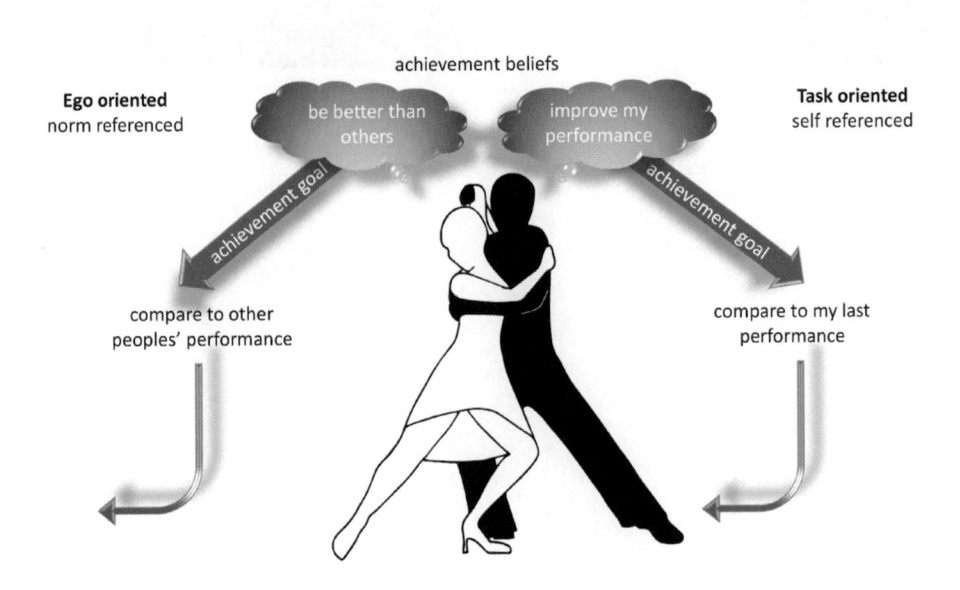

Figure 3.4
Task and ego orientation

allows them to learn, improve and gain mastery (Roberts, 2001). The behaviour is self-referenced, where we judge our performance by comparison to our personal previous performances.

The impact that this approach to performance has on behaviour is adaptive, enhancing the chances of further mastery. The resultant behaviours include increased persistence as only effort exerted will increase the chance of skill development. Those with this orientation will take on challenges as these will allow them to test their mastery by pushing themselves to the next level. The application and persistence are made possible due to their inherent interest in the task itself and the drive to master it (Roberts, 2001).

This orientation allows for the development of a healthy work ethic as success is perceived to be the product of hard work, therefore practice and training are valued. As the performance of other dancers is not a threat to their self-esteem, training is seen as an opportunity to increase group cohesion (Roberts, 2001).

Ego orientation

Alternatively, *ego orientation* is the result of differentiated beliefs about ability, where we demonstrate our competence by out-performing others, but with the minimum effort applied (Roberts, 2001). This orientation is norm-referenced where we compare our performance to that of other dancers, so we judge success or failure on our comparison to others.

Unlike task orientation, ego orientation requires a social comparison for judgements of competence to be made, but this does not mean that those who are ego oriented are necessarily competent at the tasks. Those who perceive themselves to be competent may also persist at the task as it will allow them more opportunities to demonstrate their superior ability against others. However, when a dancer believes their competence to be low, their strategies may be maladaptive. These individuals will not persist, as to do so will expose their comparative inability to others. This lack of persistence will ultimately reduce their chances to learn and improve. Their approach to challenges is twofold but with one aim – to guarantee a predictable outcome. To take on an easy challenge will guarantee success over the less competent. But equally, they may take on unachievable challenges as no one would predict success, therefore outcome is guaranteed, and if they do succeed, then all the better. Such an approach will impede learning and reduce the chance of mastery (Roberts, 2001).

There are impacts from this type of motivation. As the dancer cannot control the external factors, such as the ability of other dancers, this can lead to crises in self-confidence. It also impacts on attitudes about effort – as they believe superior ability is to expend as little effort as possible, as effort expenditure suggests a low ability. Therefore, they focus on performance opportunities and not on training, further reducing the chance of skill development.

Due to the focus that the ego oriented dancer may have on the performance of others, there is a trade-off with respect to the cognitive resources left available. When feedback for improvement is offered to ego oriented performers, its absorption is limited due to the mental resources being concentrated on the performance of others. There are other negative outcomes from ego orientation that are more sinister, where the drive to win at all costs may affect their moral compass and they are more likely to demonstrate aggressive, deceptive or immoral behaviour to demonstrate higher competence levels (Roberts, 2001).

Constructs

Nicholls (1984) argues that these are independent, orthogonal constructs. This means that we are not either task or ego oriented but may be high or low on either of the orientations. There are implications as to what impact the combinations of orientation may have on performance. It is unlikely that dancers who are low on both scales will reach great heights as they lack motivation for the activity, but it is entirely possible to be high on task and ego orientation. This dancer embraces the mastery qualities of task orientation, which allow her to develop mastery so she can demonstrate her superior ability in line with ego orientation. In addition, she may receive the admiration of others as confirmation that her mastery efforts have been successful (Carr, 2012). This suggest that ego orientation in itself is not necessarily negative, but it is the task orientation that moderates the maladaptive achievement strategies.

Motivational climate

Dancers' involvement with the task is not solely based on their own orientation towards achievement, but may be affected by their social environment (Figure 3.5). Those who are most likely to create a social environment are their parents, their peers and their teachers. Parents may have already played an instrumental role in the development of the dancer's orientation through early socialisation, and may continue to do so at a situational level, where their children adopt an involvement with the task, reflecting the type of involvement that they perceive their parents to have adopted (White, 2007). Children entering the Junior Latin Championships, encouraged by their parents to beat another couple are more likely to adopt an *ego involvement* with the competition, whereas those who are encouraged to 'go out and do their best' are more likely to be *task involved*.

Figure 3.5
Interaction between orientation, climate and involvement

Teachers are an enormous source inspiration for many dancers, so their approach to the training room may have a great impact on their learners, making them significant others, as we are driven to internalise the qualities and skills of those we greatly respect. The impact that this climate may have on the dancers' self-concept, esteem and performance is driven by the characteristics of the climate (Table 3.1).

Teachers who are perceived to be creating a *performance oriented climate* may lead dancers to adopt maladaptive achievement strategies though ego involvement. In this type of climate dancers may feel that their competency is threatened by the unacceptability of mistakes. The teacher's focus on success does not acknowledge individual's improvement. This type of climate has negative impacts on self-concept and esteem, increasing levels of anxiety and neurotic perfectionism (Nordin-Bates, 2012). Indeed, the fear of making mistakes acts as a distractor, which in itself has a negative impact on performance. The social impacts of increased competition between dancers includes peer conflict which reduces the group cohesion (an important factor that is discussed in more detail in Chapter 5) as well as distorted moral reasoning.

In contrast, teachers who are perceived to be creating a *mastery oriented climate* in their class are more likely to generate task involvement from their dancers, and the adoption of adaptive achievement strategies. On a personal level there will be greater levels of satisfaction and lower levels of burnout as dancers do not feel threatened by others and can concentrate on their own development. At a social level there are positive peer relationships with greater cohesion and a positive perception of the teacher. Research with elite and hip hop dancers has found that those experiencing a mastery oriented climate also felt that their basic needs of autonomy and relatedness had been met, increasing their satisfaction (Quested & Duda, 2008, 2009). This does not suggest that there will be no anxiety experienced in this climate. If too much emphasis is placed on the individual making improvements, anxiety may be increased at plateau periods, so care should be taken in how much this is emphasised (Carr & Wyon, 2003).

Care must also be taken in the interpretation of climates, as it is the dancer's *perception* of the climate rather than an objective assessment. It is possible that one dancer may perceive a teacher to be creating a highly performance oriented climate whereas another dancer may perceive it to be

Table 3.1 Characteristics of climates

Performance oriented climate	Mastery oriented climate
Encourages competition	Encourages self-improvement
Focus on star dancers	Supports all dancers
Does not tolerate errors	Encourages learning from errors
Success is rewarded	Effort is rewarded
Tries to out-dance the group	Dances as a group
Source: Based on Miulli & Nordin-Bates (2011).	

more mastery oriented. Such perceptions may change over time, where older dancers in Centres for Advanced Training have demonstrated an increasing perception of performance oriented climate, which does not suggest that the teacher is necessarily the catalyst for this change in emphasis, it may be the dancers' increasing focus on their career, and its competitive nature (Nordin-Bates, 2012).

> **Research in focus**
>
> **Perceptions of the Motivational Climate, Need Satisfaction and Indices of Well- and Ill-Being Among Hip Hop Dancers**
>
> **Aim** The right motivational climate needs to be created to assist dancers in maximising their potential, where a mastery oriented climate encourages skill development through task involvement, and performance oriented climate encourages social comparison through ego involvement. The climate experienced may affect motivation, where basic needs are identified as autonomy, relatedness and competence. The purpose of the research was to examine whether the climate affected dancers' basic needs, and subsequent well-being.
>
> **Method** A total of 59 hip hop dancers were questioned: 38 female and 21 male.
> The psychometric tests included:
> - Perceived Motivational Climate in Sport Questionnaire-2 (PMCSQ-2)
> - Intrinsic Motivation Inventory (IMI)
> - Positive and Negative Affect Scale (PANAS)
>
> **Results**
> - *Task-involvement:* led to feelings of autonomy, relatedness and competence which enhanced positive mood states
> - *Ego-involvement:* reduced feelings of relatedness, leading to emotional and physical exhaustion and negative mood states
>
> **Conclusions** The creation of performance oriented climates leads to dancer rivalry, therefore reducing the opportunities for relatedness and increasing feelings of tension related to the negative mood states. Mastery oriented climates fulfill all the basic needs as the focus is on mastery. This allows for feelings of autonomy in personal skill development, which leads to feelings of competence. As there is no rivalry between dancers a sense of relatedness may occur as dancers work together. Therefore a mastery oriented climates should be cultivated for maximum satisfaction and performance.
>
> (Quested & Duda, 2009)

Hierarchy of Needs

The *Hierarchy of Needs* was developed by Maslow (1970) as an extension to previous biological explanations of motivation, as he felt that humans were motivated by different needs than the rest of the animal world. Although he believed we are primarily motivated by basic biological drives (deficiency needs), once those needs have been fulfilled, we are driven by needs that are not linked to our survival, but with satisfaction (meta needs), outlined in Figure 3.6.

MOTIVATION

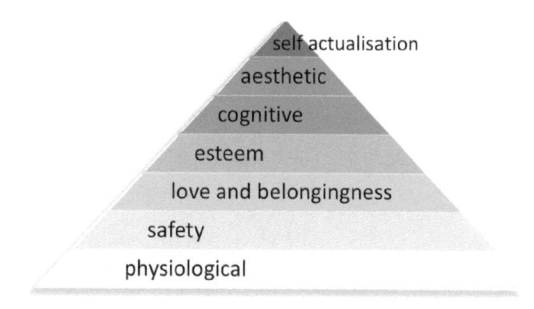

Figure 3.6
Hierarchy of Needs

Deficiency needs

Physiological needs

The most fundamental needs are those dictated by homeostasis and appetite; the drive to maintain the relevant levels of water and nutrients, sugar and salt, vitamins and minerals, in order to function effectively (Maslow, 1970). Being deficient in these needs will drive us towards achieving them. This suggests that if we are hungry or thirsty, we will be distracted from the task at hand, as well as lacking the required level of energy to sustain physical exertion in training or performances.

Safety needs

Having met our physiological needs, we are next concerned with our safety needs. In a dancing context these may include security, stability, protection, and freedom from fear, anxiety and chaos (Maslow, 1970). The need for stability and avoidance of chaos suggests that a predictable training routine, where there are clear expectations and requirements, will help dancers focus on the task at hand. The need for protection and freedom from fear means that bullying colleagues or authoritarian teachers may compromise our ability to work towards our performance potential. The freedom from anxiety may also relate to a dancer's perception of a mastery oriented climate where they can concentrate on their own progression, rather than fear of not measuring up to the class standard. Those working in a performance oriented climate may feel the need to compete in order to receive positive feedback from their teacher, which may lead to performance anxiety.

Love and belongingness needs

Once we feel safe within our dancing environment, then we may feel the need to make strong connections to members of the group, and may fear loneliness and rejection from within. This, similar to the physiological and safety needs, is a biological drive – humans are social creatures and function best in group contexts (Maslow, 1970). This need also reflects the relatedness element of Basic Needs Theory where we are driven to be part of a group that respects and supports us, with mutual respect reducing intragroup threats. The value of this will be considered in more detail with respect to group cohesion in Chapter 5. Suffice to say that our dance performance and experiences are improved when we bond together as a group.

© Shutterstock

Esteem needs

Esteem is the degree to which we value ourselves, of which there are two sources: self-esteem and the respect we are paid by others (Maslow, 1970). Self-esteem may be increased by feeling competent and gaining mastery in our field of dance. Feelings of self-esteem may increase our self-confidence, worth and strength. A lack of self-esteem is related to helplessness, and therefore is negatively related to performance. Esteem may be derived from the appreciation, recognition or attention received from others that give the dancer status or even fame. This may be productive if it is deemed to be deserved respect, based on competency, rather than unwarranted adulation.

Meta needs

Cognitive needs

The desire to know and understand drives us forward as children, but the desire to learn does not disappear with the onset of adulthood (otherwise you would not be reading this book today!). As part of personal progression, developing mastery is the drive to improve on what we already know, maintaining mental stimulation (Maslow, 1970). In a dancing context it may be learning more about the historical or cultural context of dance genres, or developing a widening repertoire of dance styles, or a deeper understanding of how anatomy or psychology relates to performance.

Aesthetic needs

Aesthetic needs are the appreciation of beauty, and although less understood, there is universal appreciation of aesthetics shown across time and cultures, suggesting beauty is an important human need (Maslow, 1970). In relation to dancing, the link is probably quite clear, that dancing is an art where movement and music create beauty. This may be demonstrated through the fluidity of physical movements, flow and synchronicity of a group, the interrelated beauty of the movement to music, through to more obvious visual satisfaction with costume, make-up and set.

Self-actualisation needs

In order to be fulfilled in life, we need to do what we feel we are meant to do, which will give us self-fulfilment. The dancer must therefore dance, but this need should only emerge when the more fundamental needs of physiology, safety, belongingness and esteem have been met. Dancing offers many opportunities to achieve self-actualisation. It may be the opportunity to work independently, to be creative, innovative or collaborative, or may be the ability to give something back to the wider community (Aujla & Farrer, 2015).

> **Research in focus**
>
> **The Role of Psychological Factors in the Career of the Independent Dancer**
>
> **Aim** Much research has been done to understand the motivational factors of dance students, but little has been done on those who have left education. Once out of dance school the professional dancer may have a varied career route with periods of instability. The purpose of the study was to examine how independent dancers maintain motivation.
>
> **Method** Semi structured interviews were undertaken on 14 professional dancers, whose job roles included performance, choreography, teaching, and administration.
> The question topics were:
> - how they maintain motivation to work independently
> - advantages and disadvantages of working independently
> - what factors, beyond their training, had helped them succeed
>
> **Results**
> - *Motivation to work independently:* they loved the autonomy of being an independent dancer, and were passionate about meeting new people and making a contribution.
> - *Challenges of working independently*: lack of structure and financial insecurity.
> - *Aiding success:* the mental skills of self-confidence, self-awareness and self-reflection aided their success. Social support from both the dance community and family were highlighted. For general well-being an ability to strike a balance between work and home life was important.
>
> **Conclusions** Success as an independent dancer requires self motivation through passion about the art, whilst grabbing opportunities as they present themselves.
>
> (Aujla & Farrer, 2015)

Burnout

Being a professional dancer requires commitment to physically and emotionally challenging training and rehearsal programmes. This demanding regime is achievable for most dancers, but for some it can become too much, and they may experience burnout. *Burnout* is a physical and psychological state that anyone may experience with respect to an area of their life to which they have committed. This state is not experienced as a result in overtraining, as those who train to the same level may not necessarily experience burnout (Roberts et al., 2007), which suggests that psychological factors must play a role.

Antecedents

Burnout is most likely to occur when there is a strong pursuit of goals and a striving for high standards, especially at times of intense training or rehearsal

(Roberts et al., 2007), but is most likely to occur when individuals are also experiencing reduced accomplishment, in spite of efforts being expended. This experience leads to devalued feelings towards dance, and the effort that is being exerted with no performance improvements leads to feelings of physical and emotional exhaustion (Quested & Duda, 2011).

There are several explanations as to why this situation may occur. The first explanation relates to stress, where the dancer may feel unable to cope with the situation, feeling overloaded, not in control, and not possessing the resources to manage the situation. The chronic stress being experienced leads to exhaustion and fatigue (Eklund & Cresswell, 2007). An alternative explanation is that the commitment we may have dedicated to dance has shifted from one of attraction (such as experienced with intrinsic motivation) to one of entrapment. The dancer may feel trapped because they have plateaued in their performance level and do not seem able to progress, but because they have invested so much time and energy into dancing, it is difficult to walk away. This may be compounded by pressure from others, adding a social dimension to a personal pressure (Eklund & Cresswell, 2007).

Research with dancers has shown that there are strong links to Basic Needs Theory, where loss of autonomy, reduced social support and reduced feelings of competency act as predictors of burnout (Quested & Duda, 2011), and there is a strong relationship between a shift from intrinsic to extrinsic motivation and burnout (Eklund & Cresswell, 2007).

Consequences

The result is a change from approach behaviours, where dancers would commit to long hours of training, to avoidant behaviours, where amotivation may become evident (Quested & Duda, 2011). As well as the evident behavioural changes, such as decreased performance and amotivation, there are other consequences, some physical and some psychological. *Physically* there may be impaired health, insomnia and reliance on drugs or alcohol (Eklund & Cresswell, 2007), and *psychologically* there may be symptoms of depression, dissatisfaction and disillusionment with dancing (Roberts et al., 2007).

PRACTICE

Motivation to join the group

The right climate

All groups are different and finding the one that suits the individual's needs is important for adherence. Often the tone of the group is set by the teacher, so their approach and the climate they create are important when considering options.

Climate selection

In order to develop a task involved approach to dance, a mastery orientated climate is needed. To establish whether this is the approach of the teacher, consider how the teacher responds to errors, how feedback is offered and how dancers are chosen for primary roles (White, 2007). If errors are punished, feedback is not considered constructive and favouritism is displayed to the more able dancers, then this is probably a performance oriented climate.

Group bonding

One of the most wonderful experiences of dancing is the camaraderie felt from the group members when the group are highly bonded to each other. If the group is not bonded, it may compromise our need for belongingness (Maslow, 1970).

Creating the bond

The sooner the bonding process takes place, the quicker the group will work together as one entity, therefore, it is important to ensure that new members are integrated into the group quickly. This can be managed initially by putting new members under the wing of long-term members so they can start to make connections, be introduced to others and feel there is someone they can ask questions of.

Allowing time for the dancers to interact will encourage bonds to be made as they will have time to learn more about each other, finding out what they have in common. This can be done at the start or end of a session, or though more social means. Organising a social activity or an evening out will also allow more time for the dancers to interact, and being away from the training room will encourage different forms of conversation, without the need to feel that they should be discussing dance.

To create an atmosphere of equity within the group, ensure that feedback is balanced, and that there is not constant praise of one skilled dancer. Perceived biased feedback or preferential treatment may lead the other dancers to resent this dancer, instead of respecting their ability. This can create intragroup conflict and lead the skilled dancer to be alienated from their colleagues.

Reducing the cliques

It is important that the group are bonded as a whole, and that there are not groups within groups, as this may lead to division and intergroup rivalry. To limit the chance of this occurring, mix up dancers into smaller groups regularly. This will help reduce cliques forming, and also encourage dancers to interact and get to know each other better.

Motivation in training and rehearsal

Being energised

Dancers must remember that their body is their tool and it requires attention and maintenance. Performance is the expenditure of energy, so if we do not have sufficient energy, then it makes performing to our potential difficult, therefore, ensuring our physiological needs are met is primary (Maslow, 1970). Ensuring that sufficient energy has been ingested, with an appropriate nutritional balance, is key to sustaining the physical demands. Hydration also plays an important role as dehydration leads to fatigue, which will impair performance and stamina, but dehydration also impacts on balance, which can be dangerous. Getting this balance requires an understanding of our physiology, but as the remit of this book is that of psychology we recommend supplementary texts, such as Quin, Rafferty, & Tomlinson (2015), see the Further Reading section for the specifics. The focus here is the behavioural patterns that support physiological fitness and performance.

Energy ingestion

In order to perform, the body needs a balanced diet and to be sufficiently hydrated, so some habits need to be adopted to ensure that you are always sufficiently energised.

First, have a water bottle with you at all times. Even when you are not doing physical work doesn't mean that energy is not being consumed – the brain needs a lot of energy to keep it going, so ensure you are hydrated even when sedentary. Bear in mind the amount you need to drink will vary greatly dependent on exertion rates and temperature, feeling thirsty is a sign of dehydration so try to avoid this state.

Never skip breakfast. Get used to eating regularly, planning your meals and times to ensure that you are never running on empty. Ensure that the right balance of protein and carbohydrates are being consumed to reflect your energy output.

Keep it natural. Although there are many products on the market that suggest they can help rehydrate and energise, these are rarely as good as the basics. Water is an excellent hydrator, it's readily available and free. Likewise, between-meal energy top-ups of fruit and nuts ensure that you know exactly what you are consuming, rather than energy bars and drinks that can lead to energy peaks, but may not be effective in gradual energy release, and may contain excessive levels of sugar and salt.

Energy maintenance

Regardless of how much energy-dense food is consumed, the body can only sustain so much exertion, so know your limits and listen to your body. Throughout the day, ensure that you have sufficient rest breaks to physically and mentally recharge, and at night ensure that you allow yourself enough sleep time to recuperate. Working harder and later to perfect something will be counter-productive if you are tired, and resultant plateaus in performance may increase the chance of burnout.

Confidence to commit

Dance is highly physical, and through the process of learning new choreography or manoeuvres the dancer may be concerned as to whether they believe that the move is achievable. If safety needs are not being met (Maslow, 1970), this may lead to lack of self-confidence, which may be exacerbated by previous experiences, or even injury.

Instilling confidence

Dancers are less likely to commit to a new move if they feel they may injure themselves in the process, so steps need to be taken to ensure that the environment is safe. Initial demonstration of the move from someone the dancer perceives as similar to themselves will model the behaviour and increases their self-confidence.

More practical efforts may be made to ensure safety through the use of crash mats for new partnered lifts or tumbles.

Injury concerns

Some concerns may originate through worries about previously sustained injuries. Having been through the injury and recovery process, it is perfectly natural to feel apprehensive as this is not an experience anyone would want to repeat. Unfortunately the worry the dancer may feel might increase the chance of a repeat injury, as stress leads to muscle tension, therefore, restricting movement. Educating the dancer regarding this dilemma, and utilising some of the stress reduction techniques from Chapter 6 may help them move towards a more relaxed engagement with the action.

Motivation to perform

Having a voice

There may be features of the performance that dancers do not feel satisfied with, in the training room or on stage. This may be based on the roles assigned or how they feel they will look when under the public scrutiny. Not having the opportunity to discuss such features may exacerbate them and lead to amotivation.

Aesthetics

The dancers' job, when performing on stage, is to recreate the vision of the choreographer and director, but it must be noted that it is the dancers who are seen by the audience, and it is the dancers who may feel judged, which will impact on their self-confidence. On this basis, it is important that the dancers feel invested in the project, especially when it comes to the vision, linking to Maslow's (1970) aesthetic needs. This may be expressed through elements of the choreography, where they do not feel confident in their ability to perform the manoeuvre or feel that it does not fit with the phrasing. Alternatively, it may be felt through costumes and make-up, which might be perceived to be too revealing or inappropriate.

It is important that the choreographer's vision is realised, and it is the dancers' job to create this vision, but this will best occur through dialogue. If they are feeling highly uncomfortable about the piece, dancers can be offered the opportunity to express concerns and choreographers should explain why the problematic features are essential to the success of the piece. Through open conversation a deeper understanding may be achieved and this increases the likelihood of engagement within the dance.

Opportunity

Although not all members of the group may be of equal ability, continued attention given to the most able is demoralising for the others, and may lead the more able to have an inflated view of their abilities. Therefore, consideration should be made to allow equal opportunities to shine (Miulli & Nordin-Bates, 2011). It may be that the opportunity for a less able dancer to take a leading role will enhance their performance as shown with the Pygmalion Effect, where belief by significant others increases self-belief and improves performance.

Motivation in performance

Imagery

Imagery has a potent effect on performance, helping the dancer to develop skills and technique (which will be discussed in more detail in Chapter 4). Imagery has other psychological effects, one of which is the ability to motivate and increase self-efficacy (Cumming & Williams, 2012). This can be a vital technique to apply at times when motivation lags, when tired or finding a task too demanding.

Motivation in the moment

When in a moment of declining motivation, and the temptation is to give up, the dancer needs to stop the thought process, and reflect on why they are involved in the activity. From this they should generate an image that relates to task success or completion (Gregg, Hall, & Nederhof, 2005).

What to imagine

Imagery sessions can be done after successful events. This might be a public appreciation of your efforts, such as receiving a standing ovation, or the satisfaction of a good show review. Alternatively, it might be the satisfaction that others might derive from your success, such as the elation felt by the group, or the pride felt by the teacher or director. This might equally be the individual's satisfaction through the visualisation of receiving a medal for competition success or being presented with a certificate of achievement. Such positive images help to motivate when sustaining the performance becomes difficult.

How to imagine

Encourage dancers to remember the experience in a multisensory manner. This must include as much visual information as possible, but must also include auditory information – the judge calling out their name or the applause of the audience. Try to include olfactory cues too – the smell of the dust on the stage or hairspray in the air. Now include emotional sensations, the pride and joy at having achieved this milestone. Once this image is easily visualised, it can be recalled at times of doubt to help recreate the feelings of prior success, converting anxiety to excitement.

Motivation for self-confidence

At times when confidence generally starts to lag, or you have a challenging performance ahead, then imagery can help boost self-confidence as part of your preparation for the event (Fish, Hall, & Cumming, 2004; Gregg et al., 2005).

MOTIVATION

Getting ready

Find a time and space where you feel comfortable and will not be disturbed. Loosen restrictive clothing and lie or sit in a relaxed position.

Close your eyes and concentrate on your breathing, trying to clear your mind of unnecessary thoughts.

Recreating the situation

Now imagine yourself arriving at the venue. Look at the building, imagining what amazing performances will be seen by the audiences coming to the show. Now imagine entering the building, noticing the energy and buzz of the atmosphere as everyone is rushing around preparing for the performance.

Imagine being in the dressing room, it is busy with dancers chatting and laughing. You have your costume on and are touching up your make-up. Look at yourself in the mirror. You see your character staring back at you, lose yourself in the character.

Managing the performance

It's your call. You file out, all chattering subsides. In the relative quiet, listen to your heart beating. Focus on its rhythm, now switch your attention to your breathing. Focus on this and if it's too fast, take three long deep breaths. Now listen to your heart rate decline gradually until you are breathing at the ideal rate.

Imagine you are standing in the wings waiting for the end of the previous number. Watch the faces of the dancers, see their control and ease of movement. Watch them embody their characters.

They exit, smiling and nodding to you as they pass. They are handing you the power to spellbind the audience with these exchanges. Grab that power, ready to use. Breathe in your character and breathe out yourself. You enter the stage and hear the opening notes to your music. Take your position, claim your position, claim your character. Give your character the permission to dance on your behalf.

Imagine the audience and acknowledge them, remembering that you have the power to spellbind them. You are taking them with you on the journey and you are in control. As the music starts, let the character lead, being totally immersed in the moment. Imagine your motion around the stage paying no conscious attention to choreography. The audience is following in your wake.

The music comes to an end. Imagine taking your final position, letting the audience float back to their seats. Breathe out your character and breathe in yourself. Imagine the applause and embrace it. It's for you. All the hard work was for this very moment – all the tears and worry have resulted in this praise – enjoy it, bottle it!

Becoming aware of your breathing again, feel the sensations of appreciation and try to keep these feelings with you. Gradually bringing yourself back into the present, open your eyes.

Self-talk

As will be discussed in more detail in Chapter 4, adopting self-talk helps us learn and master choreography, but it is also a technique naturally used to boost or maintain motivation when taking part in demanding physical activity (Gammage, Hardy, & Hall, 2001). Self-generated self-talk phrases relate to autonomy, enhancing the intrinsic motivation.

Positive boost

If you feel that you are lagging, possibly due to exertion, then energising phrases may help boost motivation, and see you through to the next break. Such phrases might be simple 'keep going', 'nearly there', 'you can do it'.

Using second-person references might help mimic the voices of those you find motivating, such as recreating phrases that your teacher may use when pushing you on. Such applications of self-talk not only can offer a mental energy boost, but may refocus attention that has drifted due to fatigue.

Avoid negativity

Self-talk is not always positive, so you need to be aware of what the voice is saying, and ensure that a positive focus is maintained, over-talking negative comments with positive ones (Hardy, 2006).

Post-performance self-reflection

It is productive to have a reflective discussion with yourself after a performance, where the strengths and weaknesses of the event are considered, showing insight. Consider how the limitations may be managed in future events, but then ensure that the self-talk concludes with reflecting positively about the successes of the experience.

Identifying needs

Performance profiling

Performance profiling is a technique that allows dancers to reflect on their own performance and, through discussion with their teacher, create an individual performance profile which can be used as the basis for goal setting (Weston, Greenlees, & Thelwell, 2013). As this method is dancer-led with the support of the teacher, it increases intrinsic motivation as it autonomy-supportive.

MOTIVATION

Profiling

The dancer should create a list of the most important facets of dance for them as an individual, where teachers emphasise that there are no right or wrong answers. The list may include technical issues, fitness issues or behavioural issues.

Having created a list, the dancer then indicates how *important* each of these facets are, ranking them from 1 (not very important) through to 10 (highly important). The dancer then rates their own *abilities* for each of the facets, from 1 (very poor) to 10 (the best I can be). For each facet, calculate the following:

> minus the ability score from 10 x the result by the importance score

	Importance	Ability	Score
Punctuality	5	5	25
Stamina	3	6	12
Concentration	7	4	42
Ganchos	7	3	49
Vuelta Por Detras	6	7	18

Those facets with the higher scores are the facets that the teacher and dancer may want to focus on as priorities, and may form the basis of goals to be set. In this case, the dancer's level of concentration and their inability to perfect the ganchos are areas of concern, so these should be prioritised.

This process can be repeated at different time points so the dancer can see progression.

Goal setting

A goal is the aim of an action, and to achieve the goal we need to be motivated to behave in a way that will lead to goal achievement, so goal setting is the strategy employed to achieve the goal. Goal setting relies on four mechanisms (Locke & Latham, 2002).

1. Goals give our behaviour direction, focusing our thoughts and behaviour on what we need to do, and distracting us from the irrelevant.
2. Goals energise us, leading to increased effort.
3. Goals increase levels of persistence, although this needs to be balanced with effort to avoid burnout.
4. Goals increase our cognitive application to a task, where higher levels of strategizing are applied.

Through the setting and monitoring of goals, the dancer can make meaningful evaluations of their progress.

Goal identification

In order to create meaningful and actionable goals several important features need to be included – and can be remembered by the acronym SMART (Doran, 1981):

- *Specific* – It is not helpful to ask a dancer to 'try harder' or 'do your best' as they are not measurable outcomes and so impossible to tell if the goals have been met. Therefore, it is important to set something concrete, such as 'complete a triple setenta'. The goal comprises a measurable action, therefore the dancers knows exactly what they are aiming for, but this in itself does not explain how to achieve the goal, therefore explicit instruction is required to move the performance forward. This may require a breakdown of task components, such as starting position, footwork and armography.
- *Measurable* – the action needs to be measurable in some way so the dancer knows whether they have met their goal. If quantifiable, it can be used throughout the process to offer feedback regarding progress and achievement.
- *Assignable* – in group goal setting it is important to know who has been assigned what goals, so individuals can take responsibility for their own behaviour.
- *Realistic* – the person setting the goal needs to consider the dancer's potential, and set goals that are within their capabilities. This is why it is helpful for the teacher to become involved in the goal-setting process as their experience may allow them to make more realistic assessments than the dancer may be able to make. If the goal is unachievable, failure to reach this goal will act as a demotivator, and may impact on self-efficacy and self-esteem.
- *Time-related* – a timeframe should be devised, including dates for summary feedback, and then a final date for goal achievement. It is important to set the right pace for goal achievement as not everyone will progress at the same rate. If a month has been given to achieve the triple setenta, and by week three the dancer is not completing a double setenta, then they can see that the goal may not be met. This may either require the dancer to work harder if they have not applied themselves sufficiently, or to review the goal period to increase persistence and reduce feelings of failure.

Goal type

Performance goals are those focused on the development of mastery, where the goal is set relative to the dancer's previous performances to allow for incremental improvements. These goals are controllable as the focus is on the self and not the performance of others. These goals may be used for events such as competitions or gradings.

Similarly, *process goals* are performance-related, but focus on very specific features of performance. These goals are skill-focused and so are used more commonly in training. They would combine through the mastering of the setenta (process goal) to ensure successful performance of a new routine (performance goal).

Alternatively, *outcome goals* focus on the result of the performance, such as winning the regional Salsa competition by the successful performance of the new routine, which would require ego involvement. These goals should be treated with care as they can become sources of negative psychological states as the dancer does not have control over the performance of others, therefore may feel frustrated and angry at losing. This may lead to demoralisation or anxiety at the public exposure of their diminished level of competency.

If a dancer tends to focus on outcome goals, it is important to help them see the value in making the goal personalised through a more performance- or process-based focus, as a way to increase their task involvement. Refocusing on the excellent execution of the new routine will help the dancers see that they have accomplished their goal (positive), rather than did not win (negative).

Goal difficulty

It is important that the goals set involve a challenge through increasing levels of difficulty (Locke & Latham, 2002). If goals are perceived to be too easy, there will be a lack of motivation to achieve. This undermining of the dancer's competence devalues the dancer's self-efficacy as the teacher is not showing confidence in their abilities.

Alternatively, it is important not to set difficult tasks in a way that makes the goal sound threatening. Difficult goals must be framed as a challenge in order to increase the dancer's focus on effort and technique, and not fear of failure (Locke & Latham, 2006).

Collaborative goal setting

Goal setting has shown to be most effective if the individual is committed to the goal. The purpose of the goals should be explained for maximum engagement, and they should be framed in a positive way to enhance motivation, rather than as a punishment of unachieved levels.

To enhance commitment, two factors have been shown to play an important role: importance and self-efficacy (Locke & Latham, 2002). To enhance the *importance* of the goal, it should be personalised, a process that may occur in two ways. First, that the dancer has been party to the construction of the goal. If the dancer has been involved in the goal choice and construction, they will be intrinsically motivated to achieve it, whereas goals assigned by a teacher, without consultation, will be experienced as extrinsic motivation which will impact negatively on performance. Second, that the goal is specific to that individual dancer and not to the entire group. Group goals should also be the product of negotiation and discussion, but personal goals should be devised which feed into the group aims.

Other people's expectations of us can have a positive effect on our *self-efficacy*, their confidence in you to achieve increases your self-confidence, and ultimately performance (Locke & Latham, 2002). The teacher can enhance self-efficacy by referencing previous achievements to create a performance baseline, and increasing the goal's level of challenge by increasing difficulty to an achievable level.

Collaborative goal setting relates to all the features of Basic Needs Theory. Feelings of autonomy are increased as the dancer has been instrumental in the process of devising personalised goals. The reinforcement of the goals from the teacher enhances the dancer's perception of competence, and the collaborative nature of the process shows relatedness.

Goal reinforcement

Feedback

Summary feedback is information given to indicate how well one is doing with respect to achieving a long-term goal (Locke & Latham, 2002). Without feedback we cannot monitor our performance, and therefore do not know how to adjust our performance if necessary. Feedback that suggests that we are not on track to achieve leads to adaptive behaviours, such as increasing effort or persistence, or employing an alternative strategy. To maintain motivation for long-term goals, and to maximise the use of summary feedback, set sub-goals so the monitoring process has more meaning, and modifications can be made based on the achievement of sub-goals.

Types of feedback

As well as the intrinsic feedback that the dancer receives from pursuing a goal, feedback may be required from external sources in order to maintain motivation and redirect behaviour. Feedback from the teacher can greatly enhance the chance of dancers achieving their goals, but the type of feedback and its delivery can mediate its effectiveness.

The most effective form is *corrective* feedback. This feedback identifies the problems within the performance but in an informational manner – suggesting how improvements can be made. This should include not only the issues with a performance, but also the strengths, as this it is just as important to know what to continue as to know what to avoid.

This is different from *negative* feedback, which also identifies the problems within the performance, but in a manner that is critical and relates the performance to failure. Care must be taken that even the body language used to deliver the corrective feedback is positive and encouraging, considering the tone of voice and non-verbal cues such as frowning (Mouratidis, Lens, & Vansteenkiste, 2010).

Rewards

Consideration needs to be made of what is being offered as a result of goal achievement. In essence, the reward from successful goal achievement should be intrinsic, that we experience satisfaction in our achievements (Locke & Latham, 2002).

Avoid offering extrinsic rewards such as prizes or league tables. This reinforcement can introduce external regulation of behaviour, leading to performance-limiting strategies, such as lack of satisfaction at not winning, although improvements may have been made, or ego involvement with the task set.

Pressure to perform related to the needs of others can also act as an external introjected regulator, but with the additional psychological stresses that may result from failure to achieve. Shame at having let the group down, or guilt for not living up to the teacher's expectations can be counterproductive. Achievement of goals that are intrinsically motivated will lead to pride in our performance, as opposed to the relief of succeeding.

Key concepts glossary

Autonomy Having control over our behaviour.

Burnout A physical and emotional state of exhaustion in an activity to which you have committed yourself.

Competence Self-belief that you have the ability in a specified activity.

Ego orientation An approach to performance where the aim is to outperform others.

Extrinsic motivation A drive to perform for reasons that are unconnected with the activity.

Intrinsic motivation A drive to perform for the love of the activity.

Motivation An internal drive to achieve needs and goals.

Motivational climate The motivational direction set by the teacher.

Relatedness A feeling generated by the support and respect received from others.

Task orientation An approach to performance where the aim is to gain personal mastery.

References

Adie, J., Duda, J. L., & Ntoumanis, N. (2008). Autonomy support, basic need satisfaction and the optimal functioning of adult male and female sport participants: A test of basic needs theory. *Motivation and Emotion, 32*, 189–199.

Aujla, I., & Farrer, R. (2015). The role of psychological factors in the career of the independent dancer. *Frontiers in Psychology, 6*(1688). doi:10.3389/fpsyg.2015.01688.

Carr, S. (2012). High task/high ego oriented students' reasons for endorsing task and ego goals in the context of physical education. *Applied Psychology, 61*(4), 540–563. doi:10.1111/j.1464-0597.2012.00505.x.

Carr, S., & Wyon, M. (2003). The impact of motivational climate on dance students' achievement goals, trait anxiety, and perfectionism. *Journal of Dance Medicine & Science, 7*(4), 105–114.

Cumming, J., & Williams, S. E. (2012). The role of imagery in performance. In S. M. Murphy (Ed.), *The Oxford handbook of sport and performance psychology*. New York: Oxford University Press.

Deci, E., & Ryan, R. (2008). Facilitating optimal motivation and psychological well-being across life's domains. *Canadian Psychology, 49*(1), 14–23. doi:10.1037/0708-5591.49.1.14.

Doran, G. T. (1981). There's a S.M.A.R.T. way to write management's goals and objectives. *Management Review, 70*(11), 35–36.

Eklund, R. C., & Cresswell, S. L. (2007). Athlete burnout. In G. Tenenbaum & R. C. Eklund (Eds.), *Handbook of sport psychology* (3rd ed.). Hoboken, NJ: Wiley.

Fish, L., Hall, C., & Cumming, J. (2004). Investigating the use of imagery by elite ballet dancers. *Avante, 10*(3), 26–39.

Gammage, K. L., Hardy, J., & Hall, C. R. (2001). A description of self-talk in exercise. *Psychology of Sport and Exercise, 2*(4), 233–247. doi:10.1016/S1469-0292(01)00011-5.

Gillet, N., Vallerand, R. J., Amoura, S., & Baldes, B. (2010). Influence of coaches' autonomy support on athletes' motivation and sport performance: A test of the hierarchical model of intrinsic and extrinsic motivation. *Psychology of Sport and Exercise, 11*, 155–161.

Goulimaris, D., Mavridis, G., Genti, M., & Rokka, S. (2014). Relationships between basic psychological needs and psychological well-being in recreational dance activities. *Journal of Physical Education and Sport, 14*(2), 277–284.

Gregg, M., Hall, C., & Nederhof, E. (2005). The imagery ability, imagery use, and performance relationship. *The Sport Psychologist, 19*(1), 93–99. doi:10.1123/tsp.19.1.93.

Hardy, J. (2006). Speaking clearly: A critical review of the self-talk literature. *Psychology of Sport and Exercise, 7*(1), 81–97. doi:10.1016/j.psychsport.2005.04.002.

Locke, E. A., & Latham, G. P. (2002). Building a practically useful theory of goal setting and task motivation. *American Psychologist, 57*(9), 705–717. doi:10.1037//0003-066X.57.9.705.

Locke, E. A., & Latham, G. P. (2006). New directions in goal-setting theory. *Current Directions in Psychological Science, 15*(5), 265–268.

Maslow, A. H. (1970). *Motivation and personality* (2nd ed.). New York: Harper & Row.

Miulli, M., & Nordin-Bates, S. M. (2011). Motivational climates: What they are, and why they matter. *International Association for Dance Medicine & Science Bulletin for Teachers, 3*(2), 5–8.

Mouratidis, A., Lens, W., & Vansteenkiste, M. (2010). How you provide corrective feedback makes a difference: The motivating role of communicating in an autonomy-supporting way. *Journal of Sport and Exercise Psychology, 32*(5), 619–637. doi:10.1123/jsep.32.5.619.

Nicholls, J. G. (1984). Achievement motivation: Conceptions of ability, subjective experience, task choice, and performance. *Psychological Review, 91*(3), 328–346.

Nordin-Bates, S. M. (2012). Performance psychology in the performing arts. In S. M. Murphy (Ed.), *The Oxford handbook of sport and performance psychology*. New York: Oxford University Press.

Ozdemir Oz, A., Lane, J. F., & Michou, A. (2016). Autonomous and controlling reasons underlying achievement goals during task engagement: Their relation to intrinsic motivation and cheating. *Educational Psychology, 36*(7), 1160–1172. doi:10.1080/01443410.2015.1109064.

Quested, E., & Duda, J. L. (2008). The experience of well- and ill-being among elite dancers: A test of basic needs theory. Paper presented at the Annual Conference of the British Association of Sport and Exercise Sciences.

Quested, E., & Duda, J. L. (2009). Perceptions of the motivational climate, need satisfaction, and indices of well- and ill-being among hip hop dancers. *Journal of Dance Medicine & Science, 13*(1), 10–19.

Quested, E., & Duda, J. L. (2011). Antecedents of burnout among elite dancers: A longitudinal test of basic needs theory. *Psychology of Sport and Exercise, 12*(2), 159–167. doi:10.1016/j.psychsport.2010.09.003.

Quested, E., Duda, J. L., Ntoumanis, N., & Maxwell, J. P. (2013). Daily fluctuations in the affective states of dancers: A cross-situational test of basic needs theory. *Psychology of Sport and Exercise, 14*, 586–595. doi:10.1016/j.psychsport.2013.02.006.

Roberts, G. C. (2001). Understanding the dynamics of motivation in physical activity: The influence of achievement goals on motivational processes. In G. C. Roberts (Ed.), *Advances in motivation in sport and exercise*. Champaign, IL: Human Kinetics.

Roberts, G. C., Treasure, D. C., & Conroy, D. E. (2007). Understanding the dynamics of motivation in sport and physical activity: An achievement goal interpretation. In G. Tenenbaum & R. C. Eklund (Eds.), *Handbook of sport psychology*. Hoboken, NJ: Wiley.

Ryan, R., Williams, G. C., Patrick, H., & Deci, E. (2009). Self-determination theory and physical activity: The dynamics of motivation in development and wellness. *Hellenic Journal of Psychology, 6*, 107–124.

Ryan, R. M., & Deci, E. L. (2000). Intrinsic and extrinsic motivations: Classic definitions and new directions. *Contemporary Educational Psychology, 25*(1), 54–67. doi:10.1006/ceps.1999.1020.

Thogersen-Ntoumani, C., Shephard, S. O., Ntoumanis, N., Wagenmakers, A. J. M., & Shaw, C. S. (2016). Intrinsic motivation in two exercise interventions: Associations with fitness and body composition. *Health Psychology, 35*, 195–198. doi:10.1037/hea0000260.

Vallerand, R. J. (2001). A hierarchical model of intrinsic and extrinsic motivation in sport and exercise. In G. C. Roberts (Ed.), *Advances in motivation in sport and exercise*. Champaign, IL: Human Kinetics.

Weston, N., Greenlees, I., & Thelwell, R. (2013). A review of Butler and Hardy's (1992) performance profiling procedure within sport. *International Review of Sport and Exercise Psychology, 6*(1), 1–21. doi:10.1080/1750984X.2012.674543.

White, S. A. (2007). Parent-created motivatonal climate. In S. Jowett & D. Lavallee (Eds.), *Social psychology in sport*. Champaign, IL: Human Kinetics.

Further reading

Biddle, S., Wang, C. K. J., Kavussanu, M., & Spray, C. (2003). Correlates of achievement goal orientations in physical activity: A systematic review of research. *European Journal of Sport Science, 3*(5), 1–20.

Goodger, K., Gorely, T., Lavallee, D., & Harwood, C. (2007). Burnout in sport: A systematic review. *The Sport Psychologist, 21*(2), 127–151.

Quin, E., Rafferty, C., & Tomlinson, S. (2015). *Safe dance practice*. Champaign, IL: Human Kinetics.

Teixeira, P. J., Carraça, E. V., Markland, D., Silva, M. N., & Ryan, R. M. (2012). Exercise, physical activity, and self-determination theory: A systematic review. *International Journal of Behavioral Nutrition and Physical Activity, 9*(1), 78.

CHAPTER 4

Skill acquisition

Learning outcomes

By the end of this chapter readers should be able to:

- recognise a variety of influences on the learning process
- define key cognitive terms
- describe how different cognitive theories can aid the learning process
- explain how imagery and self-talk impact on dance performance
- propose methods that can help dancers of different levels and styles to learn and recall choreography

CONTEXT

Dance is a highly complex activity. It requires physical technical abilities, which rely on fitness, flexibility and stamina, but it also requires great mental application in the ability to store and recreate the choreography and demonstrate consistent technique. Unlike other performing arts, dancers need to remember a vast amount of information in order to perform without error. Actors deliver lines of meaningful speech that relate to what is occurring in a scene, lines which are often pre-empted by the previous line. Singers may not have lines fed to them in the same was an actor, but they do have the pattern of the music to cue their memory, and songs tend to have a clear narrative structure. But dancers are required to recall sequences of movements that may seem abstract to the novice, without structure or narrative. Through engagement with the dance genre there will emerge meaning to the sequences which will, in time, aid recall.

Due to such complexities any strategies that a dancer can employ to enhance their physical and mental skills will be valuable. The strategies may range from how to embody a new style of dance to the learning of the basic steps. This will progress on to the learning of the vocabulary of the dance genre and complex choreographed pieces. This culminates in the recall of the choreography when under pressure to perform, showing technical skill while also letting the character shine through, seamlessly and without apparent effort.

THEORY

Information Processing Model

In order to learn we must absorb new information, which is done through a range of cognitive processes (Figure 4.1). We must start with a stimuli (S), which may be the demonstration of a new step. The first stage is to *perceive* this step, so we may watch the teacher's demonstration and we may hear the tap making contact with the floor. If we are not paying *attention* to the teacher throughout the demonstration we will not have perceived the new information, therefore the information will not be processed. Having paid attention, we need to absorb the new information by *encoding*. Encoding takes external information and helps us to integrate it within the cognitive structures of our mind. Once *stored* in our memory, we need to be able to *recall* the step as a response (R) to instruction.

Figure 4.1 Information Processing Model

S → perception → attention → encoding → memory storage → memory recall → R

Attention

Attention can be defined as a process of 'selecting one aspect of the complex sensory information from the environment to focus on, while disregarding others for the time being' (Statt, 1998, p. 10). We may attend to external stimuli through sensory experiences. We may concentrate on the new step by watching and listening to the teacher, or we may be distracted by the pinching of new tap shoes on our toes. We may notice the smell of polish from the studio floor or be aware of the taste of coffee from break time.

In addition, we can attend to internal stimuli. These can be cognitive stimuli, such as thinking and problem-solving, or even daydreaming. Alternatively, they may be emotional distractors, more of which will be covered in Chapter 6. We may also have our attention drawn to physiological changes, such as pain, discomfort or hunger, as part of the body's way of letting us know there is problem.

Theory of Attentional and Interpersonal Style

The *Theory of Attentional and Interpersonal Style* was developed as a framework to explain how aspects of attention may affect an individual's ability to perform physically or mentally to their potential (Nideffer, 1976). There are two interacting dimensions: directional and bandwidth (Figure 4.2). The *directional* dimension relates to the focus of attention, where an *external*

SKILL ACQUISITION

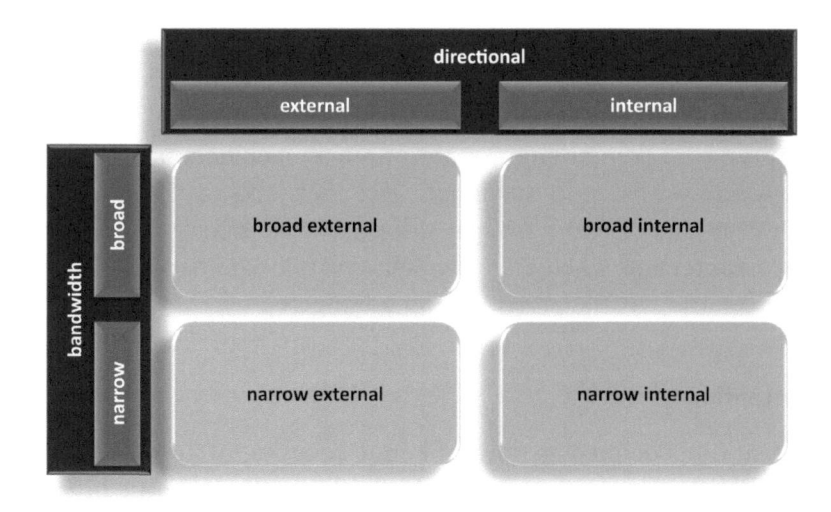

Figure 4.2
Dimensions of attentional and interpersonal style

focus refers to what is happening in the environment, outside of the body. The *internal* focus is a concentration of what is happening inside the individual. The internal focus may include cognitive, emotional or physiological factors. The *bandwidth* dimension refers to the breadth of focus, *broad* taking in a vast array of information through multiple senses, whereas *narrow* suggests a focus.

What is important is that the attentional style being used at any one moment must be the most effective to maximising performance. Table 4.1 offers examples of activities that may affect the effectiveness of each attentional style. To ensure performance is maximised, it requires that the directional aspects can be done simultaneously, which means you need to be able to divide your attention between internal and external stimuli at the same time. You also need to be able to switch quickly between a broad and narrow focus (Nideffer, 2002).

Table 4.1 Examples of effective and ineffective attentional styles

Attentional style		Effective	Ineffective
Broad external		Considering where you are on stage	Being transfixed by the audience
Narrow external		Focusing on a step being demonstrated by a teacher	Reading a text message in class
Broad internal	Cognitive	Visualising how the choreography will look onstage	Daydreaming when learning a new sequence
	Emotional	Embracing the applause at the end of a performance	Being overwhelmed with fear as you step on stage
	Physiological	Acknowledging exhaustion at the end of a long day in training	Ignoring symptoms of thirst
Narrow internal	Cognitive	Mental rehearsal of a new step	Worrying about performing in front of classmates
	Emotional	Ignoring the pre-performance panic	Being distracted by praise
	Physiological	Concentrating on calf muscle tension when warming-up	Trying to ignore sensations of pain

In addition, Nideffer (2002) believes that we have a *dominant attentional style,* where we tend to function most effectively, but when under pressure we may defer to this dominant style even though it may not be appropriate at that time. The approach taken at emotional times may include a narrow internal perspective where we listen to our inner voice that talks of failure when feeling anxious. Or at points of panic we may adopt a broad external style scanning for an escape route, and when angry we may be taking a narrow external perspective by staring at the person who had angered us.

Selective attention

Selective attention is defined as the 'deliberate focusing of attention on something to the exclusion of competing stimuli' (Statt, 1998, p. 119), and is necessary in order to learn and perform effectively. There are different types of selective attention as shown in Figure 4.3.

Distraction

Distraction is a negative form of attention because it takes your concentration away from the chosen stimuli in order to focus on an irrelevant stimuli. Distractions can take many forms. They can be internal. This may include daydreaming, or the inner voice creating a sense of worry. Internal distracters can also be emotions, such as anxiety, and even positive emotions like elation or excitement can be distracting. Some internal distractors are helpful though, such as pain, which is a warning to stop the activity, likewise listening to your body's cry for hydration, nutrition or rest are also advisable.

Distractions can also relate to external sensory factors. We may be distracted by visual stimuli such as lighting, auditory stimuli such as conversations, or even peculiar smells. These types of distraction are quite natural. Evolutionarily, we are hard-wired to respond to vivid stimuli in the environment as they would have been a source of danger, but we have evolved to be distracted by social factors too. This would be the distraction of others watching you perform, or concerns about what other people may think of you – issues covered in Chapter 2.

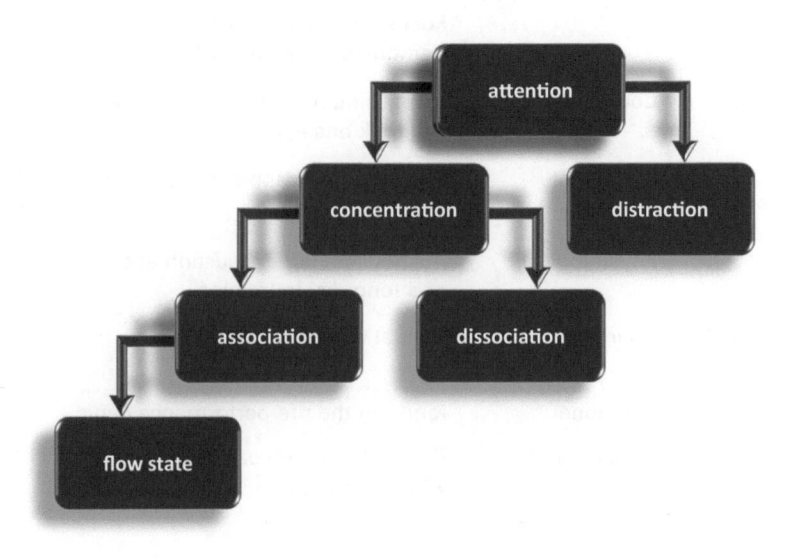

Figure 4.3
Types of selective attention

SKILL ACQUISITION

Concentrating too much on one of the multisensory components may distract from other important information that needs to be processed. There may also be conflict between internal stimuli, such as the inner voice, drowning out the external instruction of the teacher.

Concentration

The attentional state that you should be aiming for is concentration. *Concentration* is the ability to focus on what is important without being distracted by irrelevant stimuli. It is a skill to be developed as concentration cannot be forced – forcing your attention is in itself a distraction (Wilson, Peper, & Schmid, 2006). Concentration can be difficult to achieve when there is a vast array of information that requires attention. Figure 4.4 shows that within the scope of auditory attention the dancer needs to focus on the music so the right chorography can be applied, but must also be listening for director corrections. Even hearing corrections, the dancer will then need to establish to whom they have been directed before making any necessary changes. In addition, they will also be concentrating visually on fellow dancers' positions.

Dissociation

Dissociation is where the dancer may choose to focus on a task-irrelevant stimuli, often used when undergoing activities that are arduous and when performance quality is not important. This may be a technique employed during gruelling gym sessions where the ability to dissociate may help reduce physical and mental discomfort. Dissociation may be internal, such as daydreaming, or external, by focusing on incidental music or chatting with others (Stevinson & Biddle, 1999).

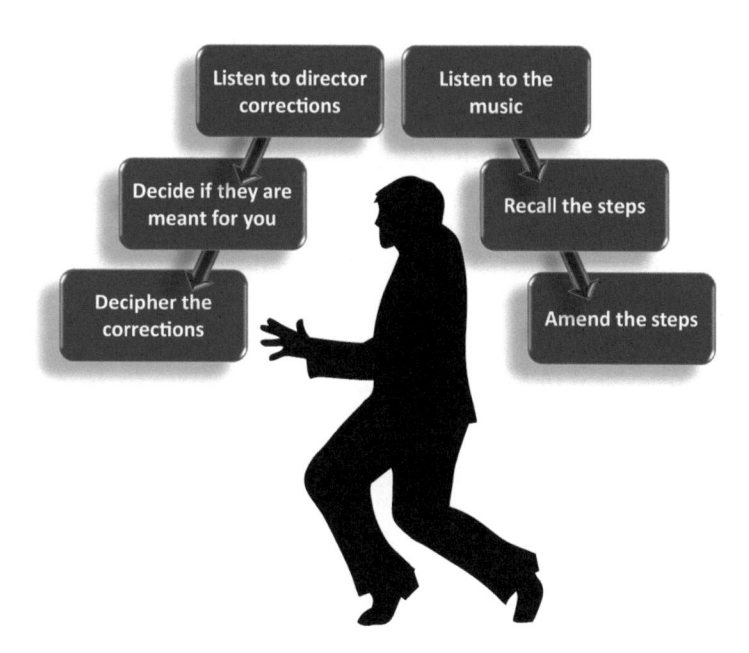

Figure 4.4
Divided attention

Association

To *associate* is to focus wholly on task-relevant stimuli as a way of examining how you are managing the performance. Again, this may be internal or external. Internal association may be the focus on heart or respiration rate, or monitoring pain to ensure maximum performance but prevent injury. External association would be ensuring that your positioning or pace matches that of co-dancers (Stevinson & Biddle, 1999). The ultimate state of associative concentration for optimal performance is Flow State.

Flow State

Flow State, sometimes referred to as *being in the zone*, is where one is completely absorbed in the activity, and this state is characterised by nine features (Nakamura & Csikszentmihalyi, 2014):

1 **Skill-challenge balance:** Being in a situation where there is a balance between your skills and the needs of the performance. The task is therefore achievable, but requires effort and concentration. There must be a perfect balance, because if the task is too easy, it will lead to boredom, and one that is too difficult may lead to anxiety.
2 **Clear and close goals:** The situation must have clear goals set at the outset, and the goals must be achievable in the context of the performance.
3 **Unambiguous feedback:** Having clear goals that are achievable within the performance ensures that the feedback, which is received in the moment, is absolutely clear. This will allow you to see where you are with respect to the goals set, as you perform.
4 **Being in control:** The skill-challenge balance allows you to feel that you can deal with any situation that arises, therefore being in control of the performance.
5 **Being in the moment:** You must have absolute concentration on the task at hand. This means that you will be in the moment, not considering something that has passed, or something that may occur in the future.
6 **Merging of action and awareness:** Being so immersed in the moment that you are absorbed in the performance, acting as one unit.
7 **Loss of self-awareness:** You lose any sense of self-consciousness. This aids performance as it reduces any negative impact that social scrutiny and self-awareness may have on performance (as discussed in Chapter 2).
8 **Time distortion:** An experience where time appears distorted, either by flying by, or feeling like you are acting in slow motion.
9 **Intrinsic motivation:** The activity is engaged in for the pure pleasure gained from it, as discussed in Chapter 3.

Encoding

Encoding is the process that converts external information into a format that will allow it to be stored for later use. When we are referring to actions, encoding is the creation of motor programs. *Motor programs* are the systems that generate a movement, built from templates made up from the previous attempts at that action, and once learnt, motor programs remove the need for complex planning. Motor programs can be built for the production of one action (shuffle), to more complex sequences of actions (triple time step). The motor program involves both cognitive and neural factors. Cognitive activation of the motor program comes from anticipation, that is to know *when* to perform the action. Neural activation sends messages around the body to initiate the action, therefore relates to *how* to carry out the movement. Each time the action is performed, evaluation of the effectiveness of the action refines the motor program until it becomes a learnt skill (Summers & Anson, 2009).

The mind stores information about motor programs as a *mental representation* (Schack, Essig, Frank, & Koester, 2014). Mental representations are made up of Basic Action Concepts (BACs), which are the building blocks of complex actions (Bläsing, Tenenbaum, & Schack, 2009). The mental representations store cognitive information such as the name of the step, verbal descriptions of its component parts, and the procedural elements that initiate the movement (Bläsing et al., 2009).

BAC for a shuffle
- Foot suspended above the floor
- Push foot forward striking the floor with the toe plate
- Bring foot back quickly striking the floor with the toe plate

Once we have a mental representation of an action, it can be triggered by just watching a dance sequence, which in turn triggers neural activity that corresponds to the production of that movement. As mental representations can be triggered through both visual or verbal cues (Bläsing et al., 2009), this suggests that the movement has been encoded as knowledge into more than one form of memory.

Research in focus

The Cognitive Benefits of Movement Reduction: Evidence From Dance Marking

Aim The learning of motor programs is a complex phenomenon as it comprises of both cognitive factors in the retention of the movements, and physical factors of the actual performance. If the cognitive aspect is important then marking a routine may be an effective form of rehearsal. The purpose of this study is to identify what role marking plays in learning routines.

Method A total of 38 advanced ballet students were split into two experimental groups (independent variable).
Day 1: Both groups learned two routines (independent variable routine A and B)
Day 2: Group 1 – dance routine A, mark routine B
Group 2 – dance routine B, mark routine A
Day 3: Perform both dances which were scored on accuracy and performance quality (dependent variable)

Results
In both routines those learnt through marking were significantly more accurate and of higher quality than the danced routine.

Conclusions The findings suggest that marking is a powerful tool to use in the learning of new routines. The cognitive function of the process is more important than the physical effort alone. Adoption of more marking could help reduce energy exertion, injury and burnout, whilst having better choreographic retention.

(Warburton, Wilson, Lynch & Cuykendall, 2013)

Memory storage

Memory is made up of a series of structures and processes that not only store information but allow us to manipulate the information. The most notable stores which relate to information storage are the working memory and the long-term memory. These memory stores link to the learning process to show how motor programs are developed (Figure 4.5).

Working memory

Functions of the working memory

The *working memory* is a store that has two main functions. Originally the working memory was labelled the short-term memory, as one of its functions is to hold information temporarily. More recent research has shown that the working memory is operating while dealing with complex situations. It is made up of a central executive that organises problem solving through three components. The *episodic buffer* combines visual information (through the visuo-spatial sketchpad) and auditory information (through the phonological loop), with memories stored in the long-term memory in order to manage situations (Baddeley, 2010).

The working memory processes different types of information in different ways. Research has shown that when trying to lay down memories of a spatial nature, such as how the dancer moves around the stage, the working memory uses resources from the visuo-spatial sketchpad. Alternatively when trying to remember body configuration, such as the sequence of steps, the working memory relies more on the phonological loop. This suggests that body movements are stored based on the names of the steps or sequences (Smyth & Pendleton, 1990).

Working memory capacity

The working memory has a limited capacity in the amount of information that it can retain at any point, but what constitutes a bit of information? A bit can be considered a concept; so it may be a letter, a word, an idea or an image.

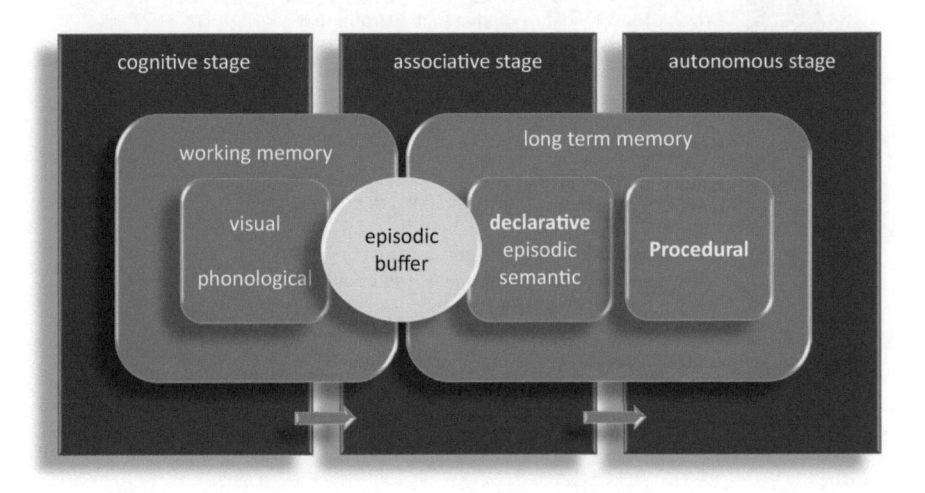

Figure 4.5
Representation of memory stores

SKILL ACQUISITION

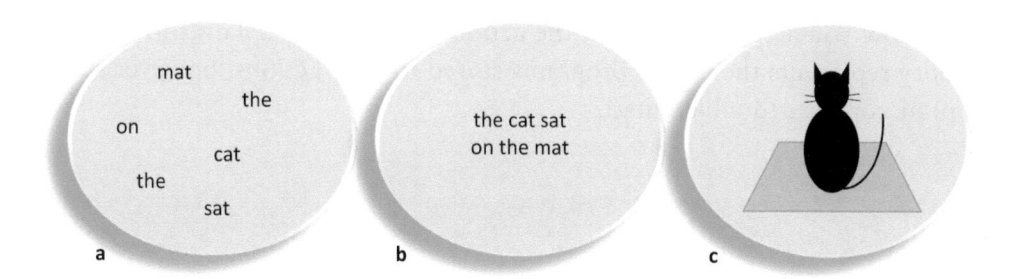

Figure 4.6 Capacity of the working memory

Although Figure 4.6 represents the same principle within each section, the section that would require the most storage is the set of six random words (a) as this constitutes six bits. If we can construct them into something meaningful, like a sentence, they become one bit (b), or we can represent them as a mental image, also being one bit (c).

As we learn the basics of a new dance genre, we start to learn its vocabulary. We can create something that equates to a meaningful sentence (triple time step), from something that was originally a set of random steps (such as: brush, hop, shuffle, step, flap, ball-change). Understanding the structure of dance helps professional dancers to predict or anticipate sequences to come, a skill that develops over time (Bläsing et al., 2009). By combining sequences based on the grammar of different dance genres allows for a *chunking* of information, reducing the number of concepts to be stored (Poon & Rodgers, 2000).

Knowledge structures of the long-term memory

Knowledge is held in the *long-term memory*, within which there are two types of memory store: (1) the *declarative store* holding memories that can be spoken about, including episodic and semantic memory; and (2) those that cannot be put into words are held in the *procedural store* (Squire, 1992).

Declarative store

Episodic memory is information stored about perceptual events in your life, and links to other autobiographic experiences stored about you. These memories may fade over time or become distorted by newer life experiences (Tulving, 1972). This might include life experiences such as your memories of your first appearance on stage.

Semantic memory is the storage of general knowledge, related to language or symbols, independent of the experience of learning the facts (Tulving, 1972). This would include your recall of the plot of *Billy Elliott* as well as being able to name the Basic Action Concepts of a sequence of steps used as a double-time step.

Procedural store

Procedural memories are those that relate to how we do something – the mental representations. They differ from semantic memory as they are the non-verbal component, for example, you might be able to do a ball-change but putting into words how you actually carry out the action is problematic. This form of memory represents the motor programs stored for our actions, however simple (hop) or complex (double wing).

Memory recall

Context-dependent memory

Once memories have been stored, they will need to be recalled at appropriate times. One way to assist in recall is to mimic the situation at encoding. *State-dependent memory* refers to internal aspects, such as your state of mind at the point of learning, whereas *situation-dependent memory* refers to being in the same environment or exposed to the same environmental cues at recall, as had been present at the encoding stage. Being exposed to such triggers enhances the level of recall (Godden & Baddeley, 1975). One of the most effective cues to recall is the music (Stevens, Ginsborg, & Lester, 2011). This is most effective as it underpins the learning process (encoding), the phrasing within the music suggests actions (cues), and most importantly it will be playing during the performance (recall). Expert dancers utilise a range of musical cues, such as high and low notes, rhythm and chorus to aid chorography recall (Poon & Rodgers, 2000).

Stages of skill acquisition

Learning is a process that occurs through a combination of:

- direct perception, such as watching the teacher (cognitive processes);
- mirroring, where the brain triggers already stored motor programs (neuronal);
- implicit learning through the already learnt step names and dance vocabulary (association) (Stevens & McKechnie, 2005).

Fitts and Posner proposed a model of *skill acquisition* that breaks the learning process into three stages: the cognitive, associative and autonomous stages (cited in Beilock, Wierenga, & Carr, 2002), which is underpinned by information processing (see Figure 4.5).

Cognitive stage

The *cognitive stage* is sometimes referred to as the verbal stage as it is the time where we gather information about the new skill to be learnt, and this new information will initially be expressed through language. Through learning the range of terms used to express steps and combinations (vocabulary), a grammar is built (Stevens & McKechnie, 2005). This language may include the application of non-dance-related terms to help suggest force or dynamism, or they may be sounds that represent rhythm (tum-tee-tum-tum). Gathering of

© Shutterstock

declarative information occurs in this stage, where information about *what* and *how* is stored in the semantic knowledge store.

The way that information is processed at this stage is referred to as controlled processing. *Controlled processing* is the conscious effort to process new information through the working memory. As the effort is conscious, only one factor at a time can be concentred on, making the process very slow and inconsistent (Abernethy, Maxwell, Masters, van der Kamp, & Jackson, 2007). As we become more proficient as dancers, we may bypass this stage when there is sufficient vocabulary already stored (Stevens & McKechnie, 2005).

Associative stage

As we develop the skills we start to make associations between stimulus and response, learning production rules where we understand that 'if I do this – then that will happen', for example, 'if I spot when turning – then I will keep my balance'. As we start to grasp the basics we no longer need to pay attention to them, and can focus on the more difficult aspects. This leads to more fluid and efficient movements.

Autonomous stage

The *autonomous stage* is the point of accomplishment, where the skill has been learnt. This is now stored as a motor program of procedural knowledge. In the autonomous stage we are using *automatic processing*, bypassing the working memory as the action no longer requires any conscious thought. As a result, movements are now effortless and fluid as a different area of the brain is now responsible for the movement. As no conscious attention is required, the mind has capacity to focus on other things such as characterisation (Abernethy et al., 2007).

Although an autonomous stage might have been reached, this does not mean that the action will always be automated. If we start to pay conscious attention to the movement, this will make our brain revert to controlled processing and the movement will lack fluidity. This may occur if we overthink something, especially in action. This may also occur when we are stressed because we become more aware of our performance.

Imagery

Imagery theory

In the same way that we store different types of knowledge separately in the mind, the brain also uses different areas for these different functions, but with overlap (Figure 4.7). Motor programs (how to create a movement) are represented in a different area of the brain than the area which deals with mental representations, be it actual visual perception such as watching an action, or when imagining a movement. There are also separate areas for visual and spatial processes (Jeannerod, 1994). As these different activities are dealt with separately within the brain, so are our mental images of these activities.

SKILL ACQUISITION

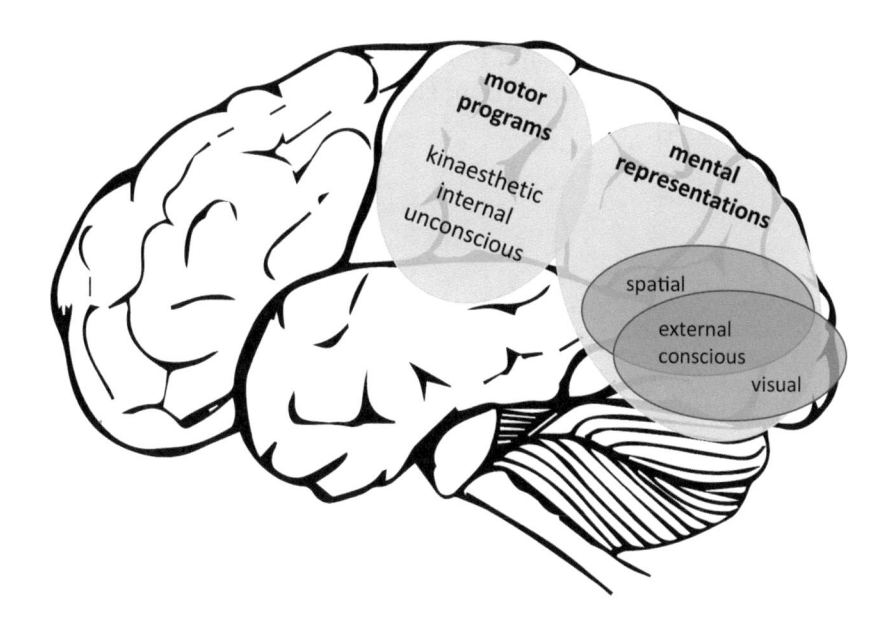

Figure 4.7
Representation of imagery within the brain

Mental imagery

Mental imagery is the creation of pictures in our mind. When we undertake mental imagery we do this at a conscious level, where we are able to describe what we imagine. At a *visual* level we can manipulate the image through rotation and through time, whereas at a *spatial* level we can rotate the perspective or imagine movement through space. These images are therefore taking an external perspective, as if we were watching ourselves on screen.

Motor imagery

Motor imagery is imagining carrying out a specific movement. When we carry out motor imagery, we do it from an internal perspective – as though we are looking through our own eyes. This means we experience the imagery at a more sensory level; a kinaesthetic feeling of the action, including sensations of force and pressure (Jeannerod, 1994). Motor imagery is different from visual imagery as we cannot verbalise our motor programs because they relate to procedural knowledge.

Action, observation and images

Due to the overlapping nature of knowledge stores and brain functions, we do not have to rely on doing the movement for this neural trace to be activated in the brain. An observation of the activity will mirror this neuronal activity triggering the same areas of the brain as if we were actually carrying out the movement (Gallese & Goldman, 1998). This suggests that once a skill has been attempted and an initial neural trace has been created, watching others demonstrating the action can enhance this trace in your brain.

In addition, the same neurons that are used to undertake an action are also activated when we mentally recreate the action. Therefore, motor and mental imagery are considered *functionally equivalent* – that within the brain the same neural activities take place whether we execute the movement or just imagine doing it. This not only occurs within the brain, but research has shown that there are minute eye movements and muscle contractions that correlate with actually carrying out the physical action, showing its impact throughout the body (Jeannerod, 1994).

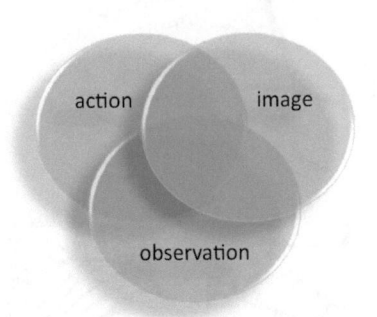

This means that once learnt, an action can be practised mentally as well as physically, but it also means that if we create an incorrect version of the action, we will mimic this incorrect action when we return to physical action. Research has also shown that there needs to be a functional equivalence between the time required to undertake the action, and the time taken to imagine it (Jeannerod, 1994).

Functions of imagery

Imagery has many different functions, as can be seen in Figure 4.8 (Gregg, Hall, & Nederhof, 2005). The purpose of the imagery may be either general or specific, and this perspective may be applied not only to skill-based activities, but may have motivational functions:

- *Learning*: Cognitively the dancer may want create specific images to help master a certain step – referred to as *cognitive specific* (CS). While learning, the most common use of imagery is during the training process, imagining the step before trying. This can be taken out of the studio and used as an additional means of the skill acquisition.
- *Rehearsing*: Imagery can be used to gain a more general grasp of character or choreography – referred to as *cognitive general* (CG). It can be used prior

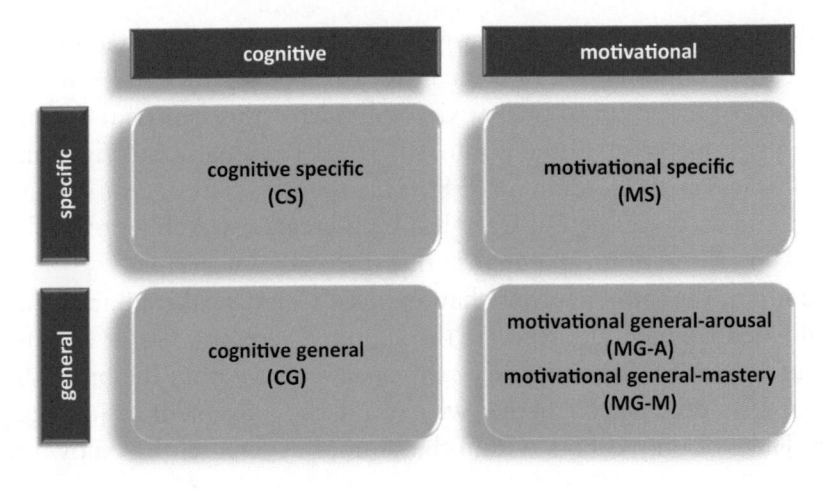

Figure 4.8
Functions of imagery

Source: Based on Hall, Mack, Paivio & Hausenblas (1998).

to assessments or performances to reassure or recap on choreography. Imagery can also be applied during movement, especially the use of metaphorical images to enhance the motion.
- *Self-confidence*: There may be a motivational purpose to the imagery with a particular aim in sight, such as winning a competition – *motivational specific* (MS), or *motivation general-mastery* (MG-M) for general confidence boosting, as discussed in more detail in Chapter 3.
- *Emotional regulation*: Imagery can also be used to manage your emotional state through *motivation general-arousal* (MG-A). It can be used to help achieve the right state of arousal prior to performance, or it may be used to manage pre-performance anxiety (see Chapter 6 for more details).

Content of imagery

Multisensory

Imagery adds a more concrete experience to something that could otherwise be quite abstract, and the more detail that can be included, the more effective imagery will be (Bolles & Chatfield, 2009). Although the term *imagery* suggests a visual perception, there is much more to imagery than this. The purpose of imagery is to recreate the real environment within the mind, and the nearer this internal mental representation is to reality, the more effective it will be. Therefore, all senses should be utilised, as shown in Figure 4.9.

- **visual** – anything that can be seen when performing, including steps, performers, stage or audience
- **auditory** – anything that can be heard when performing, such as music and footsteps
- **haptic** – anything that creates a sense of touch, especially in partner work
- **olfactory** – anything that you can smell when performing
- **gustative** – anything that you can taste when performing
- **kinaesthetic** – all the feelings of movement experienced when performing

Figure 4.9
Multisensory imagery

The expert dancer is more likely to create multisensory images (Bolles & Chatfield, 2009), which in time will increase in quality, over which they will have greater control (Nordin & Cumming, 2006).

Perspective

Imagery content is likely to change over time. As a novice, the images are more likely to be visual in nature, and often from an external perspective – as if you are looking at a video of yourself (Nordin & Cumming, 2006). This is because when learning, dancers spend more time looking at the external images of teachers demonstrating steps, so this is how they recreate their images. As dance proficiency increases, there is a tendency to use internal perspective as if looking through your own eyes. This generates more kinaesthetic and less metaphorical images (Nordin & Cumming, 2006). This is a result of the skills having been acquired, so there is no need to see them at a literal or metaphorical level. The dancer is now working on whether it *feels* right.

Research in focus

**Where, When and How:
A Quantitative Account of Dance Imagery**

Aim Although imagery has been shown to be a useful technique in a range of different physical activities, there are differences between dance and sport, as dance is a preforming art. The purpose of this research was to establish when dancers are more likely to use imagery, whether this is situation-dependent, and how the imagery is generated.

Method A survey was completed by 250 dancers, from leisure through to elite, from thirteen different dance genres.
The Dance Imagery Basics survey was used to collect data about:
- Dance genre, level and years of experience
- Scaled questions indicating how, where and when imagery is most likely to be used

Results
- *Frequency:* higher level dancers used imagery more frequently than leisure dancers
- *When:* higher level dancers were more likely to use imagery in motion
- *Sources:* higher level dancers were more likely to get images from teachers and each other
- *Image type:* higher level dancers were more likely to produce complex images

Conclusions There were no differences in imagery outside of the studio, regardless of level and genre, which suggests that although elite dancers are using it to their advantage in practice, much more use of imagery could be made by all dancers outside of the dance context.

(Nordin & Cumming, 2007)

SKILL ACQUISITION

Sources of imagery

Images can be gathered from a range of sources. They may be from the direct observation of teachers, professional dancers or colleagues. They may be from media sources, such as videos or stage productions, or they may be dynamic or static, such as referring to photographs or books. Alternatively, the images may be internally produced from memories of previous performances (Nordin & Cumming, 2007).

Image range

Images can be of actual content, such as imagining the correct posture or a specific step. Imagery can also help dancers to grasp a movement or force through using metaphorical images. Metaphorical images help create a movement which is difficult to explain in words. Metaphorical images can be used to create motion, 'imagine you are being blown by the wind', or to create a sense of pressure or dynamism.

Self-talk

Self-talk can be described as talking to oneself, where the conversations are dynamic and of a motivational or instructional nature, where the interpretation of the message is as important as the sending of the message (Hardy, 2006).

Dimensions of self-talk

Self-talk can be described through six different dimensions, each having a different impact on performance (Hardy, 2006) as can be seen in Figure 4.10.

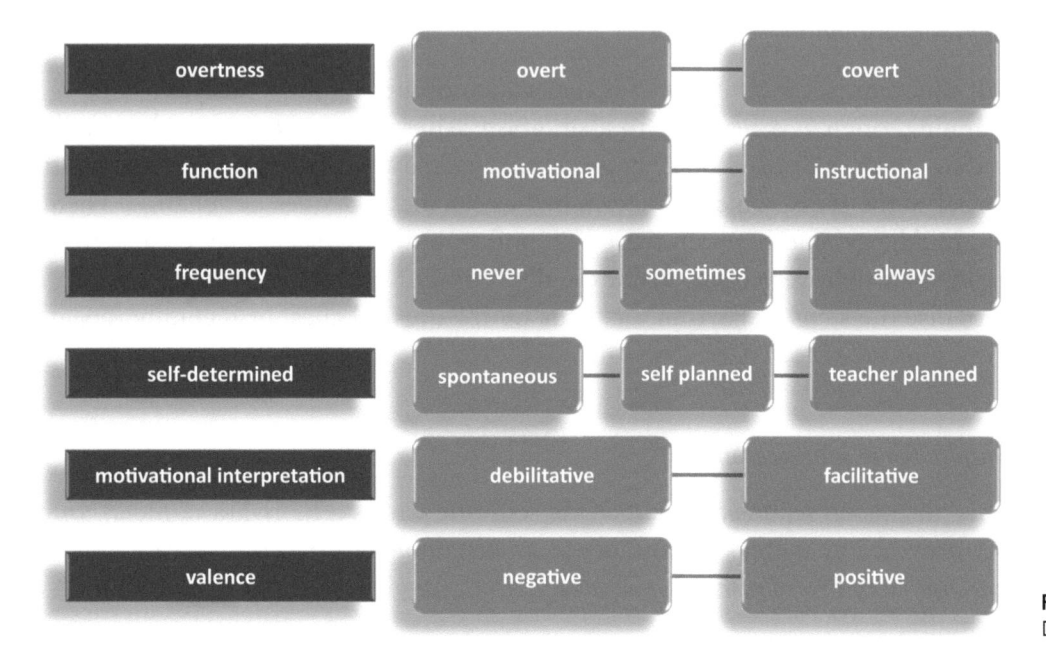

Dimension			
overtness	overt	covert	
function	motivational	instructional	
frequency	never	sometimes	always
self-determined	spontaneous	self planned	teacher planned
motivational interpretation	debilitative	facilitative	
valence	negative	positive	

Figure 4.10 Dimensions of self-talk

Overtness

The *overtness* of self-talk is whether the verbalisations are private messages spoken aloud for your ears only, or whether the message is *covert*, where the conversation is held in your mind. Although the content of the messages may be the same, the effect may not be. When engaging in overt self-talk, other senses are at play, the fact that you need to articulate the statements requires different cognitive processing than purely thinking. And once the message has been articulated, it is then received through the phonological loop by listening to the message you have sent. You are therefore having to receive and process the message sent, a process that does not occur when the message is covert.

Function

There are two functions of self-talk: instructional or motivational. *Motivational* self-talk can affect your level of arousal, concentration, desire to pursue the activity and the effort you apply, whereas *instructional* self-talk can improve skill, timing and accuracy, especially of fine muscle control. The instructions may be verbalised as a *preparation* for performance to achieve the right level of activation or recalling the first few steps, *during* the action to maintain concentration or timing, or even as a *result* of the action as a form of reinforcement.

Frequency

The dimension of frequency falls between *never* using self-talk, through to using it *all of the time*. Research suggests that those who use self-talk more frequently are likely to benefit from it, although this is dependent upon the positivity of the other dimensions.

Self-determined

Self-talk that is *self-determined* is that which occurs spontaneously without planning, often as a response to a situation. Alternatively, *determined* self-talk is that which is devised by someone else. This may be the teacher telling you to verbalise the steps, which is determined as the message does not change. There is a middle ground between these two points, in that dancers may choose to make their own verbalisations of the dance in different ways. You might verbalise the steps or rhythm, or focus on the musical cues, or mentally repeat the count.

Motivational interpretation

This dimension relates to whether the self-talk acts as a motivation, *facilitating* performance by increasing confidence or sustaining effort. Alternatively, the message may be *debilitative*, encouraging you to give up either physically or mentally.

Valence

The valence of self-talk refers to whether the content of the message is deemed as *positive*, such as praise, or *negative* such as reprimanding yourself. The valence dimension is different from motivational interpretation, as praising ourselves may lead to conceit and a lack of effort, whereas reprimanding ourselves may motivate us to work harder as demonstrated in Figure 4.11.

Content of self-talk

Instructional

Instructional self-talk can include a range of content for different outcomes (Gammage, Hardy, & Hall, 2001). In preparation for a performance, it can be used to set the level of arousal by calming phrases, such as 'and breathe', or confirmation of what is to be performed, such as verbalising the initial step sequence. During performances there may be the continued dialogue of steps or counts, or it may be applied when reaching the trickier sequences. Self-talk may also be used to adjust pace throughout the performance with instructions like 'take it easy' or 'don't rush'.

Motivational

Motivational self-talk can be used prior to performances as a confidence booster, 'let's go', or during 'keep it up' and 'we're nearly there'. After performances it can be used to reinforce behaviour through praise or confirmation. Other self-talk may reflect feelings 'I'm loving this', or even appearance-related content, 'looking good'.

Structure of self-talk

Self-talk may be comprised of single word (Gammage et al., 2001). This might be pre-determined instructions, such as 'focus' or technique-related 'extend', or it might be spontaneous motivational responses, such as a celebratory 'yes!'.

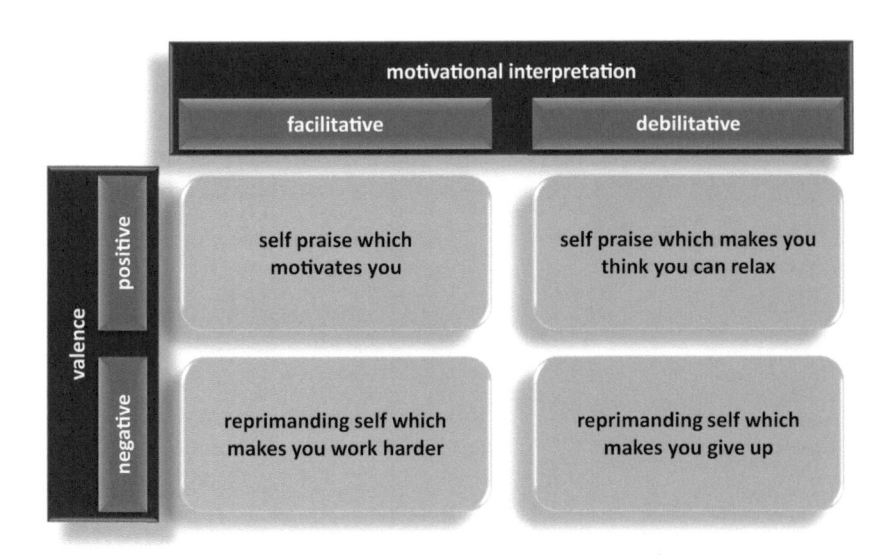

Figure 4.11 Interaction of motivation and valence dimensions

© Shutterstock

The self-talk may extend to whole sentences. These may be naturally occurring such as reprimanding yourself with 'why did you do that?' or specified, such as step sequences.

The self-talk may also vary in how the speech is addressed (Gammage et al., 2001). It may be first person references 'I'm on it' or second person references 'you knew you could do it.' When it is a second-person reference, it may be a phrase that your teacher regularly uses, or even the voice of the teacher that is being heard, bringing the teacher to the performance within your head.

PRACTICE

Imagery

Teaching imagery

Imagery is not necessarily a natural function, dancers who have been taught by someone who encouraged imagery use were more likely to use imagery in their practice than those who had not been encouraged (Bolles & Chatfield, 2009), therefore dance teachers should use directed imagery to enhance retention of information and performance expression.

Directing dancers

Nordin and Cumming (2006) found that teachers could make imagery more prominent in their classes. This can be achieved through explicitly directing dancers to visualise specific skills or feel certain moves. Movements that are difficult to describe could be expressed through metaphorical imagery. They also suggested that teachers should encourage dancers to use imagery outside of the studio.

When introducing dancers to imagery, it is important to consider what types of imagery they will respond well to, and what images they are capable of creating. The age of the dancer is important as asking teenagers to 'bounce like Tigger' will not be as effective as using this image with young children. Equally, children who have never seen Tigger will not be able to engage with the imagery activity, so consideration needs to be made of what is being asked.

When working with novice dancers (or even those new to imagery), try using words or phrases that relate to visual imagery, such as '*see* how the arm rotates'. Those with more experience should be encouraged to undertake kinaesthetic imagery '*feel* that upward stretch' (IADMS, 2011).

Introducing imagery to dancers

On the face of it, imagery does not sound as though it can be as effective as practice, so some dancers will need to be convinced as to the validity of the technique. To help convince dancers to adopt the technique as part of their skills development repertoire, there are several steps that can be taken (Morris, Spittle, & Watt, 2005).

Engaging with the idea

Starting with anecdotal evidence will help personalise the validity of the technique. These personal accounts could be those of the teacher's or may be accounts given by professional dancers which are widely available from interviews in the media.

Understanding the mechanisms

Dancers may be curious how thinking about a physical action can make you perform it more effectively. Therefore, a simple explanation as to how the brain and mind work with respect to overlapping functions will help inform. Offer further reading for those who are curious (see Further Reading section for recommendations).

Engaging with the process

Once the dancers can see that there are scientific explanations and there are examples of dancers they admire benefitting from imagery, they will be more likely to take the process seriously. Start with simple imagery exercises, building as their proficiency increases.

Building imagery skills

Imagery is a complex skill which needs to be developed over time (Cumming & Ramsey, 2010), adults are more successful at creating and controlling images than children (Morris et al., 2005). The only prerequisite is that the dancer needs to have tried to execute the move before the imagery is applied (Williams, Cumming, & Edwards, 2011). This ensures that there is a motor representation of the movement for the image to associate with.

Start with easy aspects, such as a simple skill, from an external perspective, concentrating on purely visual perception. This can be gradually developed by increasing the complexity of the skill from a step to a sequence. More sensory elements can be added to increase the completeness of the experience. Finally, make the transition from an external to an internal perspective to introduce kinaesthetic sensations.

Personalisation

To maximise the technique, dancers can identify issues that are specific to their practice and focus on these particular factors. This will increase performance techniques, and will subsequently increase the motivation to engage in the process due to the meaning the dancer has attached to the focus of their imagery (Cumming & Ramsey, 2010).

Scripts

Creating scripts to help dancers with their imagery can be a useful way to ensure that they are engaging in the process. Audio-recording scripts ensures that the dancer can try their imagery in a comfortable place with their eyes closed – focusing on the directions within the script. Recording the scripts ensures that you have control over the type of language used, and that the pace of the imagery exercise allows sufficient time for images to be created without the dancer rushing through the process, and ensures that the timing is correct for performance pieces. This also offers the option to really personalise the script to meet each dancer's needs (Cumming & Ramsey, 2010).

Multisensory imagery

The word imagery suggests a visualisation – as though sight is the perception that is being used. Although this is often the essence of imagery, especially in the early adoption of the technique, this should be expanded to increase the completeness of the mental recreation.

Visual

Skill acquisition

Visual representations of the skill are often the starting place. When learning a new step, an external perspective can really help the dancer understand what the step should look like. Once this is done, then the dancer should try to rotate the image to increase its completeness within the mind.

Performance

When progressing on to an internal perspective, different visual cues may become important. The mental images will not tend to be of the self or the steps, but on what is occurring around. It may be visualising the stage and audience as a way of familiarising yourself with the environment to control emotions. Alternatively, it may be a recreation of the dancers' places on the stage as the choreography progresses, through spatial visualisation.

Auditory

One of the most prominent auditory features of the performance is going to be the music, offering the most specific cues to action. This can be augmented by other sounds. Obviously in tap routines there is the tapping to complement the music, reinforcing the retention and recall of choreography. There are also other auditory cues that may help with confidence-building, such as audience applause at the end of the piece.

Haptic

There are many ways that the sensation of touch becomes evident, from the feel of your shoes to the weight of your costume. There may be the use of props that add to the touch sensation. Human touch may also feature, where dancers interact with each other, especially important in hold or if lifts are involved.

Olfactory

Although not the first thing that comes to mind when considering dance – smell may feature in some ways. It may be the smell of hairspray and make-up when getting ready, or the dust catching in the heat of the stage lights that creates the sensation of place. All of these add to the atmosphere and may help when using imagery to manage emotions.

Gustative

Probably the least important sense in dance imagery, but when considering the personalisation of dance imagery, if you commonly eat a specific food on a performance day or chew gum, then these are tastes that can make the image complete.

Kinaesthetic

This is the most advanced sensory experience when undertaking dance imagery. It is the ability to feel body posture, dynamism, flow and movement, rather than just view it. This is the type of sense that dancers should be aiming for as they become proficient in their technique.

Skill acquisition

Step learning

Having identified that memory is not a singular store, but a series of processes that link to different stores, then it makes sense to relate new information to as many of the knowledge stores as possible in order to maximise the learning potential.

Working memory

To activate as many areas as possible within the working memory, we need to bring together the visuo-spatial sketchpad with the phonological loop. To do this, learners need to know what the step looks like to activate the visuo-spatial sketchpad, and link this visual image with the name of the step.

When connections can readily be made between the name of the step and the movement, then the learner has reached the *associative stage* of learning.

Long-term memory

Once we have learnt to associate the name of the step with what it should look like, we need to develop this into a longer-term memory by creating a motor program. Breaking the step down into parts creates a verbal framework in the semantic element of the declarative store, while trying to carry out the step will produce a motor program within the procedural store.

Once this can be done without conscious attention being paid to it, the *autonomous stage* of learning will have been achieved.

Verbal

Using language when teaching activates the declarative store, within which the semantic stores holds fact-based information.

Chunking

The name that we give a step acts as a verbal shorthand, when we combine them into a name that represents a sequence, the shorthand is even more effective. In cognitive terms the combining of concepts such as step names is called *chunking*, as it is the chunking together of complex information into a meaningful code. Saying 'basic cramp roll' is more meaningful and efficient than saying 'right toe, left toe, right heel, left heel'. The earlier dancers learn the vocabulary of their dance, the more efficient use of class time (Poon & Rodgers, 2000).

Instructional self-talk

Using language activates both phonological and procedural elements of memory, both can help trigger the correct motor programs. Using covert self-talk, where you say the steps in your head, can act as instructional self-talk. This may even be the hearing of your teacher's voice calling the steps, if this is what is recalled from training. Additionally, it may help to sing the steps in your head to add timing, rhythm and sequence.

Sound patterns

We can also help dancers learn steps through verbalisations that recreate the sound of the step. Trying to remember an abstract set of movements may be difficult, and in some cases we may remember the actual movements but not the rhythm. Choosing phrases that are appropriate to your particular learner group can help underpin the rhythm of the step. For example, a ladies' recreational tap class might use the phrase 'would you like white or red wine?' as a rhythmic template for a time step, whereas 'will you come for a picnic?' would be more appropriate for a children's class. This verbalisation will help link declarative information with procedural knowledge.

Spoken imagery

To help dancers create shapes or hold postures, imagery can be used as metaphors for movements that are not always easy to describe verbally. These images can be adapted to work with learners of all ages. A wing step can be described as trying to wipe chewing gum from the sole of your shoe, or to correct posture, try asking the dancers to imagine being pulled by a string from the top of their head.

Visual

There are various opportunities to store visual information when learning. This may be an observation of a teacher demonstration, an observation of yourself in the mirror, or looking at your limbs in action.

Observation

Generally the first point of learning is through the observation of others, often a dance teacher. This activates the visuo-spatial sketchpad within the working memory, and the more frequently we observe the action, the more we start to create a motor program within the mind, even though we are not practising the movement while watching. It is the motor program that will form the foundation of the procedural knowledge when it is developed into a long-term memory.

Mental imagery

The visualisation of a skill is the mental recreation in the mind of what a movement looks like, and as such it tends to be an external view of the movement (Holmes & Collins, 2001). This external view allows you to look at the image from different perspectives; what it looks like to the audience (front view), how it looks to fellow dancers (back or side views), even how it looks to you (internal, top view). The ability to manipulate images will allow more control over your imagery skills and a much deeper understanding of the action. Those who undertake skill visualisation have lower levels of anxiety (Fish, Hall, & Cumming, 2004).

Kinaesthetic

There is only so much that can be learnt in terms of technical knowledge or the recognition of steps – the rest is really down to practice. The ultimate aim is to remove the mind from the activity and let the body take over. When you reach this stage, you are in the autonomous stage of learning.

Imagery

When learning a step, it is best imagined from an internal perspective as this is how it will be performed. Try to imagine what you would see through your own eyes while you were dancing (but resist the temptation to look down!). There should be very little reliance on the visual component of imagery through this perspective, as the emphasis should be on the kinaesthetic feel of the action. This is what you are aiming to create as this is how it will be when performing – the knowledge that it *feels* right.

Remembering choreography

In the studio

Much of the dancer's life is spent in the studio with the aim of remembering dance sequences for competition, assessment or performance. However technically accomplished you may be, if you cannot remember the steps, your technical ability will never be discovered. Therefore, anything that can be done to help the retention of choreography must be utilised.

Marking

Marking is any reduced movement of a target sequence, diminishing size, height or extension of steps, or substituting hand gestures for foot movements. Marking has many functions, and as it has been found to be as effective as physical rehearsal, teachers should consider the integration of marking more strategically into their classes, especially when leaning new choreography (Warburton, Wilson, Lynch, & Cuykendall, 2013). It is important to finalise any session with fully danced performance to reinforce the marking, creating the necessary motor programs.

Energy conservation

Having grasped the sequence, marking can be used to reinforce memory traces without having to expend more energy. This means that class time might be better utilised as fatigue reduces cognitive attention and physical skills, which in turn may increase errors and frustration.

Preparation

Marking can be done at the start of each class. This will prepare the brain with the relevant motor programs to be used, and refresh the memory of the step sequences.

Refinement

Once the choreography is learnt, marking can be used to improve dancer's spatial understanding of the set piece by moving through the space to the music. Static marking can now be used to emphasise aspects of choreography that need more attention, and to correct timing issues.

Demonstrations

Teacher's demonstrations act as a model for learner behaviour, and are effective for several reasons.

Modelling

In a social context, demonstrations promote social learning as the dancers are observing someone they perceive as a role model due to their dance expertise. Through the desire to internalise this level of proficiency, they will aim to retain the information received so they can reproduce it, to the satisfaction of the teacher (Bandura, 1977). This relational aspect indicates why teacher feedback is vital to reinforce good or improving representations of the steps.

Observational impact

At a cognitive level, the observation of known steps activates the same neural pathways as those used when undertaking the actions, therefore, building up stronger neural connections with the motor program. Due to this strong cognitive link to physical reproduction, it is important that what is observed is exactly what is required to be reproduced, as incorrect observations go deeper than a cognitive level. Teachers may want to dissuade helpful students from demonstrating to struggling colleagues as any errors in their demonstrations may be counter-productive to the learning of others.

Perspectives and mirrors

Although much of the research already presented has suggested that observation and imagery are important techniques to learn choreography, there are caveats to this. At some point there will be the need to perform the sequence without other visual aids, so the choreography will need to be stored and recalled, without reliance on watching the dance teacher. When in the studio, dancers often gauge their progress by watching their own performance in the mirrors. It is important that they can perform without the mirror as they may be using the reflections of the other dancers to aid recall.

For the highest quality performance the choreography needs to be learnt so well that it requires no conscious attention, being performed automatically. In order to ensure this occurs, external visual cues must be removed. Covering the mirrors is one way that reliance on them can be reduced, but to really establish whether the sequence is remembered, try performing the dance in different situations. If there are no other venues available, just changing the orientation within the studio can be very effective.

Associations

Creating associations between verbal references to choreography and the physical motion has been shown to enhance recall. During the learning phase this can be done by saying (or singing) the names of the steps (in your head or aloud) (Poon & Rodgers, 2000). Conversely, making small physical marking gestures while recounting the steps verbally helps embed the memories (Starkes, Deakin, Lindley, & Crisp, 1987).

As dancers become more proficient, they are able to derive a great amount of information from cues within the music, so the use of music as a trigger for recall can be highly beneficial (Poon & Rodgers, 2000). Therefore, it may help to make associations to elements of the music or sing the lyrics internally when practising a routine to create associations from steps to features of the music.

Imagery

Imagery can be used during the learning process to help absorb different elements of choreography at an action and spatial level.

Learning

For sequences within the dance that are less well learnt, imagery can be used to slow these sections down, allowing a focus on the intricate aspects of the movement. When the problem area has been understood, imagery should continue at the correct performance speed (Holmes & Collins, 2001).

If there is a complex interaction between the dancers on stage, imagery can be manipulated through adopting an external perspective. Trying to visualise how all the dancers move around the space will help individuals see where they need to be and when. Once the spatial aspects are learnt, then return to an internal perspective (Holmes & Collins, 2001).

Preparation

Both the observation of others and the personal imagery of movements prior to undertaking the movement prime the brain with the motor program that is required (Williams et al., 2011). This can be used as preparation for a difficult step or sequence, or it can be used as preparation for a dance performance for reassurance.

Maintaining concentration

Long sessions in the studio are not only physically tiring, but they can be mentally tiring too. To make the best of the time spent in training or rehearsal, there needs to be maximum concentration, but this cannot be sustained indefinitely.

Keeping it fresh

One way of helping sustain concentration is to vary the tasks, spending limited intervals of time on each activity. This can give both body and mind a rest, so practice can be returned to refreshed. This can be achieved through interspersing technical drills with choreographic content, or physical dance time with marking. Using time for discussions about problematic sequences or creative input refreshes the dancers physically and mentally, and may help iron out aspects that are holding dancers back.

Self-talk

Self-talk can be used to correct the attentional style. If dancers are drifting into daydreams (broad internal), self-talk (narrow internal) can help refocus their attention. Teachers can support dancers by using motivational phrases that the dancers can internalise, or can encourage them to find their own voice to maintain their concentration. Phrases like 'back in the room' or 'focus' can help them adopt the correct attentional style.

External attention may need to be paid to broad aspects, such as using the space on stage, or narrow features such as a specific step. Suggesting cue words at key times may help dancers adopt self-talk techniques at the relevant times.

> **Outside the studio**
>
> Although many a long hour may be spent in the studio, there may be times when there is insufficient time to learn the pieces for a new production. At these times it may be useful to use time outside of the studio to help the learning process.

Musical cues

To recreate the context of dance, music is the greatest cue. Elements of its construction, such as chorus or highlights, should help jog the memory and dictate emotional expression and changes in dynamism. Another vital component of using music to augment imagery of choreography is that it offers functional equivalence for the timing of the performance by setting the correct pace (Holmes & Collins, 2001). Once the choreography is learnt, it can be mentally rehearsed anywhere. Using earphones, dancers can rehearse while sitting on the bus or waiting for a class to start. Even putting the music on before drifting off to sleep.

Video

To ensure that the choreography that is being memorised outside of rehearsal is correct, then using video footage as an aide-memoire is a reliable source of information. Out of studio access to the video can fill in gaps in the memory, increasing the dancer's confidence when memory of the steps match those on the video. Watching the video can increase memory retention through the motor neurons mirroring what is being observed. The video may also recreate the actual environment if shot in the actual performance space, which enhances the learning process (Holmes & Collins, 2001).

When taking videos as a memory aid, it is important that the performance being recorded is to the level that the dancers are expected to reach, as this will be used to set the bar. In addition, it may help to have the video filmed from behind the dancers modelling the sequence, as this recreates the perspective that the dancers will have, and reduce right-left confusion.

Injury

Being injured can be a very stressful period for a dancer. Not only is there the stress of having the pain and discomfort of the injury, and the effects this may have on your daily life, but there are professional stresses that come with being injured. With competition for roles, and tight rehearsal schedules, dancers want to be back on their feet as soon as possible. This urgency to return to the studio needs to be balanced with being fit enough to dance for fear of further injury.

One way that this drive to return too early can be tempered is through imagery. Being in the studio, watching the demonstrations, listening to the instructions and absorbing the movements with the music, start to create memory traces within the brain. This has the effect of reducing stress as the choreography is being learnt at the same rate as the other dancers, and feeling involved in the dance and its development (IADMS, 2011).

Performance enhancement

Performing

Although it is essential to remember the choreography and be as technically accurate as possible when performing, it is also important to remember that the audience are there to be entertained. Concentration on the steps and focus on technical prowess may rob the performance of the character, distract from the storytelling, or reduce engagement with the audience.

Self-talk for performance

Motivational

When performing for an audience or assessment, you do not have the teacher or director there for support, so self-talk is a way of bringing them to the performance within your mind. Recreate their voice in your head saying the phrases that you know will support you when nervous.

If the task is exhausting, then the adoption of motivational self-talk can help maintain effort throughout the performance. Use your inner voice to give you the momentum to carry on.

Instructional

If the task is technically challenging, then using cue words can help maintain high technical ability. Even the tone of voice used within self-talk can act as a cue to action. Emphasising or elongating a word can remind the dancer of pace, height or force.

Embodying the dance

Walk the genre

When learning a new dance genre, especially if already proficient in another, it is difficult to leave information from other genres behind. Although there are some helpful transferable skills and knowledge that will be of benefit, this can sometimes be problematic.

To embody each dance, one needs to adopt the character of the genre, and a way that we judge characters in real-life situations is often from first impressions – what someone looks like. Adopting the physical posture of the dance style, and learning to walk in this way help you create the character of the dance genre. Consider the slouched loose walk of the street dancer compared to the poise of the ballerina.

This can be extended by the adoption of a character which can be embodied by wearing the relevant clothes and even adopting a character name that links to that dance.

Self-talk

Having reached the time of the performance, the dance should be automated, meaning that there is no need to pay conscious attention to the choreography. At this point the dancer needs to embody the dance, not the technique. Self-talk to remind yourself that this is a dance which needs to be felt by the audience, and this will only occur if *you* are feeling it in the performing. Phrases like 'dance it' or 'feel it' can help remind the dancer to engage in the emotion or storytelling, as the technique should already be in place.

Embodying the character

Having learnt the choreography, then you must ensure that the character is being portrayed, using imagery to create a richness to your character (Hanrahan & Vergeer, 2001). The images can involve factors not necessarily related to dance, such as their clothes or the way they speak or the places they would visit. Creating a deep understanding of the character you are portraying will help you capture this essence within the dance – adding authenticity.

Imagery

Having established that imagery can be used as a means of learning steps and choreography, it may also be used to enhance performance elements. There are many ways that imagery can be employed depending upon what the dancer is trying to achieve (Hanrahan & Vergeer, 2001).

Inspiration imagery

Before launching into new choreography, imagery can be used to set the scene, so the dancers understand their characters within the piece. This may include how they walk and move, and how they interact with each other:

You are playing Roxie Hart. Think about why she has murdered her lover, what does this tell you about her character? How would this affect her interactions with the world?

Atmospheric imagery

By imagining a particular atmosphere, dancers can adapt their movements based on the restrictions or allowances of the chosen atmosphere:

Imagine you are moving through syrup, how would this restrict your movement?
You are in space, in zero gravity, how light would your movements be?

Emptying out/filling up images

A means of preparation for performance, images can be used to rid the body of unwanted tension by breathing out the negative energy, or by breathing in good air. Particular features may be added to the air being inhaled or exhaled:

Breathe out the fog that is weighing you down.
Inhale the yellow of the sun, feel its radiance shining out of you.

Meditative imagery

When learning new choreography, there will be plateau points when the dancers are too tired to progress any further within that session. Take this opportunity to relax and recoup energy by considering other elements of the performance, such as height, direction, interaction and dynamism. Listening to the music with closed eyes will allow associations to be made between musical cues and these performance features.

Key concepts glossary

Attention A concentration of sensory effort towards stimuli.

Concentration A focus of sensory effort towards a chosen stimulus.

Distraction A removal of concentration of sensory effort towards a chosen stimulus to an irrelevant stimulus.

Encoding The integration of external stimuli into the mind for further processing.

Imagery The creation of mental pictures in the mind.

Information processing The processes used to take external stimuli from the environment and integrate them into the mind for future use.

Memory The ability to receive, store and recall different information for future use.

Recall The ability to draw from the mind information previously stored.

Self-talk A conversation occurring with the self.

Skills acquisition The learning of a motor program so the performance can be demonstrated consistently.

References

Abernethy, B., Maxwell, J. P., Masters, R. S. W., van der Kamp, J., & Jackson, R. C. (2007). Attentional processes in skill learning and expert performance. In G. Tenebaum & R. C. Eklund (Eds.), *Handbook of sport psychology*. Hoboken, NJ: John Wiley & Sons, Inc.

Baddeley, A. D. (2010). Working memory. *Current Biology, 20*(4), R136–R140. doi:10.1016/j.cub.2009.12.014.

Bandura, A. (1977). *Social learning theory*. Englewood Cliffs, NJ: Prentice-Hall.

Beilock, S. L., Wierenga, S. A., & Carr, T. H. (2002). Expertise, attention, and memory in sensorimotor skill execution: Impact of novel task constraints on dual-task performance and episodic memory. *The Quarterly Journal of Experimental Psychology: Human Experimental Psychology, 55*, 1211–1240.

Bläsing, B., Tenenbaum, G., & Schack, T. (2009). The cognitive structure of movements in classical dance. *Psychology of Sport and Exercise, 10*(3), 350–360.

Bolles, G., & Chatfield, S. J. (2009). The intersection of imagery ability, imagery use, and learning style: An exploratory study. *Journal of Dance Education, 9*(1), 6–16. doi:10.1080/15290824.2009.10387379.

Cumming, J., & Ramsey, R. (2010). Sport imagery interventions. In S. Mellalieu & S. Hanton (Eds.), *Applied sport psychology: A review* (pp. 5–36). London: Routledge.

Fish, L., Hall, C., & Cumming, J. (2004). Investigating the use of imagery by elite ballet dancers. *Avante, 10*(3), 26–39.

Gallese, V., & Goldman, A. (1998). Mirror neurons and the simulation of mind reading. *Trends in Cognitive Sciences, 2*, 493–501. doi:10.1016/S1364-6613(98)01262-5.

Gammage, K. L., Hardy, J., & Hall, C. R. (2001). A description of self-talk in exercise. *Psychology of Sport and Exercise, 2*(4), 233–247. doi:10.1016/S1469-0292(01)00011-5.

Godden, D. R., & Baddeley, A. D. (1975). Context-dependent memory in two natural environments: on land and underwater. *British Journal of Psychology, 66*(3), 325–331. doi:10.1111/j.2044-8295.1975.tb01468.x.

Gregg, M., Hall, C., & Nederhof, E. (2005). The imagery ability, imagery use, and performance relationship. *The Sport Psychologist, 19*(1), 93–99. doi:10.1123/tsp.19.1.93.

Hanrahan, C., & Vergeer, I. (2001). Multiple uses of mental imagery by professional modern dancers. *Imagination, Cognition and Personality, 20*(3), 231–255. doi:10.2190/RLBE-XQK9-C65F-X05B.

Hardy, J. (2006). Speaking clearly: A critical review of the self-talk literature. *Psychology of Sport and Exercise, 7*(1), 81–97. doi:10.1016/j.psychsport.2005.04.002.

Holmes, P. S., & Collins, D. J. (2001). The PETTLEP approach to motor imagery: A functional equivalence model for sport psychologists. *Journal of Applied Sport Psychology, 13*(1), 60–83. doi:10.1080/10413200109339004.

IADMS. (2011). Handout 3(2)B: Dance imagery. *International Association for Dance Medicine & Science Bulletin for Teachers, 3*(2), 12.

Jeannerod, M. (1994). Motor representations and reality. *Behavioral and Brain Sciences, 17*(2), 229–245. doi:10.1017/S0140525X0003435X.

Morris, T., Spittle, M., & Watt, A. P. (2005). *Imagery in sport*. Champaign, IL: Human Kinetics.

Nakamura, J., & Csikszentmihalyi, M. (2014). The concept of flow. In M. Csikszentmihalyi (Ed.), *Flow and the foundations of positive psychology* (pp. 239–263). New York: Springer.

Nideffer, R. M. (1976). Test of attentional and interpersonal style. *Journal of Personality and Social Psychology, 34*(3), 394–404. doi:10.1037/0022-3514.34.3.394.

Nideffer, R. M. (2002). Theory of attentional and personal style vs. test of attentional and interpersonal style (TAIS). *Enhanced Performance Systems*, 1–34.

Nordin, S. M., & Cumming, J. (2006). The development of imagery in dance part I: Qualitative findings from professional dancers. *Journal of Dance Medicine & Science, 10*, 21–27.

Nordin, S. M., & Cumming, J. (2007). Where, when, and how. *Research Quarterly for Exercise and Sport, 78*(4), 390–395. doi:10.1080/02701367.2007.10599437.

Poon, P. P. L., & Rodgers, W. M. (2000). Learning and remembering strategies of novice and advanced jazz dancers for skill level appropriate dance routines. *Research Quarterly for Exercise and Sport, 71*(2), 135–144. doi:10.1080/02701367.2000.10608891.

Schack, T., Essig, K., Frank, C., & Koester, D. (2014). Mental representation and motor imagery training. *Frontiers in Human Neuroscience, 8*, 328. doi:10.3389/fnhum.2014.00328.

Smyth, M. M., & Pendleton, L. R. (1990). Space and movement in working memory. *The Quarterly Journal of Experimental Psychology Section A, 42*(2), 291–304. doi:10.1080/14640749008401223.

Squire, L. (1992). Declarative and nondeclarative memory: Multiple brain systems supporting learning and memory. *Journal of Cognitive Neuroscience, 4*(3), 232–243.

Starkes, J. L., Deakin, J. M., Lindley, S., & Crisp, F. (1987). Motor versus verbal recall of ballet sequences by young expert dancers. *Journal of Sport Psychology, 9*(3), 222–230. doi:10.1123/jsp.9.3.222.

Statt, D. A. (1998). *The concise dictionary of psychology*. London: Routledge.

Stevens, C., Ginsborg, J., & Lester, G. (2011). Backwards and forwards in space and time: Recalling dance movement from long-term memory. *Memory Studies, 4*(2), 234–250. doi:10.1177/1750698010387018.

Stevens, C., & McKechnie, S. (2005). Thinking in action: thought made visible in contemporary dance. *Cognitive Processing, 6*(4), 243–252. doi:10.1007/s10339-005-0014-x.

Stevinson, C. D., & Biddle, S. J. H. (1999). Cognitive strategies in running: A response to Masters and Ogles (1998). *Sport Psychology, 13*, 235–236.

Summers, J. J., & Anson, J. G. (2009). Current status of the motor program: Revisited. *Human Movement Science, 28*(5), 566–577. doi:10.1016/j.humov.2009.01.002.

Tulving, E. (1972). Episodic and semantic memory. In E. Tulving & W. Donaldson (Eds.), *Organization of memory*. New York: Academic Press.

Warburton, E. C., Wilson, M., Lynch, M., & Cuykendall, S. (2013). The cognitive benefits of movement reduction. *Psychological Science, 24*(9), 1732–1739. doi:10.1177/0956797613478824.

Williams, S. E., Cumming, J., & Edwards, M. G. (2011). The functional equivalence between movement imagery, observation, and execution influences imagery ability. *Research Quarterly for Exercise and Sport, 82*(3), 555–564. doi:10.1080/02701367.2011.10599788.

Wilson, V. E., Peper, E., & Schmid, A. (2006). Training strategies for concentration. In J. N. Williams (Ed.), *Applied sport psychology: Personal growth to peak performance*. Boston: McGraw-Hill.

Further reading

Hardy, J. (2006). Speaking clearly: A critical review of the self-talk literature. *Psychology of Sport and Exercise, 7*(1), 81–97. doi:10.1016/j.psychsport.2005.04.002.

Holmes, P. S., & Collins, D. J. (2001). The PETTLEP approach to motor imagery: a functional equivalence model for sport psychologists. *Journal of Applied Sport Psychology, 13*(1), 60–83. doi:10.1080/10413200109339004.

Krasnow, D. (2015). *Motor learning and control for dance: Principles and practices for performers and teachers*. Champaign, IL: Human Kinetics.

CHAPTER 5

Social factors

> **Learning outcomes**
>
> By the end of this chapter readers should be able to:
>
> - recognise how social factors link to dance performance
> - define key terms related to leadership and group cohesion
> - describe different theories of leadership and group cohesion
> - explain how different forms of communication may impact upon dance performance
> - propose how to encourage group cohesion within dance practice

CONTEXT

So far we have been concentrating on the dancer as an individual, but as dance does not occur in a social vacuum, so now we need to consider the group and social factors.

Human behaviour is created through the interaction of the individual's psychological state with their environment, therefore our dance performance may be greatly dictated by the social interactions within the class or company (Carron, Widmeyer, & Brawley, 1988). There are additional social factors to consider, first, that the group will tend to be led by someone experienced in this dance genre, and, second, that the dance may be performed for the consumption of others, be they judges or members of the public. With so much emphasis on these varied social interactions it is vital to achieve the right social environment to maximise enjoyment and performance quality.

Every dancer is an individual, but individuals create groups that have a personality of their own. Think about the different dance groups that you have been part of over the years and reflect on the different qualities and emphases of each group. Ensuring that there is in-group harmony is important, as conflict and antagonism may lead to communication breakdown and potentially dancers may leave, if they do not find the atmosphere conducive. One way to ensure that this is not the case is to create a group that is well bonded, as this has been shown to enhance adherence and performance.

One important factor that may impact on how well the group bonds is the quality of the leadership, which, in the case of dancing, is generally the teacher, choreographer or director (but will be referred to as the teacher for the remainder of this chapter). They have the potential to make or break a group through their leadership approach, and therefore are an important area of study. How the teacher affects the group is through their communication with the group, and the degree to which they encourage communication within the group, as the lack of intragroup communication will decrease the chances of group bonding. This requires the leader to be flexible considering the needs of different types of group (professional company, leisure class or affiliate class) to ensure that group goals are met.

THEORY

Leadership

Multidimensional Model of Leadership

The *Multidimensional Model of Leadership* is made up of three levels: characteristics, behaviours and outcomes (Chelladuria, 2007). These levels interact as can be seen in Figure 5.1.

Situational factors

The *situational characteristics* may vary greatly dependent on situation type (training for exams, developing choreography for competitions, or rehearsal for a show), and performance type (solo or group pieces). The *required behaviour* will be an amalgamation of these situational demands combined with the dancer characteristics, such as dancer ability (novice or professional), and dancer motivation (leisure, student or professional).

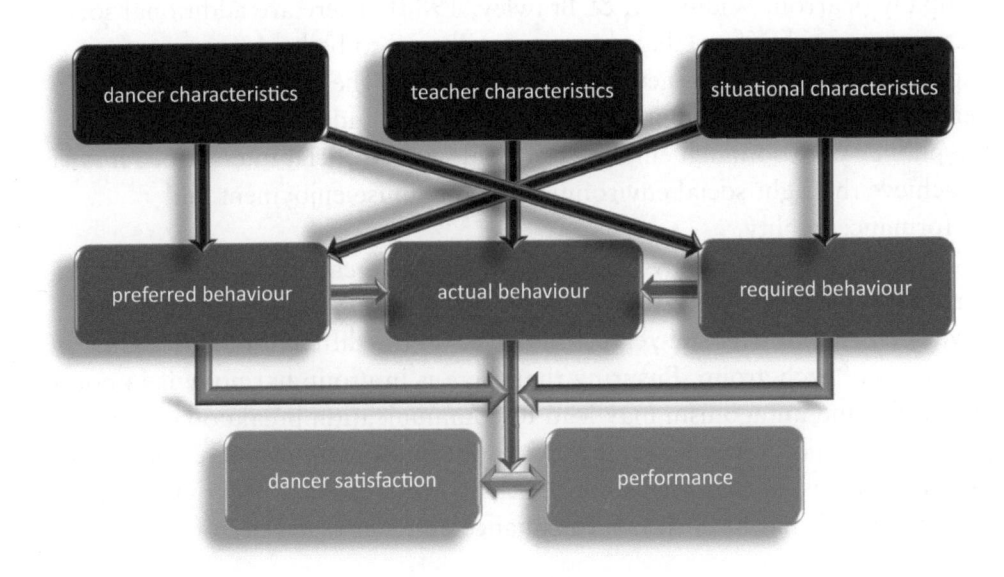

Figure 5.1
Multidimensional Model of Leadership

Source: Based on Chelladurai (2007).

Dancer factors

The *dancer characteristics* may be their age, gender, personality, motivation and ability of the individual or group. These in turn will affect the dancer's *preferred behaviour*, considering whether there is a need for instruction, social support or feedback. For example, those working recreationally may not feel the need to undertake repeated drills during their evening class, where equally a professional dancer might prefer to focus on the nuances of choreography. The onus is on the dancers to appreciate that different leadership behaviours may be necessary at different times to meet the needs of the situation.

Teacher factors

Bearing in mind the *teacher's characteristics* (personality, expertise and experience), the *actual behaviour* must balance the dancer's preferred behaviour with that required by the situation in order to maximise the outcome. This requires the teacher to be flexible, adapting to new and evolving requirements.

Outcomes

The choice of *actual behaviour* will impact on the quality of the *performance* and the *satisfaction* that the dancers experience. The feedback from these two sources will affect the current and future behaviour of dancers and teachers. If rehearsals for an important show are not progressing on time, the teacher may forgo the dancers' satisfaction as the performance quality needs to take priority, whereas if there is an increasing level of dropout from a recreational class then the teacher may change their behaviour to increase dancer satisfaction.

This model highlights the complexity of the leadership situation. The varied social factors must be balanced alongside the situational factors for the optimum outcome. This model explains why a change in one variable, such as company members, a different director or time pressure can have a great impact on the dance quality or in-group feelings. Those leaders who can adapt their style to balance the preferred and required behaviours will be more successful than those who use a universal approach to all situations.

Leadership qualities

Based on the Multidimensional Model of Leadership, Chelladuria (2007) developed five dimensions of leadership behaviour, which, if adopted correctly, increase performance and satisfaction. Two dimensions relate to task orientation (*training and instruction* and *positive feedback*), two dimensions relate to decision-making (*autocratic* and *democratic behaviour*), and the final dimension relates to social factors.

Training and instruction

This is considered the most desirable behaviour of the leader as it is the factor that will enhance a dancer's ability and ultimately the group performance and satisfaction. Training and instruction underpin skill development and technical enhancement, encouraging a focus on training and a positive work ethic.

Positive feedback

The leader's ability to recognise good behaviour and offer appropriate feedback based on what they observe will increase performance quality and respect from the learners.

Democratic behaviour

Democratic behaviour suggests the degree to which the teacher allows group members to be involved with decision-making. This may be decisions about practice and training, it may be about the group goals, or it may be about productions. Such involvement leads to the dancers feeling more invested in the project, therefore more likely to internalise the mission.

Autocratic behaviour

Alternatively, autocratic behaviour is demonstrated through the degree to which the teacher discourages group interaction and retains all decision-making powers. This form of leadership may be useful in important and stressful situations as a means of completing tasks quickly and efficiently, but is not necessarily positive for long-term group cohesion.

Social support

This is the teacher's consideration of the welfare of their group, and is a leadership behaviour that can increase group cohesion and harmony. Understanding how the dancers' mental state can affect performance quality is important. Offering social support and empathy regarding life issues may help the dancer to regain the required state of mind, by treating the whole dancer.

Teachers who demonstrate high levels of instruction and positive feedback and social support, while favouring a democratic, rather than an autocratic, approach create groups that are highly bonded with increased self-efficacy and enjoyment levels, and low levels of anxiety and burnout (Chelladuria, 2007).

Transformational Leadership

Unlike other forms of leadership, such as *Transactional Leadership* which is a form of power based on external rewards and punishment, *Transformational Leadership* relies on the relationship between teachers and the group (Burns, 1978). A transformational leader considers the needs of the group members alongside the goals of the group, and aims to integrate both. This type of power does not use threats and coercion, but relies on the power to motivate the group through understanding them and supporting them (Fairholm, 2001). There are five characteristics that are linked to transformational leadership (Bass, 1995).

© Shutterstock

Charisma

A *charismatic leader* is self-confident and assertive, leading to strong emotional attachments within the group. These emotional bonds will increase the levels of trust that the dancers have in the teacher and their mission.

Individualised consideration

Individualised consideration requires that the leader gives personal attention to each group member so no one feels neglected. This interaction emphasises the leader's understanding of each individual, and sets roles or tasks that link to their ability or preferences.

Intellectual stimulation

To create intellectual stimulation the leader must develop an environment which encourages creativity and innovation, helping the group members think in different ways.

Inspirational motivation

Through emotional identification the group are motivated to action based on the teacher's skills of communication and persuasion.

Idealised influence

The leader's ability in communicating their mission leads the group members to internalise these beliefs and actively promote them to others.

The impact that transformational leadership has on individual group members is to increase self-confidence through the individualised consideration, and the encouragement to be creative and to take responsibility for elements of decision-making. If the teacher sets high standards of performance, they will create a working culture that leads to the group adoption of such standards. The resultant group cohesion, work ethic and self-confidence increase resilience when in times of adversity (Hardy et al., 2010).

Groups

Groups are complex and diverse, but generally include some overlapping qualities. Groups require a level of interaction where views or instructions are exchanged with other group members and leaders. Groups will have goals, either *task* focused, *socially* focused or a combination of the two, which give the group direction. There will be a structure based on roles allocated to different group members, which creates interdependence through the reliance on different group members to fulfil their assigned roles (Forsyth, 2014). How these features are expressed within the group may be highly dependent on whether the group is a leisure class, professional company or competitive group.

Group formation

A dance class, troupe or cast are a collection of individuals that make up a group, but the construction and maintenance of groups are a complex process, comprising stages referred to as forming, storming, norming, performing and adjourning (Tuckman, 2001).

Forming

When a group first comes together, the members are often experiencing a mixture of excitement of the new challenge ahead, blended with some anxiety as to whether they will be able to meet the expectations. Often there are occasions where boundaries are tested as a means of establishing what the parameters are for acceptable behaviour regarding both the leader and other group members (Bonebright, 2010). These may include attitude to work, formality of interaction and the type of language used.

Storming

Once established, there will be a process of gradual interaction where individuals start to divulge information about themselves to others, varying the degree of disclosure in order to present the image of themselves that they wish to present. As discussed in Chapter 2, this is where impression management may occur where the edited version of the self is portrayed. Once individuals start to get to know one another, there may be jostling for position in any potential hierarchy, with polarisation around issues or individuals. The basis for power may be reliant on dance prowess, experience or even personality. The desire to be at the top of any group hierarchy may be driven by the influence this power may have on future group decisions and direction. There is the potential for conflict and power struggles, and jealousy and subgroups may develop as part of this process (Bonebright, 2010).

Norming

Once any conflict has abated, the group can become bonded, and a group identity will develop. There will be acceptance of individuals' idiosyncrasies and in a coherent group the interaction will be positive, cooperative and helpful. The group will have found its level and there will be agreement about the acceptable levels of behaviour within the group (Bonebright, 2010).

Performing

The group can now focus on the business for which it was created where issues can be discussed and resolved. There will be group cohesion and a team approach through mutually agreed targets and roles (Bonebright, 2010). The group can celebrate successes together or reflect on poorer performances without a blame culture, all taking responsibility for their part in the performance.

Adjourning

In some cases the group will have a specified duration, such as with the cast of a show. Adjourning can be a very emotional period dependent upon how well bonded the group are and how they perceive the success of the performance. Close groups who believe the performance to be successful will find this period the hardest, whereas others feel change is a positive state and the excitement of moving on to a new challenge may soften the blow (Tuckman & Jensen, 1977).

Although this model may offer a framework for some dance-related situations, this is not necessarily how all groups develop, as in some cases the group may have been established for many years and have a transient membership as people join and leave. In such cases there may be intermittent periods of storming, norming, performing and individual adjourning. How well any aspect of this process goes is often down to how well the group leader manages the evolving situation.

Group cohesion

Cohesion can be defined as the sum of forces that cause a group to remain together (Carron, 1982). This can be quite difficult to capture as group cohesion is dynamic, changing in form and intensity for each dancer as circumstances change. Each dancer needs a motive to stick with the group and positive feeling for doing so. Carron, Widmeyer, and Brawley (1985) developed a conceptual model to highlight the multidimensional nature of group cohesion.

Dimensions

There are two dimensions that interrelate to show the complexities of group cohesion; one dimension focuses on how the group is perceived by individuals, and the second dimension focuses on the functions of the group (Carron, Eys, & Burke, 2007). These dimensions can be combined to create a multidimensional model as illustrated in Figure 5.2.

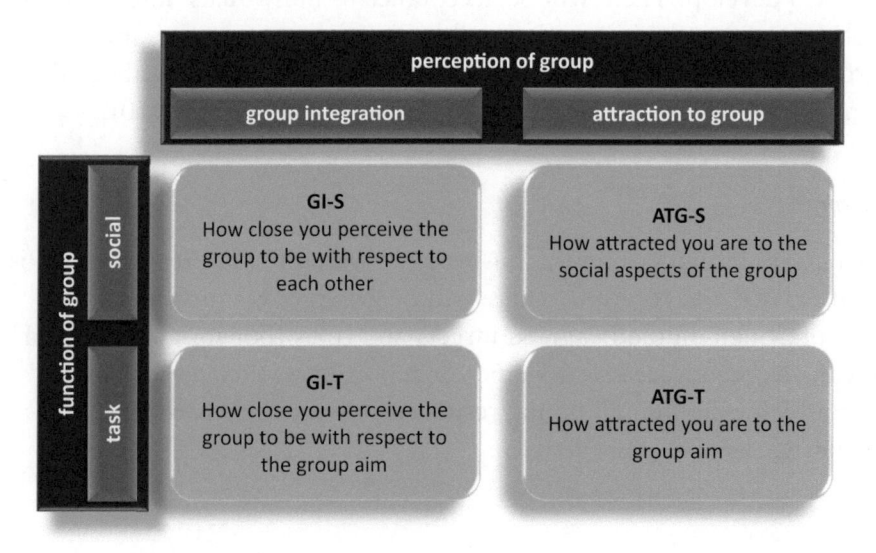

Figure 5.2
Conceptual Model of Group Cohesion

Source: Based on Carron et al. (1985).

	group integration	attraction to group
social	**GI-S** How close you perceive the group to be with respect to each other	**ATG-S** How attracted you are to the social aspects of the group
task	**GI-T** How close you perceive the group to be with respect to the group aim	**ATG-T** How attracted you are to the group aim

(perception of group / function of group)

Dancers assess the group using the *perceptions* they have of the group. The first perception is cognitive and relates to the dancer's view of how close the group members are, referred to as *group integration*. This may range from a tightly knit group to a group with very loose associations with each other, possibly due to a lack of opportunity to interact with one another. The second perception is affective as it is the dancer's *attraction to the group* through an assessment of how the group might meet their needs. This may include factors such as the degree of friendship and belongingness felt, the value that they attach to the group through empathy with each other, and the enjoyment derived from the activities undertaken with the group (Carron, 1982).

The next consideration is based on what the perceived functions of the group are. A group high in *task orientation* will be focused on achieving group goals, whereas a group high on *social orientation* works towards maintaining social harmony within the group (Carron et al., 2007).

Consequences

Cohesion is important as it affects the performance of the group in many ways. Higher group cohesion is positively related to:

- success, which is stronger in female groups
- taking responsibility for one's own actions
- disruption management
- sacrifice behaviour
- group efficacy
- punctuality

and is negatively related to:

- absenteeism
- social loafing
- role ambiguity
- depression, anger and tension (Carron et al., 2007)

Leadership role in cohesion

Research has shown that the group climate that the teacher creates (as discussed in Chapter 3) plays an important role in cohesion. A climate encouraging task involvement predicted enhanced cohesion, whereas an ego-involved climate was negatively related to individual satisfaction with the group (García-Calvo et al., 2014). Therefore, it is vital for the teacher to consider the impact they have on the group attitude to successful performance in order to enhance the chance of group cohesion. Transformational leadership qualities of individual consideration, acceptance of group goals and teamwork through intra-team communication have been shown to enhance task cohesion (Smith, Arthur, Hardy, Callow, & Williams, 2013).

> **Research in focus**
>
> **Group Cohesion Effects in Exercise Classes**
>
> **Aim** Group cohesion is a potent indicator of the likelihood of a group remaining as one and doing so through times of disruption. There are different draws to a class, it may be for the enjoyment of the activity (task) or it may be because of the people that attend (social). If we do not feel that the group is meeting these needs then the resultant behaviour is to drop-out. The purpose of this research was to identify what factors predict absenteeism and drop-out in exercise classes.
>
> **Method** An aerobic dance class was used as the context, where 46 females attended an hour class three times per week.
> Independent variable:
> - high attendees (attending more than 66% of classes)
> - drop-outs (not attending 12 of the sessions)
>
> Dependent variables:
> - Group Environment Questionnaire (GEQ)
>
> The research commenced in week 4 where the GEQ was used to collect baseline data and was applied again four weeks later.
>
> **Results**
> - *Task cohesion:* both groups rated task cohesion equally as high as each other.
> - *Social cohesion:* the dancers who dropped out did not perceive the group to be well integrated at the outset, whereas the attending dancers did, and those who dropped out were less attracted to the group than the attenders.
>
> **Conclusions** By week three it is possible to predict the factors that lead to drop-out of exercise classes, that being the social aspect. Those who dropped-out did not feel the group was well integrated from the outset, therefore it is important to implement activities that will help group members get to know each other.
>
> (Spink & Carron, 1994)

Interactions

Teacher-dancer relationship

Types of dependency

The relationship between a dancer and the teacher is based on the level of responsibility that the individuals feel they have to each other, and the degree of freedom that the dancer is allowed (Figure 5.3). Where the dancer has a low level of responsibility and no freedom, they are therefore reliant on the teacher (*dependent*), whereas when allowed total freedom, the role of the teacher has been marginalised and the dancer's progress may be restricted by not acting as part of a group (*independent*). Where there are high levels of reliance on each other but there is no freedom, the relationship is co-dependent and therefore restricted in its ability to grow.

SOCIAL FACTORS

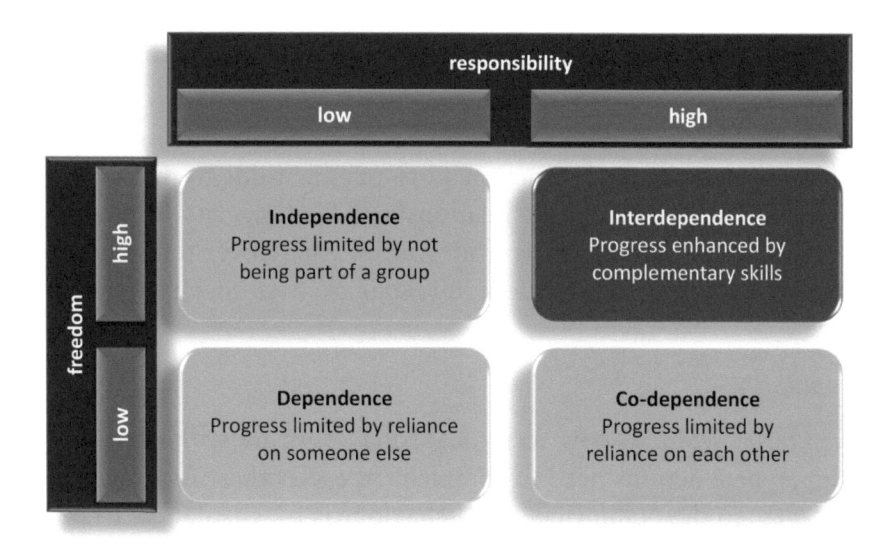

	responsibility	
	low	**high**
freedom high	**Independence** Progress limited by not being part of a group	**Interdependence** Progress enhanced by complementary skills
freedom low	**Dependence** Progress limited by reliance on someone else	**Co-dependence** Progress limited by reliance on each other

Figure 5.3
Impact of types of dependency

Where there are high levels of freedom as well as a responsibility to each other, the teacher-dancer relationship is *interdependent*, where each is reliant on the other for different reasons. The dancer is reliant on the teacher to provide instruction to maximise their progression, whereas the teacher is reliant on the dancer to learn and develop. The interdependence is required for the successful completion of the task, but also for the development of the self (Jowett, 2007). If a teacher sees her students progressing, it reaffirms her competency as a teacher, and a dancer's success confirms that she has the right teacher.

Interaction outcomes

The interdependence is based on *interaction outcomes*, where both parties apply a cost-benefit analysis to ensure that the relationship is of benefit to them both. The positive elements of satisfaction and motivation are weighed up against the negative elements of conflict and frustration for a decision to be made. The decisions may be focused on the nature of their current experience of the teacher-dancer relationship, or it may be a comparison with opportunities outside of this relationship (Jowett & Nezlek, 2012).

The 3+1Cs model

Jowett (2007) developed a model to explain the interdependent relationship based on four constructs (one was added to the model at a later date, hence the unusual name): closeness, commitment, complementarity and co-orientation.

Closeness

Closeness is affective, and refers to the mutual feelings of liking, respect and trust which result from teacher-dancer interactions. The higher level of disclosure from both parties, the greater understanding that dancer and teacher have of each other. This suggests that conversations need to go beyond that of just dance, but there is an understanding of the dancer as a whole.

Commitment

Commitment is cognitive, and is the degree of attachment felt to each other, expressed by the motivation to remain in the relationship. The longer the relationship, the stronger the commitment to pursue it due to the investment that both parties have made in the relationship. The longevity of the relationship also changes the needs from within, where over time the dancer may require less technical instruction, in favour of more social support.

Complementarity

Complementarity refers to how reciprocal behaviours are within the relationship, where actions need to complement each other. At a basic level the teacher *teaches*, so the complementary behaviour is for the dancer to *learn*. This complementarity may express itself in other more fleeting situations, for example, if the dancer is becoming *angry* at being unable to master a step, then the complementary behaviour adopted by the teacher should be to *pacify*, where a match in mood might be dangerous.

Complementarity needs to be considered carefully as in most dance situations there is not an even power balance, therefore, the complementarity of dancer's *submissive* behaviours should not be driven by *domineering* teachers. Although this does show complementarity, it is not experienced in a positive way to allow the dancer to flourish.

Co-orientation

Co-orientation is the degree to which each party understands the feelings of the other. Authentic disclosure, where both parties feel that they can be honest about how they feel, can enhance the chances that there is a real empathic understanding between dancer and teacher.

In order for a relationship to be interdependent, there must be closeness, commitment and complementarity, a finding that has been shown to be particularly strong for female dancer-teacher interactions, suggesting similarity may play a role (Jowett & Nezlek, 2012). If dancers do not feel that there is closeness, it may be that a lack of disclosure is being interpreted as a lack of commitment to the relationship. Alternatively a lack of positive complementarity might suggest that the teacher does not understand the dancer as they do not react in a helpful manner.

Communication

Communication is more than just the words we use – all of our behaviour communicates something, even the decision not to communicate communicates something. Communication can be:

- *verbal*
    - what we say – the actual word used
    - how we say it – intonation and emphasis
    - the meanings drawn – sarcasm or humour

- *vocal*
  - unconscious noises – laughing
  - conscious noises – sighing
- *non-verbal*
  - posture
  - eye contact
  - facial expression
  - unconscious hand gestures
- *symbolic*
  - hand signals
  - demonstrations
- *cognitive*
  - attitude
  - decision-making

It is important to bear in mind the impact that non-verbal factors have on the interpretation of the message sent and the emotional state of the sender. Even the teacher's most positive words of praise will not be interpreted as such if they are delivered with a negative posture and regular eye rolling. Equally, monotonous agreements and lacklustre postures of the class may suggest that they are not impressed with the suggestion of extended rehearsal – regardless of what they are saying verbally.

Teacher communication types

During any group interaction there are many types of communication that may occur, and how each situation is handled will impact on group cohesion and self-efficacy. Smith, Smoll, and Hunt (1977) devised a system of coding teacher behaviour into 12 different interaction types as shown in Figure 5.4.

Reactive behaviours

Reactive behaviours are those that correspond to situational factors such as a good performance or errors. When a high degree of skill has been demonstrated or an increased level of effort is detected, it is important to ensure that this is acknowledged by the teacher, as the dancer needs to know that the execution was correct so it can be added to the dancer's technical knowledge as well as increasing their self-confidence.

Responses to errors can be managed in positive and negative ways. Positive interactions can include technical assistance on how to correct the error, or encouragement when the dancer knows what to do, but has not achieved it at that moment. Negative responses will work to undermine the dancer's confidence and self-efficacy, through punishment or hostile feedback. Not responding to errors can work in two ways. If it is not mentioned, then the dancer may be unaware that an error has been made. Alternatively, it may be kinder not to respond to every error as the dancer may be having a bad day.

Figure 5.4
Teacher behaviours

Source: Adapted from Smith, Smoll & Hunt (1977).

Reactive behaviours		
Responses to required performance	Reinforcement	A positive reaction to a desired skill, performance or application of effort
	No reinforcement	Not responding to a desired skill, performance or application of effort
Responses to errors	Error-related encouragement	Encouragement given after an error
	Error-related technical instruction	Explanation as to how to correct an error
	Punishment	A negative verbal or nonverbal reaction to an error
	Punitive technical instruction	Instruction given on error correction in a hostile manner
	Ignoring errors	Not responding to an error
Response to misbehaviour	Keeping control	Managing group behaviour
Spontaneous behaviours		
Dance related	General technical instruction	Spontaneous instruction on skills and techniques
	General encouragement	Spontaneous encouragement not related to performance
	Organization	Administrative communication
Dance irrelevant	General communication	Communications with group that is not dance-related

The final form of reactive behaviour is to acknowledge and manage undesirable behaviour in the studio that undermines the authority of the teacher or is counterproductive to completion of the task at hand. This may be more likely to occur when going through the storming stage of group formation, or where there is complacency within the group.

Spontaneous behaviours

Spontaneous behaviours are communications that occur that are not a response to a specific event. These may be practical, such as technical instruction, or general encouragement to enhance motivation. They may also be unrelated to dance performance, such as administrative information or references to topics outside of dance.

Immediacy

Immediacy can be described as behaviours that reduce physical and psychological distance between people, where non-verbal immediacy reduces physical distance through interactions involving touching, eye contact, length of interaction, informal dress or relaxed posture. Verbal immediacy reduces psychological distance through signalling openness for communication and use of inclusive language such as 'we' or 'our'. Verbal and non-verbal immediacy of teachers has been shown to relate positively to satisfaction, and all measures of cohesion (Turman, 2008).

Conflict

Types of conflict

Conflict can be described as a struggle between parties due to incompatible goals or limited resources. The conflict can be *content*-based where the disagreement may be related to problem-solving or task completion, which can be a productive situation as better solutions may be created as a product of any interaction that occurs once the conflict has been settled. Alternatively, the disagreement may be *relational*, taking on more personal aspects, therefore more likely to become emotional. Even this form of conflict may have positive outcomes if those involved learn more about themselves and tolerance of other as a result (LaVoi, 2007).

Conflict is a complex phenomenon which may occur in a variety of different forms often based on unrealistic expectations (Figure 5.5). Conflict does not always require a social interaction, as observed in Chapter 2, we may experience *intrapersonal* conflict where we are battling with ourselves. Conflict may be at an individual level, such as *interpersonal* conflict, such as dancer and teacher arguing about punctuality. Conflict may occur at group levels such as *intragroup* conflict which may happen at the storming stage of group development, or may happen between groups such as the *intergroup* conflict between two street dance troupes at a competition. Each form of conflict requires managing in different ways for effective resolution.

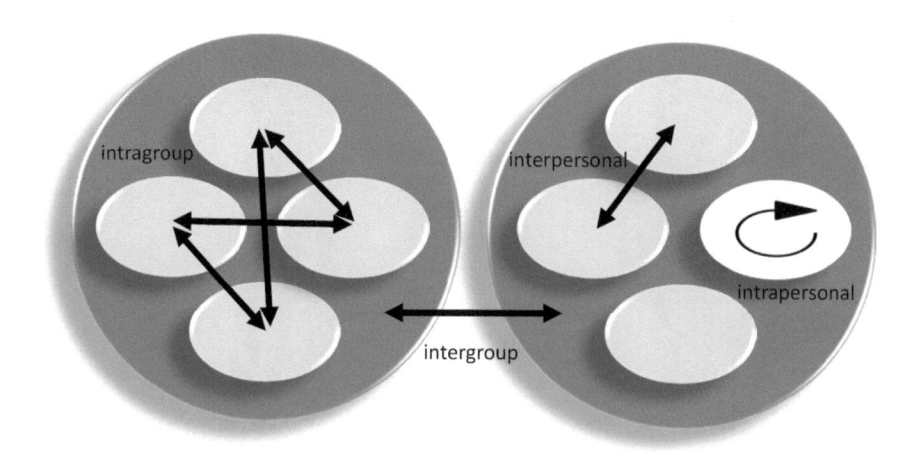

Figure 5.5
Types of conflict

Competence-Based Model of Interpersonal Conflict

The Competence-Based Model of Interpersonal Conflict examines the communication that occurs *within* the conflict rather than examining the causes leading to the conflict. This model focuses on the judgements made about the communication that occurs within the conflict episode and the means employed to resolve the conflict. The judgement of our own communication and that of other parties are assessed for communication competence and satisfaction (Canary, Cupach, & Serpe, 2001). The judgement of the episodic communication from all parties may then affect future outcomes for the individual and the relationship (Figure 5.6).

© Shutterstock

SOCIAL FACTORS

Figure 5.6
Competence-Based Model of Interpersonal Conflict

Using an example it is possible to see how different forms of communication used by the different individuals within the conflict can affect satisfaction and impact the direction of the future relationship. Consider this situation:

> A dancer has high hopes of being chosen for the solo role in this year's show. She has been with the company for several years and believes she has served her time in the chorus. She has just found out that the role has been given to a relative newcomer to the company. She doesn't think this is fair as she has been there longer so it is her turn. She approaches the teacher and complains bitterly about the injustice.

For a positive outcome for all, communication competence is required (Figure 5.7):

- *Teacher communication*: As the dancer makes her feelings known, the teacher listens to her full complaint in order to make an informed judgement about all aspects of the situation, such as identifying whether this is a personal disappointment or a dislike of the newcomer. The teacher then explains that the newcomer is a seasoned performer and is familiar with the piece, the style of which would not suit our complainant. The teacher suggests that there are more appropriate roles on the horizon and in the meantime to work on a specific aspect of her technique.

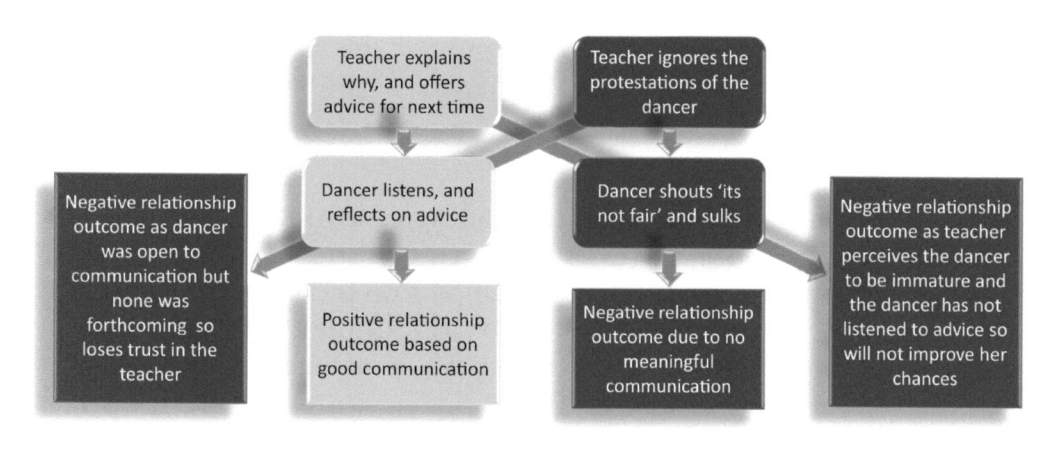

Figure 5.7
Outcomes from the Competence-Based Model of Conflict

- *Dancer communication*: The dancer's response is to listen to the explanation, acknowledge the points being made, reflect and act on the advice.
- *Dancer outcome*: The dancer will feel that competent communication has occurred, her complaint was met with a balanced and logical response, therefore, she feels motivated to work and is satisfied with all the parties' role in the situation.
- *Teacher outcome*: The teacher has seen the passion of the dancer through the complaint, and the subsequent maturity of her response to the interaction, and, therefore, will keep her in mind for future roles.

Negative behaviour from any party may have negative consequences for the future relations:

- *Teacher negative communication*: Poor communication competence from the teacher, through angry outbursts or avoidance of the issues, will leave the relationship in deficit. Aggressive outbursts may make the dancer feel that the teacher is unapproachable or lead to increased anxiety. Avoidant responses mean that problems will not be solved, which has a gradual eroding effect on the relationship.
- *Dancer negative communication*: Aggressive or sulky responses from the dancer will give the impression that the dancer is not one of the group, but self-centred. This may indicate the dancer's immaturity or the breakdown of group cohesion.

PRACTICE

Communication

Avoiding negative forms of communication

There are many ways that the same message can be communicated, and many interpretations can be made of the same words based on other non-linguistic factors. An awareness of the impact of these various forms of communication can prevent the deterioration of the relationship between dancer and teacher.

Types of language

Abusive language can be highly demeaning to anyone, and when used in a group setting increases the levels of distress by creating embarrassment (Turman, 2003). The impact on other group members is also negative as it leads to feelings of pity for the individual and feelings of anxiety for the group members observing such behaviour.

Although this may enhance cohesion through feelings of solidarity within the group, this is no longer a group that members may feel attracted to, leading to loss of respect for the teacher and increasing the chances of attrition.

Tone of voice

It is not just the words used that convey meaning, but how they are delivered. Simple voice control, such as not shouting can reduce the levels of anxiety experienced. Tones of voice that indicate exasperation, disappointment and disbelief can all have negative effects on individuals and the group.

Before adopting a negative tone, consider the intention of the act that you are responding to. If there was a positive intent but unfortunately resulted in a poor performance, then what purpose does a negatively intoned response have? It will probably just serve to make the dancer feel worse than they already do. On the other hand, if the behaviour to which you are responding was intentional, then indicating disappointment may be relevant as a means of showing the consequences of actions. When dealing with negative behaviours, remember that you must maintain a professional presence and not revert to the poor behaviour that you are responding to.

Meaning behind the messages

In groups of equals, sarcasm and teasing may be a way to bond and show colleagues that the relationship is close enough that this form of communication is meant affectionately (Turman, 2003). When the relations are asymmetrical, such as with teacher and dancer, this form of communication can be problematic. Even if the dancer seems to respond well to the jibe in front of the group, this may well be a strategy to save face, this may not be how they feel inside. The younger the dancer and the newer the relationship, the more problematic this interaction type may be.

Non-verbal communication

So much of what we communicate does not come from the words, but from the body language that accompanies them, which is received at an unconscious level. Offering positive verbal feedback, if our facial expression suggests pity or despair, will lead to confusion or lack of trust, therefore leading to ineffective communication, so it is important to maintain congruence within all forms of communication.

What is often clearer is when the recipient does not have the distraction of verbal feedback and therefore relies on visual cues. Great damage can be done from sighing, hunched posture, eye-rolling and frowning. In such cases, encouragement or instruction is more relevant as the damage done can be hard to repair.

Consider how you interact with others, and when dealing with poor performance, take a breath for a second before you act, to consider how to maintain a professional demeanour, regardless of what you are feeling on the inside.

Videotaping a class or training session can give real insight into the impact that *your* communication has on the group. It is not always an easy thing to watch, but may help with reflection and future communication.

Non-communication

Having highlighted the importance of communication, sometimes it is better not to communicate. If dancers are not behaving properly and you feel this may be an attention-seeking behaviour, then responding to the behaviour will encourage the dancer to repeat the negative behaviour. Ignoring this behaviour will lead to its eradication as your lack of response is not having the desired effect.

Motivational speeches

The influence teachers have over their group is often underestimated by those in charge, therefore it is important to remember that as a teacher you are setting the standard for the group. Performance quality may vary over time so to help the dancers achieve their potential, the teacher must lead from the front.

Enthusiasm

The teacher not only directs the activities of the group but sets the atmosphere, therefore it is incumbent on them to create the right atmosphere and mood regardless of how they may feel inside. Enthusiasm is contagious, so utilising motivational speeches to bring the group together, especially in times of difficulty, challenge or fatigue can have restorative effects.

Encouragement

There will be times when a dancer is trying as hard as they can but are not yet hitting the mark. When no progress has been made upon which to comment, then it is vital to offer encouragement to keep the dancer motivated to continue – not all feedback needs to be performance-based, it can be effort-related (Rhind & Jowett, 2010).

SOCIAL FACTORS

Instruction

A group may be motivated to perform but in order to progress, it is important that technical instruction is delivered appropriately.

Personalise

Ensure that some time is spent giving personalised instruction and feedback. This will not only increase the dancer's technical skills but allows more personal bonds to be made through the feelings of individualised consideration (Burns, 1978).

Types of instruction

Ensure that constructive feedback is given for both good and poor performance.

If feedback is not received for a good performance, the dancer may not be aware of its quality and may not know to reproduce it again.

Equally, positive feedback of poor performance allows the dancer to be aware of errors made, and corrective instruction can help the errors to be rectified.

When the dancer is aware of the correct technique but is having problems making the move, then corrective feedback can be counter-productive. In such cases, positive encouragement or recommending a different activity to reduce the likelihood of frustration may be more productive.

Interaction

Communication should not be a one-way flow of information, but an interaction of information, ideas and feelings. Therefore, interaction should be encouraged between dancer and teacher, as well as between dancers, to help encourage group cohesion.

Openness

It is important that communication within the group is two-way, most especially in the asymmetric aspect of dancer-teacher relationship. Such two-way interaction may be easily managed when referring to technical instruction, but many other factors may affect a dancer's performance – some of which may not be dance-related. For this reason it is important that the dancer feels that she can talk to the teacher about other issues that are not dance-related (Rhind & Jowett, 2010).

For this to occur, there needs to be an atmosphere where not all conversation must be dance-related. Non-dance conversations allow a greater understanding of each group member and help develop relationships within the group. Openness will be increased if the teacher demonstrates consistent patience and positive responses when dancers need to disclose other information.

Socio-cognitive conflict

To develop dancers' cognitive capacities it is useful to put them in situations which challenge them, one such method is by inducing socio-cognitive conflict. In problem-solving activities our first answer is rarely the best one, and our final response could often be improved with reflection.

Set small groups a creative or problem solving task where their first response is to write, *in silence*, ideas that they think would answer the brief. When all group members have written their thoughts, they then share their ideas with the group. The reason for the silent consideration is that once someone has made a suggestion out loud, it may be difficult to think of any other solution. The subsequent comparison of ideas requires the development of communication skills:
- initially the explanation of your idea;
- listening to the ideas of each group member;
- not interrupting or criticising others' suggestions;
- considering the merits of all the ideas;
- negotiating the best solution based on the interaction of ideas;
- compromising when necessary.

The conflict should be at a cognitive level and not a personal level and the activity can enhance group cohesion and develop individuals as critical thinkers (Mogonea & Popescu, 2015).

Conflict management

Conflict management is the ability to accommodate tension, balancing the needs of all concerned to produce a win-win situation (LaVoi, 2007). This requires an understanding of the needs of the individuals and the situation, and the ability to listen, be objective and call on others who may have information that can contribute to the solution.

Managing expectations

A source of tension and conflict may arise when individuals feel that their expectations are not being met. In order to prevent such conflict from arising, it is important to have an open discussion about the expectations of all parties at the outset, and ensure that this conversation is repeated at important points throughout the relationship as situations change and the relationship matures.

Consequences of the expected levels of behaviour must be clearly communicated at the outset so all are aware of the agreed code of behaviour. If sanctions or punishments are a feature of the group, then they must be transparent and apply equally to all (Rhind & Jowett, 2010).

Understanding the conflict

Feelings of frustration that lead to conflict may be avoidable if the individual can reflect on the source of the frustration and consider the intention behind it (LaVoi, 2007). This is important as some conflict can have long-term detrimental effects on the relationship. Consider this situation: a teacher is angry as a dancer has missed a rehearsal. The dancer was at an audition, but failed to tell the teacher in advance.

The conflict in this situation is not *content*-based as the teacher appreciates the importance of the audition, but is angry that they were not informed in advance, therefore, it is *relational*. Content-based conflict is more easily resolved as it is an agreement about tasks, whereas in this situation the teacher feels that the relationship has been compromised due to the lack of communication.

Focusing on the task aspect of the situation, and not taking the dancer's oversight personally will help resolve the conflict without long-lasting damage to the relationship.

Dual Concern Model

According to the *Dual Concern Model* (Rahim, 2011), the approach taken to conflict management depends on our level of concern for all parties involved in the conflict, both yourself and others (Figure 5.8). The *compromise* is where there is moderate concern for self and others and will result in all parties having to give up something to find a resolution, which is a better approach than styles where there are low levels of concern. The *avoiding* style is problematic as it does not confront or manage the problem leading to low levels of

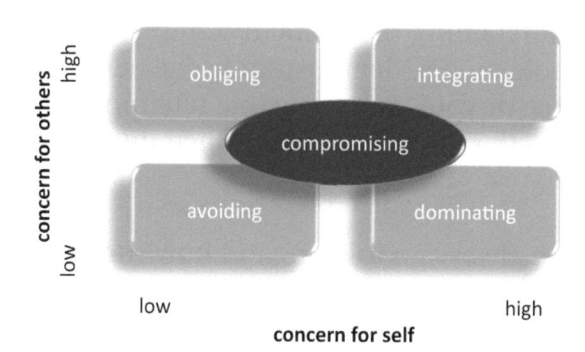

Figure 5.8
Dual Concern Model

satisfaction. Alternatively, the *dominating* style is adopted when there is only concern with the self, therefore, no satisfaction is achieved beyond the individual, as opposed to the *obliging* style where there is satisfaction for others but with self-sacrifice. The ideal approach is the *integrating* style, which seeks to reach maximum satisfaction for both parties through creativity and innovation to arrive at unique solutions (Rahim, 2011).

The integrating solution is not the easiest or quickest solution, but with investment it may be the best for all concerned in the long run. To reach this type of solution requires open and honest conversations about the needs of each party and how these relate to the group and individual goals. The solutions will often be novel and as such will require creative thinking rather than deferring to the norm. This may be seen as a brave move as professional reputation may be at stake, but it may be a case of *dare to lose to win*.

Leadership qualities

Developing the relationship

In order to maximise the commitment and performance of the dancers, the teacher needs to go beyond their role of instruction and make bonds with the dancers if they are to follow. The bonds come in the form of dancer-teacher relationships.

Relationship motivation

Motivation is not always directly related to the task but may be related to the relationship, so working towards enhancing the relationship through motivating the group may improve performance as a consequence (Rhind & Jowett, 2010). Factors that encourage the development of the relationship are the teacher's ability to demonstrate skill and effort, and a passion that motivates others while still retaining the element of fun and enjoyment.

Acting as a role model, demonstrating the behaviour that you would wish to see in your dancers, while retaining an enjoyment factor will lead to the internalisation of such qualities.

Positivity

Situations do not always go to plan, and how the teacher manages such situations will impact on the dancers' desire to maintain the relationship. When things have not gone as expected, maintaining a positive outlook is not sufficient, there needs to be positivity of action – be a leader. The positivity may be through adaptation of

Cohesion

Team-building interventions

To increase cohesion, team-building activities may be undertaken to expedite this. A framework for the implementation of team-building interventions should be considered to maximise their effectiveness.

Phases of team-building

1 *Introductory phase* – It is important to inform the group as to the purpose of the team-building exercise, and how it is effective so they engage more fully with the activities.
2 *Conceptual phase* – An overview of how the team-building intervention will work using methods that are appropriate to the group in order to get the right message across. This should demonstrate how theory will impact on their practice.
3 *Practical phase* – This session will allow the group members to set the agendas that they feel are important to work on.
4 *Intervention phase* – The programme developed based on the previous three stages is implemented (Paradis & Martin, 2012).

Focus and duration

Interventions that are focused, rather than trying to improve everything all at once, have been found to be more effective (Martin, Carron, & Burke, 2009). This suggests that there should be a decision made as to which factor needs to be prioritised and then develop an intervention focused on this.

Second, the duration of the intervention needs to be considered. In order to be meaningful and have time to become embedded, any intervention must be over two weeks long, although research has shown that the longer the intervention, the better the effect (Martin et al., 2009).

Task cohesion

To create groups with a clear purpose, it is essential that there is group agreement on the aims and goals of the group. In order to achieve the goals, each member needs to work to their remit, therefore having a clear understanding of each member's role, its associated responsibilities and behaviours, and the impact that failure to execute the role has on the group aim is vital (Eys & Carron, 2001). Such agreement and understanding will enhance group cohesion and have a positive impact on performance.

Setting agendas

It is important the groups have goals in terms of future direction and performance enhancement, but the development of such goals should be a process of interaction and agreement rather than dictated orders from a teacher. Setting goals and performance profiles (as discussed in Chapter 3) as a group can bring the group together, as the dancers will feel invested in the project.

Intergroup communication

A democratic approach to training, rehearsals and classes will allow the group the opportunity to make decisions on a range of dance-related issues. If they have made teacher-directed group decisions, they are more likely to adhere to the outcomes than from decisions made by teachers without negotiation. Teachers retain control by outlining the parameters of decision-making, but all have played a role in the ultimate decision. This may be through the teacher narrowing down the music selection to four tracks that the teacher feels are appropriate for a performance, and it is the group's job to make a final decision from these options.

Roles and responsibilities

It is important for everyone to understand not only their role, but the roles of others in order to function effectively. There needs to be task clarity, where each member knows the expectations of the role, how to achieve these aims, and what aims to prioritise. It should also be made clear what the consequences of failure to fulfil the role are to other group members (Eys & Carron, 2001).

In order to establish how clear the roles and responsibilities are, each group member writes down their perception of their own role and responsibilities, and that of one other group member. By reviewing this feedback, the teacher will able to establish where there is role ambiguity which may lead to conflict if not clarified.

Commitment behaviour

An important feature of group cohesion is that as part of being committed, group members will show sacrifice behaviour. Sacrifice behaviour is the opposite of selfish acts as it shows how much the group means to the individual.

Sacrifice behaviour can be encouraged by asking individuals to help with tasks outside of class time, and then to thank those who have helped in class. From making this behaviour normal within the group, a work ethos will be developed.

Social cohesion

Social cohesion is as important as task cohesion, especially in leisure dance classes (Spink & Carron, 1994), indeed, at times when the task is not going well, it may be the social cohesion of the group that helps sustain the motivation to continue. In order for social cohesion to occur, it requires the investment of time to allow those bonds to be made and maintained.

Having time to socialise

In order to bond, individuals within the group need to know each other, and this can only come about if they have the opportunity to talk to each other, to find out what they have in common – strengthening their attraction to the group (Burke, Carron, & Shapcott, 2008). Such commonalities are likely to be aspects of their lives outside of dance, so not only should communication be encouraged, but this should not be restricted to dance-related communication. In order to foster such interact, opportunities to discuss issues that are not dance-related should be made available to the group.

Time at the beginning or end of class should be allowed for chatting between the dancers to allow time for personal disclosure and catching up on things that have been happening in their lives. If time is tight, encourage the dancers to chat while they warm up in pairs. This allows group members to share issues of burning importance while still using their time productively.

Social events chosen by the group should be encouraged, where leadership and other formal roles are put to one side to allow for equitable interaction.

Intergroup communication

Sometimes allowing time to communicate encourages more communication between the same people, possibly leading to cliques or subgroups, therefore interaction between different group members must also be encouraged. Putting dancers into small groups to work on specific skills or create choreography will help break down any subgroups that may be developing. Asking members from any subgroups to buddy-up with new class members will further help increase integration.

Distinctiveness

One element of being in a group is that you are a member of something that others are not, which creates an *in-group/out-group* view, where the in-group view is based on what the group members have in common, and the out-group view is how your group is different from other groups. By encouraging group distinctiveness, this in-group/out-group view can be strengthened, cohesion being a by-product.

Making the group distinct could be through the use of identifying features such as devising a group name, organising matching hoodies, or even having your own group motto or chant.

Social networks

Extending the social network beyond just that of the dancers to include family and friends will help the teacher see the dancer in context, allow them to understand more about their life outside of the studio. This may also allow the family members to see their relative in a different light. They may see skills and dedication that they do not observe at home, and may feel more disposed towards supporting them in their dance careers as a result (Rhind & Jowett, 2010).

Inequity

The teacher can affect the cohesion of the group negatively by showing favouritism towards particular dancers. This behaviour can turn a previously well-cohesed group in on itself, and leave the preferred dancer isolated through no fault of their own, and destroys any respect the group may have held for the teacher (Turman, 2003). Bearing this in mind, it is vital that dealings with the group are equitable, sharing sought-after roles or having a system of selection that is entirely transparent. This will allow the group to see that all are being treated equally and cohesion can be sustained.

Life on tour

Being on tour may mean protracted time away from home, missing family, friends and loved ones. In addition to this, there is the nomadic nature of the existence, waking up in a new town each day or week can be disorientating, and the inside of hotel rooms and tour buses can be tedious. How these factors are managed may be the make or break of your show career.

Extended family

For the period of the show the cast become a big family, and just as with real families, we don't get to choose who we are related to. On this basis, there is the chance that we will not always get on with our colleagues. When confronted with a potential character clash, consider the following factors:

- Is the other person entirely to *blame* for the situation, or might you have contributed to it in some way?
- What is the *intention* of the other person? Do they mean well but act in a manner that you find irritating, in which case, accept that

you are different types of people, and bear this in mind when dealing with the individual so as to avoid conflict?
- Ensure communication is always constructive as the fallout from disagreements often affects more than those directly involved.

Time out

Although it may be fun being part of an extended family on tour, ensure that you make time for yourself, and that you respect others' need to do this too, especially if sharing a room. Utilise this time with something that absorbs you, such as reading, walking or watching a film.

Homesickness

Being away from home might sound like a glamorous time on the road visiting new cities, but it is surprising what we may miss from life at home – therefore, be prepared to feel homesick at times, this is perfectly normal.

There are several ways homesickness can be managed, and getting a balance between them can be key.

First, bring a little bit of home with you. Find an object that will help you connect with home to bring comfort in the difficult times. Keep in contact regularly using social media or emails so the distance does not seem so great.

Second, see the tour as your new family (although possibly only temporarily). As soon as you meet the group, make sure you talk to as many new people as possible, remembering all the time that they are probably as nervous as you. The quicker the group bonds, the more like a family they will feel.

Key concepts glossary

Closeness Mutual feelings of liking and trust exchanged between individuals.

Commitment The degree of attachment people may share.

Communication Methods of transferring messages between individuals.

Complementarity The use of reciprocal behaviours to balance interaction between individuals.

Conflict Tension between individuals who have opposing views.

Co-orientation A mutual understanding of each other's feelings.

Group cohesion The bonding between members of a group.

Group formation The process of individuals becoming a group.

Leadership A process of guiding individuals towards the achievement of goals.

References

Bandura, A. (1977). *Social learning theory*. Englewood Cliffs, NJ: Prentice-Hall.

Bass, B. M. (1995). Theory of transformational leadership redux. *The Leadership Quarterly, 6*(4), 463–478. doi:10.1016/1048-9843(95)90021-7.

Bonebright, D. A. (2010). Perspectives: 40 years of storming: A historical review of Tuckman's model of small group development. *Human Resource Development International, 13*(1), 111–120.

Burke, S. M., Carron, A. V., & Shapcott, K. M. (2008). Cohesion in exercise groups: An overview. *International Review of Sport and Exercise Psychology, 1*(2), 107–123.

Burns, J. M. (1978). *Leadership*. New York: Harper & Row.

Canary, D. J., Cupach, W. R., & Serpe, R. T. (2001). A competence-based approach to examining interpersonal conflict. *Communication Research, 28*(1), 79–104. doi:10.1177/009365001028001003.

Carron, A. V. (1982). Cohesiveness in sport groups: Interpretations and considerations. *Journal of Sport Psychology, 4*, 123–138.

Carron, A. V., Eys, M. A., & Burke, S. M. (2007). Team cohesion: Nature, correlates and development. In S. Jowett & D. Lavallee (Eds.), *Social psychology in sport*. Champaign, IL: Human Kinetics.

Carron, A. V., Widmeyer, W. N., & Brawley, L. R. (1985). The development of an instrument to assess cohesion in sport teams: The Group Environment Questionnaire. *Journal of Sport Psychology, 7*, 244–267.

Carron, A. V., Widmeyer, W. N., & Brawley, L. R. (1988). Group cohesion and individual adherence to physical activity. *Journal of Sport and Exercise Psychology, 10*(2), 127–138. doi:10.1123/jsep.10.2.127

Chelladuria, P. (2007). Leadership in sports. In G. Tenenbaum & R. C. Eklund (Eds.), *Handbook of sport psychology*. Hoboken, NJ: John Wiley & Sons, Inc.

Eys, M. A., & Carron, A. V. (2001). Role ambiguity, task cohesion, and task self-efficacy. *Small Group Research, 32*(3), 356–373. doi:10.1177/104649640103200305.

Fairholm, M. R. (2001). *The themes and theory of leadership: James Macgregor Burns and the philosophy of leadership*. Washington, DC: The George Washington University: Center for Excellence in Municipal Management.

Forsyth, D. R. (2014). *Group dynamics*. Belmont, CA: Wadsworth Cengage Learning.

García-Calvo, T., Leo, F. M., Gonzalez-Ponce, I., Sánchez-Miguel, P. A., Mouratidis, A., & Ntoumanis, N. (2014). Perceived coach-created and peer-created motivational climates and their associations with team cohesion and athlete satisfaction: evidence from a longitudinal study. *Journal of Sports Sciences, 32*(18), 1738–1750. doi:10.1080/02640414.2014.918641.

Hardy, L., Arthur, C. A., Jones, G., Shariff, A., Munnoch, K., Isaacs, I., & Allsopp, A. J. (2010). The relationship between transformational leadership behaviors, psychological, and training outcomes in elite military recruits. *The Leadership Quarterly, 21*(1), 20–32. doi:10.1016/j.leaqua.2009.10.002.

Jowett, S. (2007). Interdependence analysis and the 3+1Cs in the coach-athlete relationship In S. Jowett & D. Lavallee (Eds.), *Social psychology in sport*. Champaign, IL: Human Kinetics.

Jowett, S., & Nezlek, J. (2012). Relationship interdependence and satisfaction with important outcomes in coach-athlete dyads. *Journal of Social and Personal Relationships, 29*(3), 287–301. doi:10.1177/0265407511420980.

LaVoi, N. M. (2007). Interpersonal communication and conflict in the coach-athlete relationship. In S. Jowett & D. Lavallee (Eds.), *Social psychology in sport*. Champaign, IL: Human Kinetics.

Lewicki, R. J., Tomlinson, E., & Gillespie, N. (2006). Model of interpersonal trust development: Theoretical approaches, empirical evidences, and future directions. *Journal of Management, 32*, 991–1022.

Mach, M., Dolan, S., & Tzafrir, S. (2010). The differential effect of team members' trust on team performance: The mediation role of team cohesion. *Journal of Occupational and Organizational Psychology, 83*, 771–794.

Martin, L. J., Carron, A. V., & Burke, S. M. (2009). Team building interventions in sport: A meta-analysis. *Sport and Exercise Psychology Review, 5*, 3–18.

Mogonea, F., & Popescu, A. M. (2015). The role of sociocognitive conflict in academic-type learning. *Procedia: Social and Behavioral Sciences, 180*, 865–870. doi:10.1016/j.sbspro.2015.02.228.

Paradis, K. F., & Martin, L. J. (2012). Team building in sport: Linking theory and research to practical application. *Journal of Sport Psychology in Action, 3*(3), 159–170. doi:10.1080/21520704.2011.653047.

Rahim, M. A. (2011). *Managing conflict in organizations* (4th ed.). New Brunswick, NJ: Transaction Publishers.

Rhind, D. J. A., & Jowett, S. (2010). Relationship maintenance strategies in the coach-athlete relationship: The development of the COMPASS model. *Journal of Applied Sport Psychology, 22*(1), 106–121. doi:10.1080/10413200903474472

Smith, M. J., Arthur, C. A., Hardy, J., Callow, N., & Williams, D. (2013). Transformational leadership and task cohesion in sport: The mediating role of intrateam communication. *Psychology of Sport and Exercise, 14*(2), 249–257. doi:10.1016/j.psychsport.2012.10.002.

Smith, R. E., Smoll, F. L., & Hunt, E. B. (1977). A system for the behavioral assessment of athletic coaches. *Research Quarterly, 48*, 401–407.

Spink, K. S., & Carron, A. V. (1994). Group cohesion effects in exercise classes. *Small Group Research, 25*(1), 26–42. doi:10.1177/1046496494251003.

Tuckman, B. W. (2001). Developmental sequence in small groups. *Group Facilitation: A Research and Applications Journal, 3*, 66–81.

Tuckman, B. W., & Jensen, M. A. (1977). Stages of small-group development revisited. *Group and Organization Studies, 2*(4), 419–427.

Turman, P. D. (2003). Coaches and cohesion: The impact of coaching techniques on team cohesion in the small group sport setting. *Journal of Sport Behavior, 26*, 86–104.

Turman, P. D. (2008). Coaches' immediacy behaviors as predictors of athletes' perceptions of satisfaction and team cohesion. *Western Journal of Communication, 72*(2), 162–179. doi:10.1080/10570310802038424.

Further reading

Carron, A. V., & Brawley, L. R. (2012). Cohesion. *Small Group Research, 43*(6), 726–743.

Jowett, S. (2005). The coach–athlete partnership. *The Psychologist, 18*(7), 412–415.

Khan, Z. A., Nawaz, A., & Khan, I. (2016). Leadership theories and styles: A literature review. *Journal of Resources Development and Management, 16*, 1–8.

CHAPTER 6

Managing emotions

> **Learning outcomes**
>
> By the end of this chapter readers should be able to:
>
> - recognise why emotions need consideration in dance-related situations
> - define key terms related to arousal and performance
> - describe different types of anxiety
> - explain how different emotions may impact upon dance performance
> - propose how to manage emotions experienced in different dance-related situations

CONTEXT

Emotions are a vital component of life and add colour to our life experiences. Emotions are also an important form of communication, emotional expression informing others how we feel at that moment. Emotions may be so potent that they can become contagious, which is excellent news if the emotion is joy, but less helpful if the emotion is fear (Totterdell, 2000). All aspects of life can impact on our emotional state, and dancing is no different. As a dancer, life may at times feel like an emotional rollercoaster. There will be the high points, where we feel elated at achieving our next grade, or more fleeting moments of joy at having mastered the technicalities of a fouetté turn. Often it is these positive emotions that strengthen our desire to continue as a dancer. Equally, we may experience a range of less desirable, negative emotions. Although these may not be pleasant, it is sometimes these experiences that motivate us, pushing us on to the next level.

Unfortunately, we cannot always be successful in what we do within the profession, possibly because we do not yet possess the skill to achieve the task set, as might be experienced in examinations, or because we are competing against many other dancers when auditioning. Inevitably there will be times of disappointment, and how we manage these experiences may have an impact on our career trajectory. For some the negative emotions are not only self-destructive, but are counterproductive to those around them. Frustration can lead to feelings of anger, which, if outwardly expressed, can be highly problematic and create problems within the group.

Sometimes we may experience negative emotions before we have even given the performance, through stress and anxiety. This may be due to the pressure of being evaluated in an examination or audition, often referred to as pre-competition nerves or stage fright. Sometimes we may feel this in the lead-up to an event, but as soon as we start to dance, the nerves melt away, our worries seemingly unnecessary. This is not necessarily the case for everyone – some dancers may feel they have no control over their emotions, potentially impacting on their performance, in extreme cases, it may force them to leave the profession completely.

Having an understanding about how our body and mind interact at a point of high emotion may help a dancer to understand their emotional triggers. This self-knowledge may allow them to identify and control their emotions before they become problematic. To be able to do this leads to a more enjoyable and positive dance performance for all concerned.

THEORY

One of the most commonly experienced emotional states that impacts on dance performance is anxiety felt when under stress. The explanations of what happens to us physically and mentally when needing to perform are highly complex, therefore the process will be broken down into discrete elements which build into the model shown in Figure 6.1.

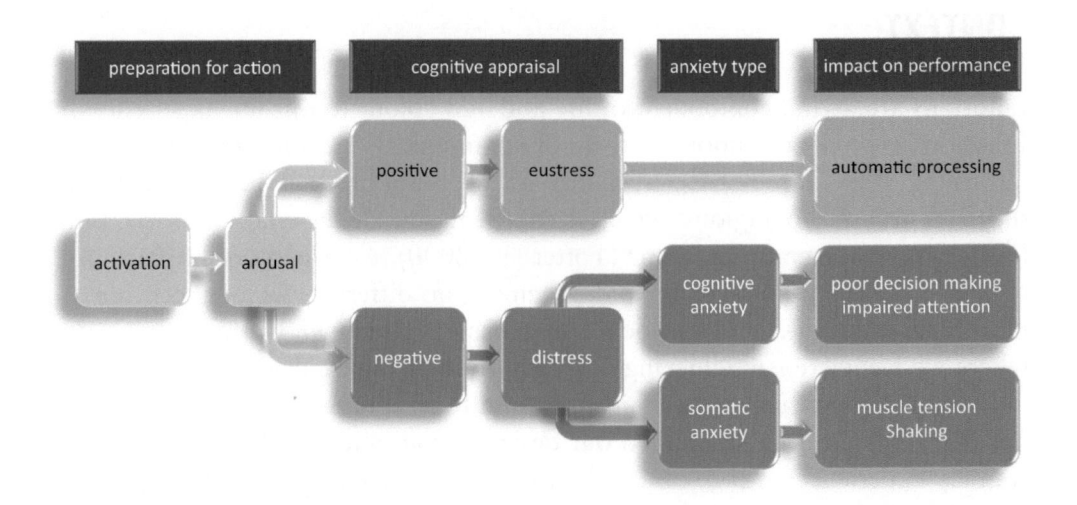

Figure 6.1
Overview of arousal and performance factors

Preparation for action

Activation, arousal and stress

To understand how emotion may impact on performance, it is important to understand how the body prepares for action when not in an emotive state. When we know that we need to perform, the body needs to enter a state of *activation* where it prepares itself for the physical and mental challenges of the task ahead. Therefore, to perform beyond that of normal activity, a range of physiological changes needs to occur to meet the demands of the performance.

The activation leads to a state of *arousal*, which is defined as 'the extent of the release of energy, stored in the tissues of an organism, as is shown in activity response' (Duffy, 1962), how poised the body is for action. This suggests arousal is a continuum where you may be comatose at one end of the scale, through to a state of high excitation at the other end. When the levels of arousal are linked to performance, there are differing effects dependent on various factors.

First, let's consider what impact arousal alone has on our performance. Imagine if you were woken up at 5 o'clock in the morning and required immediately to perform a complex ballet routine – how prepared would you feel for this, physically and mentally? You would probably have problems of concentration as you had not been awake long enough to have achieved the required level of alertness, lacking mental arousal. Equally, your body having been at rest for so long would also need to become energised for you to be able to perform to your highest potential, lacking physical arousal. The same can be seen when we give dancers a routine that is too simple, their high level of boredom leads to a lower level of performance as they are not mentally or physically challenged by the task. Likewise, if we are too excited about an event, we may not be able to control our emotions, which can have a detrimental effect on our thoughts and actions.

These extremes can be seen in Figure 6.2 which is based on Yerkes and Dodson's (1908) Inverted U Theory. This theory suggests that if we are under-aroused, physically or mentally, we display low levels of performance. Conversely if we are over-aroused, we may not be able to concentrate sufficiently or control our actions, and therefore see a deterioration in performance. The grey area shows that there is a zone of optimal functioning where our level of arousal has reached an ideal point.

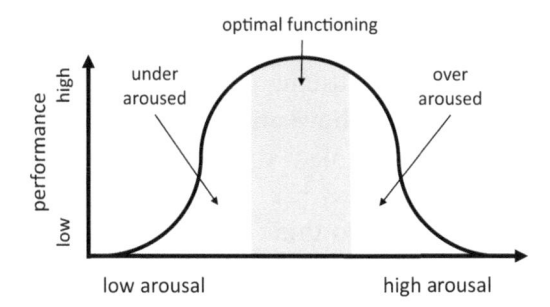

Figure 6.2
Impact of arousal on performance

The level of arousal that is relevant to a performance also varies dependent on several factors: the *experience* of the performer and the *complexity* of the activity. Dependent on how proficient we are at a task, we will require different levels of arousal to achieve our best possible performance level (Figure 6.3). A novice needs very low levels of arousal, as being too aroused may lead to an inability to control their muscles, therefore impairing the fluidity of the moves. As they are new to the activity, they must keep low levels of mental arousal as any mental interference will act as a distractor, impairing their concentration which is vital when learning a new task. However, an expert may need higher

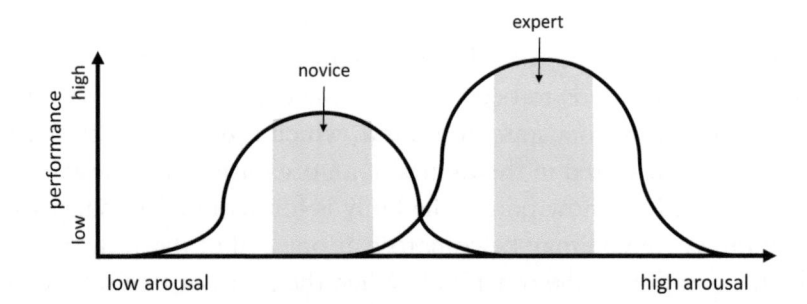

Figure 6.3
Impact of arousal based on the experiences of the performer

levels of arousal to even engage with the task, requiring more physical and mental arousal to reach their optimum point of performance.

The other important factor is the *complexity* of the skill being performed as illustrated in Figure 6.4. If the activity requires *gross motor skills*, such as speed, endurance or strength, then a high state of arousal puts you in the optimum state, as the body is primed, ready for action. Whereas, if you are undertaking a complex activity that relies on *fine motor skills*, such as concentration or hand-to-eye coordination, then a high level of arousal will interfere with your physical performance through increasingly shaky movements. Mental impairment might be experienced through *hypervigilism*, where over-arousal may act as a distractor from concentration on the needs of the task (Oxendine, 1970).

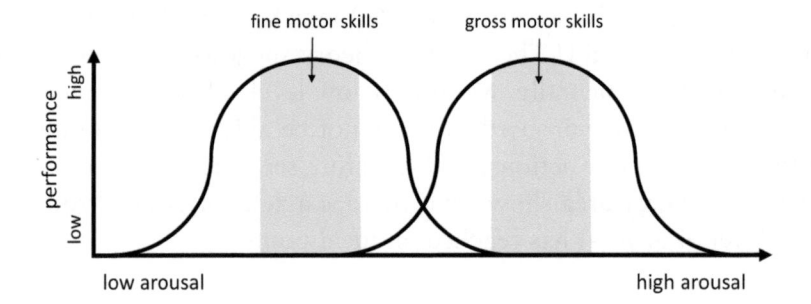

Figure 6.4
Impact of arousal based on the complexity of the skill

If we are experiencing arousal, this suggests that the situation has been perceived as more important than usual, and could be argued that the body is then put under *stress* to perform above and beyond normal levels. Stress is an evolutionary development whose role is to enhance survival prospects by preparing the body for action. In essence, stress is a physiological state, and although this is not how we tend to think about stress, it is neither good nor bad. Our tendency is to see stress as a worrying time when we cannot cope with a situation, so to make sense of this apparent contradiction, we need to define some vital concepts and understand how the mind and body relate to each other.

The physiology of stress

Stress can be defined as the physiological response to a stressor, where a stressor can be defined as a stimulus, real or imagined, that one perceives as a threat. In evolutionary terms the stressor might be a sabre-toothed tiger ready to attack, and the stress response is our *fight or flight mechanism* which primes our body to manage the situation. Unfortunately, many of today's stressors are

© Shutterstock

not the type where fight or flight are relevant, but understanding the processes that the body goes through may help us reduce its impact on our performance, and even help us harness some of the resultant energy.

Our body may have a stress response to *biogenic* stressors, such as too much caffeine, extreme temperatures or excessive exercise, where internal adaptations help the body respond to the chemical, environmental or behavioural changes. For a dancer, the stressors are more likely to be *psychosocial* in nature, where an individual may interpret an event, such as a public performance, as either a threat or a challenge. Such interpretations are based on an individual's perceptions, but before we consider the perception of stress, it is necessary to understand the physiological processes at play.

Once the stressor has been perceived, in the *hypothalamus*, an area of the brain responsible for homeostasis, hormones are released to initiate the stress response through the *sympathetic nervous system*. The hypothalamus releases the corticotrophin-releasing hormone (CRH) which informs the pituitary gland to release the adrenocorticotropic hormone (ACTH), a hormone which travels through the bloodstream to the adrenal glands where it triggers the release of two vital hormones: cortisol and adrenaline (Smith & Vale, 2006). The function of cortisol is to regulate blood glucose levels, blood pressure and heart rate (Whitworth, Williamson, Mangos, & Kelly, 2005), whereas the function of adrenaline is quicker and more varied. Its release leads to dilation of the bronchioles and increases the heart rate, ensuring a greater supply of blood to the muscles and brain. It also relaxes the stomach, intestine and urinary bladder, while also stimulating the release of glycogen from the liver into circulation (Watson, 2015).

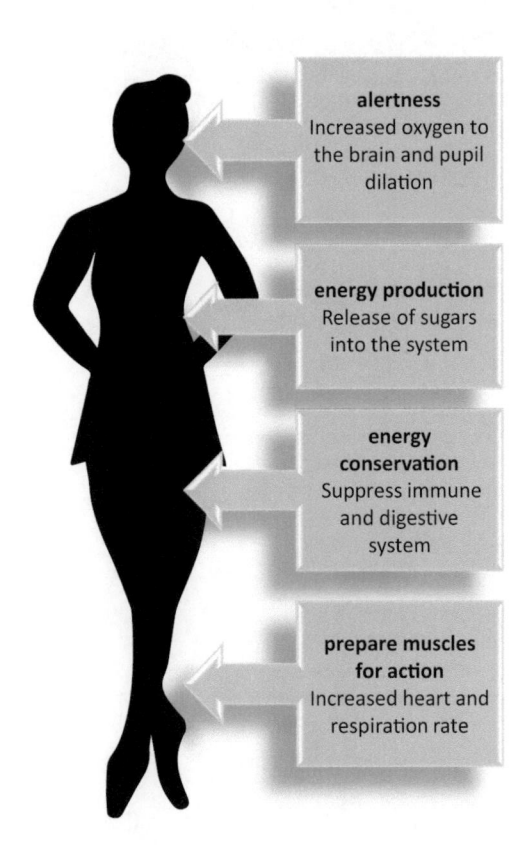

Figure 6.5
Arousal response

So, if these are the changes that are happening within, what are their consequences with respect to dance performance? To answer this question, we need to understand what the body is trying to do. We are back to the sabre-toothed tiger attack – we need to be able to fight or run to survive, so essentially the body is preparing for action. How useful this is depends upon what the stressor is. If we need a sudden burst of energy, then this evolutionary response is advantageous, because to fight or flee we need to make an energetic response, how this occurs is shown in Figure 6.5.

First, we need to get oxygenated blood to the major muscles, which have been assisted by the increase in blood pressure and respiration rate. To ensure that we have enough energy to sustain such output, we need to gather energy resources. The release of sugars from the liver adds to the store of energy available to manage the situation. The body does not solely rely on the sugars stored for energy, it also uses energy conservation techniques to assist. One energy-saving technique used is the suppression of the immune system (Rojas, Padgett, Sheridan, & Marucha, 2002), while a second technique used is that the sympathetic nervous system inhibits the digestive system (Lovallo, 2016). In times of instant emergency, the suppression of the immune and digestive systems seems logical, ensuring more energy is available to deal with the immediate threat enhances our chance of survival. Unfortunately, when we experience stress over prolonged periods, suppression of these systems can create health problems such as stomach ulcers and vulnerability to infection (Selye, 1976). For this reason, it is important to be aware of our stress responses and try to deal with long-term stress in order to avoid such health problems.

Symptoms of stress

If we understand what is going on inside our body when under stress, it can help us understand some of the symptoms we may also experience (Figure 6.6). Take a minute to bring to mind what physiological symptoms you experience when stressed:

- The dry mouth and the butterflies in the stomach we may experience are a result of the suppression of the digestive system.
- Shaking is result of having your system primed for action.
- Feeling hot and sweaty is due to the blood flowing to our major muscles.
- Rapid breathing is the result of the increased blood pressure and respiration rate.
- The need to go to the toilet more frequently is due to the relaxation of the bladder.

The physiological changes also impact on our mental capacity to deal with the situation. The adrenaline released increases the supply of oxygen to the brain which enhances executive functions, such as problem-solving and decision-making. This also leads to dilation of the pupils which allows us to be more visually vigilant. These enhanced cognitive functions will complement the increased physical strength to maximise the chances of survival.

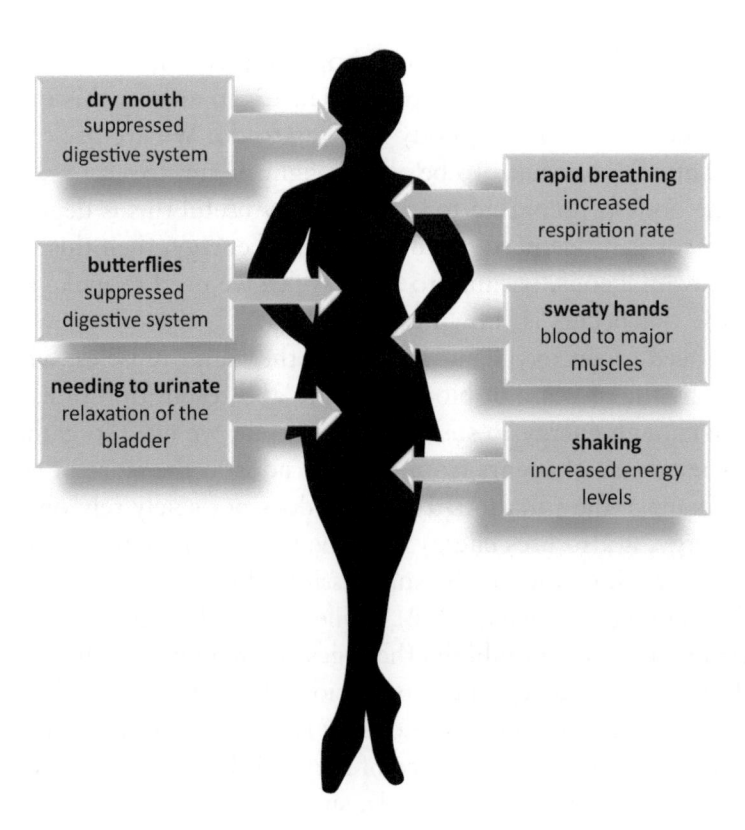

Figure 6.6
Arousal experience

Cognitive appraisal

Eustress, distress and anxiety

So it seems, stress is not stressful, it is purely a physiological response to a situation. If this is the case, why do we think of it as stress? This is where the mind comes in, it is our interpretation of the situation which may lead us to perceive the event as a stressor. Consider a rollercoaster ride, for some, this is an exciting prospect, *the speed and exhilaration at flying through the sky*, whereas for others it is a terrifying activity, 'I'll almost certainly fall to my death!' Imagine you are lining up, waiting to board – what are the sensations this situation brings to mind for you? The sensations will be similar regardless of your view of rollercoaster rides, as this is the body preparing for action. It is how you perceive the activity which will affect how you interpret these feelings.

Cognitive appraisal refers to the individual's thoughts about the impending event – whether you perceive it as a challenge or a threat. The perception is ultimately based on an assessment of the demands of the situation and the resources you believe to be available to meet those demands (Jones, Meijen, McCarthy, & Sheffield, 2009). The assessment of the resources are based on three factors:

- self-efficacy, the dancer's belief that they have the skills required to meet the needs of the challenge;
- how much the dancers believes she can control the situation, which will be highly dependent on the situation and previous experiences;

MANAGING EMOTIONS

- the goals that have been set for the performance, where the more important these goals are to the individual, the more impact this will have on the cognitive appraisal.

A positive interpretation is where we see the situation as a challenge. Where we believe we have the skills and energy required to cope with the situation, the subsequent feeling of excitement is referred to as *eustress*. Conversely, the perception of an inability to cope leads to a threat perception, referred to as *distress*.

Types of anxiety

Multidimensional Anxiety Theory

Of interest here is the negative interpretation, referred to as *anxiety*, an emotional response to the appraisal of the stressor. The Multidimensional Anxiety Theory suggests that anxiety can be experienced in two ways, through *cognitive anxiety* or *somatic anxiety*. Cognitive anxiety relates to worry and negative expectations about the situation or outcome, and negative concerns about the self. Somatic anxiety relates to emotionality, where perceptions of the physiological responses are experienced as unpleasant, leading to feelings of nerves and tension (Jones & Hardy, 1990). The interactions of these forms of anxiety are bidirectional. As can be seen in Figure 6.7, a dancer may be worried about whether she can remember the choreography (cognitive), which interrupts the fluidity of the performance (somatic) as she has reverted from automatic processing to controlled processing. Alternatively, the sensation of sweaty palms and shaky hands prior to an audition (somatic) may distract his attention from the routine and lead to forgetting (cognitive).

These forms of anxiety are orthogonal, meaning that they are independent of each other. Some dancers may be prone to higher level of cognitive anxiety, worrying about how they look or whether they will remember their solo. Others may be more likely to express somatic anxiety, possibly being fidgety or feeling sick before going on stage. Alternatively, some may experience both forms to greater or lesser extents.

However, the relationship that cognitive and somatic anxiety have with respect to performance is not as straightforward as the relationship between arousal and performance. As can be seen in Figure 6.8, the different types of

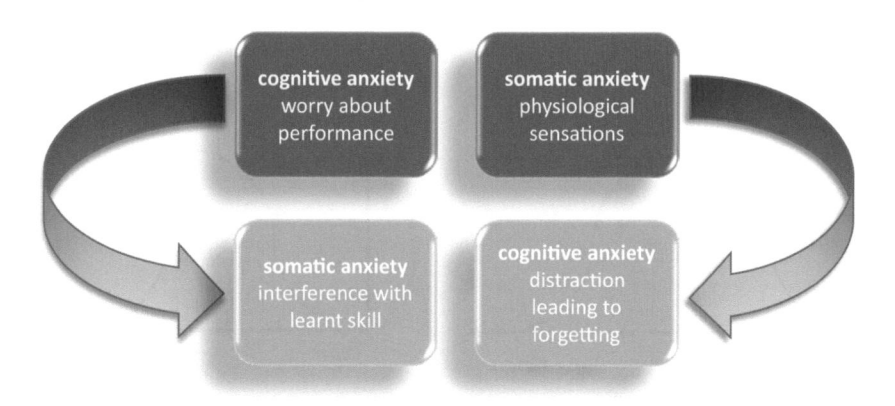

Figure 6.7
Bidirectional relationship between cognitive and somatic anxiety

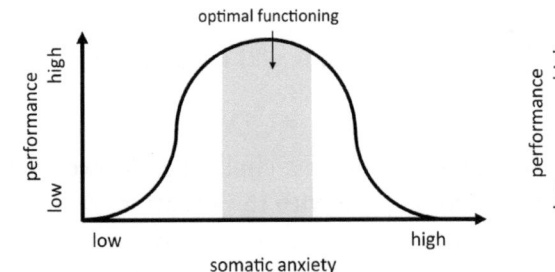

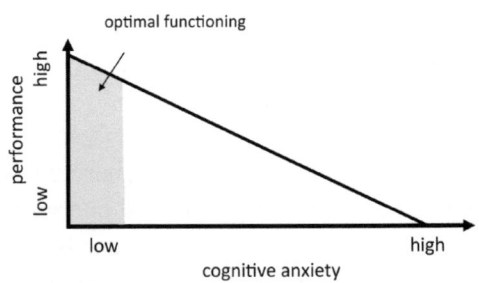

Figure 6.8
Differences in optimal functioning between cognitive and somatic anxiety

anxiety rely on different levels of arousal for optimum performance. Somatic anxiety mimics the same inverted U relationship seen with arousal and performance, whereas a different pattern is observed with respect to cognitive anxiety, which forms a negative linear relationship (Hardy, 1999). This means that low levels of cognitive anxiety will lead to optimum performance, and as the level of cognitive anxiety increases, the performance will decrease. From this we can see that performance is dependent upon what type of anxiety one is prone to.

Catastrophe Theory

One critique that has been made of the Multidimensional Anxiety Theory is that both dimensions have been treated as independent constructs, and it does not consider the interactive nature of the two forms of anxiety. Catastrophe Theory is based on Hardy and Fazey's model of the relationship between cognitive anxiety and physiological arousal (cited in Jones & Hardy, 1990). In this model (Figure 6.9), cognitive anxiety determines whether the level of physiological arousal becomes counterproductive to the required level of performance. While acknowledging the inverted U relationship between physiological arousal and performance, when cognitive anxiety is low, there will be a gradual and continuous decrease. However, where the level of cognitive anxiety is high, there is a large and disproportionate impact on performance occurring at the cusp of the catastrophe (Hardy, 1999; Monsma & Overby, 2004). Instead of the gradual reduction in performance, *hysteresis* occurs where there is a sudden and dramatic loss of form.

Explanations for this outcome combine the impacts of cognitive and somatic anxiety responses. At a cognitive level, in times of stress, we defer to controlled processing (discussed in Chapter 4), whereby we are applying conscious thought to our actions, similar to when we are in a learning mode.

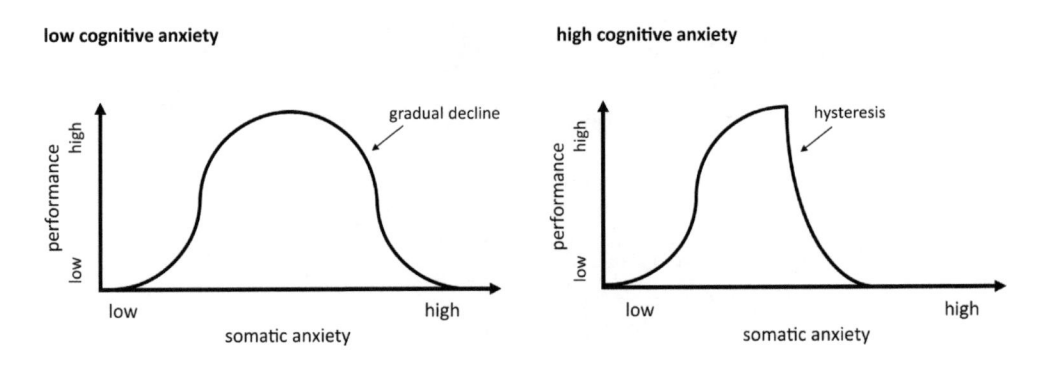

Figure 6.9
Catastrophe Theory

This may lead to forgetfulness and a lack of fluidity in movement. In addition, there is the narrowing of attentional field where we may be fixated, rather than concentrating on the needs of the task. At a somatic level the stress response may lead to the tensing of muscles which interferes with our fluidity of movement, and subsequently increasing effort is required, so we tire more quickly.

Temporal patterning

Not only does anxiety affect us in different ways but when we experience these different forms is also varied, and is referred to as *temporal patterning*. As can be seen in Figure 6.10, levels of cognitive anxiety are stable and high in the long lead-up to an event where we may be preoccupied by thoughts of the event. The levels of somatic anxiety do not start to rise until hours before the event, where we may be aware of shortness of breath and butterflies. In both cases the levels of anxiety drop as the performance commences (Martens, Vealey, Burton, & Martens, 1990).

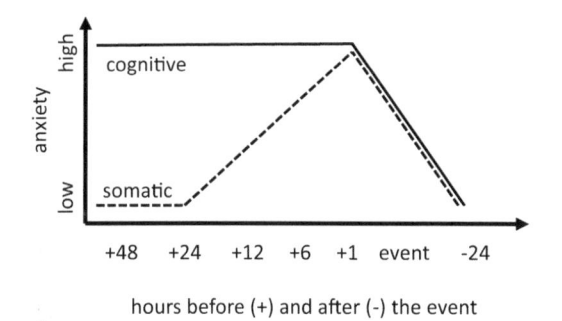

Figure 6.10
Relationship between anxiety and event

State and trait anxiety

How anxiety manifests itself within individuals is highly varied, often related to personality and previous experience, both of which will now be discussed. There are times when we consider our performance to be more important than others, so we may perform in a relaxed and calm manner in the studio when rehearsing, but as we stand in the wings we start to feel symptoms of anxiety, referred to as *state anxiety*. This is normal apprehension felt at important events. Our levels of state anxiety may be affected by *dispositional factors*, where some people are generally more likely to perceive situations as threatening, referred to as *trait anxiety*. Trait anxiety is a more habitual response to all sorts of situations, linked to personality, the result being that high trait anxiety increases levels of state anxiety (Spielberger, 1966).

Impact of anxiety on performance

Cognitive impact

There are a range of effects that anxiety may have on performance linked to cognitive processes. One feature of anxiety is *perceptual narrowing* where we

> **Research in focus**
>
> **The Relationship Between Imagery and Competitive Anxiety in Ballet Auditions**
>
> **Aim** Competition for places in dance schools and companies is high, so it is not surprising that auditions might be a source of anxiety, therefore any means of managing the anxiety would be helpful to dancers' success. The purpose of this study was to identify whether there is a relationship between imagery use and audition anxiety.
>
> **Method** A total of 131 young ballet dancers auditioning for a local ballet school and company were questioned using a range of measures:
> - Competitive State Anxiety Inventory (CSAI-2)
> - Movement Imagery Questionnaire (MIQ-R)
> - Sport Imagery Questionnaire (SIQ)
>
> The dancers completed all three measures during the three hours prior to the audition in order to assess their state anxiety.
>
> **Results**
> - *Cognitive anxiety:* was a greater predictor of failure, but decreased with experience
> - *Self confidence:* previous audition success increased self confidence. Dancers using less arousal imagery (MG-A) and more motivational imagery (MG-M), were more likely to be self confident
> - *Anxiety:* Dancers using more arousal imagery (MG-A) and less motivational imagery (MG-M), were more likely to experience cognitive and somatic anxiety
>
> **Conclusions** Imagery can have facilitative and debilitative effects on audition performance therefore it is important to guide dancers to employ deliberate performance-enhancing imagery to reduce debilitative cognitive anxiety and increase facilitative somatic anxiety and self confidence.
>
> (Monsma & Overby, 2004)

may experience tunnel vision, referred to a Cue Utilization Theory (Easterbrook, 1959) illustrated in Figure 6.11. This theory suggests that low levels of arousal may lead to lack of concentration as we become too broad in our perceptual selectivity. As arousal is increased, we narrow down our perceptual field to an optimum state of concentration, which is ideal in the case of a sabre-toothed tiger as we can focus clearly on the immediate threat, a coping mechanism. If arousal becomes too high, we will move from an optimal state to a point of fixation. This means that we are not observing other important cues in the environment.

Another cognitive impairment links to memory. Remembering choreography is at the heart of dance, so anything that impacts on this function can have profound consequences. Anxiety may negatively affect our working memory which will lead to problems of decision-making, a wrong decision being critical for performance. In addition, our long-term memory may also be affected, especially if we have become self-conscious. This focus on the self may

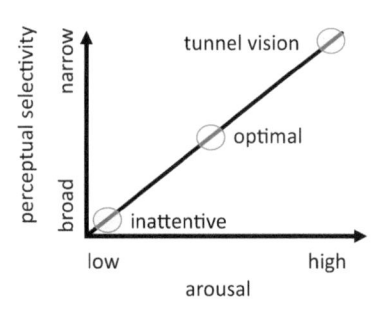

Figure 6.11 Impact of arousal on attention

increase the chance of reverting to controlled processing as discussed in Chapter 4, so routines that have been well rehearsed and that can normally be performed automatically, without the need for conscious thought may suddenly be completely absent from your mind. A positive appraisal of the situation allows the body to operate to its optimum psychological level with minimal cognitive interference, functioning at an automatic level of processing.

Somatic impact

There are also several impacts from somatic anxiety on physical movement. At one end of the scale, fine motor control and manual dexterity will be affected by reduced cognitive functioning and over-arousal leading to a highly

---

Research in focus

Psychological Recovery: Progressive muscle relaxation (PMR), anxiety, and sleep in dancers

Aim Sleep is a means to recharging energy stores and to recover from strenuous activity, therefore lack of sleep may leave us at a performance disadvantage. Sometimes problems of sleep onset may be due to anxiety, keeping us alert at a period when we should be at rest. The purpose of this research was to establish whether the stress reduction technique, progressive muscle relaxation, could help sleep onset.

Method A total of 12 elite female dance students were used in the intervention study.
Dependent variable:
- Endler Multidimensional Anxiety Scale-Trait (EMAS-T)
- Daily sleep diaries were completed

Intervention:
- Participants were to undertake a progressive muscle relaxation activity daily for the duration of the study

Results
- Dancers with particularly high trait social evaluation anxiety and late sleep onset time benefitted from the relaxation technique.

Conclusions For those who are consistently concerned about social evaluations, sleep may be a problem. Engaging in a simple one week intervention may give them the skills to reduce their physiological anxiety sufficiently to allow the onset of sleep.

(McCloughan, Hanrahan, Anderson & Halson, 2016)

energised state. With respect to more gross motor coordination, when in a threat state, the body adopts coping strategies, but these are still grounded in survival responses to sabre-tooth tiger threats. Survival strategies used in this situation would lead to protective stances and postures to avoid the stressor, which in a dance performance may lead to lack of engagement with the audience or assessor. Another survival stance is that of *freezing* where the degrees of freedom in movement become restricted, which leads to erratic or jerky moves, a disaster if in the middle of a performance (Magill, 2001), whereas the positive interpretation ensures that blood flow is increased sufficiently to maximise muscle power and speeding up decision-making (Jones et al., 2009).

Other emotions

Action tendencies

Although this chapter focuses predominantly on anxiety, this is not the only emotion likely to be experienced by dancers, although it is a frequently cited source of performance impairment. Throughout a performance the dancer may go through a range of emotional states based on their perceptions of the performance, and what they perceive from the environment. Other emotions that may hinder performance are anger, disappointment and embarrassment. Although emotions are an internal state of mind, they may lead to *action tendencies*, which are the outward expression of that inner state (Uphill, Groom, & Jones, 2014). These action tendencies may be linked to external factors, such as the performance, potentially acting as a motivational drive. They may also be linked to the inner emotion being experienced, such as celebration or aggression. Once an action tendency has been expressed, it is not just the individual who may be affected by the expressed emotion, but those around them may also be affected. If the expressed emotion is positive, this may serve to encourage others involved, but negative expression, such as aggression expressed towards other people through verbal aggression or physical violence, can have devastating effects. Even if the anger is towards items of frustration, through kicking or hitting objects, it may be equally upsetting to those who observe it, serving to increase their level of arousal and anxiety.

Positive emotional states

Some emotional states, such as happiness and excitement, have been shown to be productive in performance enhancement (Cerin, 2003; Uphill et al., 2014) due to their links with arousal and a positive cognitive appraisal. *Excitability* can also be observed in personality development and has been linked to heightened talent or ability, referred to as over-excitability. Over-excitability is a positive state of arousal linked to the enhancement of five different dimensions (Thomson & Jaque, 2016). This state produces surplus energy which drives *psychomotor* behaviour, heightens *sensual* experiences therefore reducing tension, increases the *imagination, intellectual* drive and *emotional* expression, all factors that may enhance creativity and musical interpretation.

Photograph courtesy of Kianna Stephens.

Negative emotional states

Anger may have similar impacts on performance to that of anxiety, leading to decreases in concentration, motivation, confidence, and increasing maladaptive behaviours (Martinent & Ferrand, 2009). Anger is a reactive emotional state which might include hostility, which is a negative attitude towards someone or something. The behavioural outcome of this state is aggression, which is the intention to cause physical or psychological harm (Ruiz & Hanin, 2011). As an emotional state, it reflects a level of heightened arousal, therefore affecting physical and mental aspects of performance, suggesting similar impacts upon performance as is witnessed with anxiety. In addition, anger is generally the emotional response to frustration, which suggests that there has been a level of interference on the dancer's goal, therefore, performance reduction may already have occurred, leading to a performance that might spiral out of control.

Likewise, embarrassment is generally an emotional response to a situation where the dancer may be feeling self-conscious, possibly due to having made an error. As a consequence, the dancer may be focusing on her performance of self-presentation, prohibiting automatic processing, the resultant controlled processing thus reducing flow of movement (Uphill et al., 2014).

Self and interpersonal regulation

Emotional regulation is the deliberate strategy to decrease, maintain or increase the experiences of specified emotions, through an ability to identify and process their emotional states, then comprehend and manage their emotional behaviours (Tamminen & Crocker, 2013). As part of their communicative power, emotions will affect those around you. On the one hand, they have the power to become contagious, infecting those around you, which, depending on the emotion, can have positive or negative outcomes. This is especially important as dancers are often required to work closely as a group, therefore, how you manage your emotions may well impact on the emotions, and potential performance, of others.

A range of factors may affect the impact that your emotions may have on the group. Some of these factors relate to long-held features of the group, such as how long the group have been together and their current levels of cohesion (as discussed in Chapter 5). Other factors may be context-dependent, linked to the importance of the situation. Therefore, a recreational class may generate high levels of joy due to the lack of pressure and high levels of fun being experienced, whereas a final, time-pressured rehearsal prior to a dance competition may see levels of anger running high due to frustration.

How these emotions are dealt with may vary. At an individual level there may be the need to quash any outward signs of the feelings, through self-censorship or a consideration of how these emotions are expressed through body language. At a group level these emotions may be dissipated in different ways, through social interaction, either by practical or social support of a colleague, or by changing the atmosphere from a negative emotion to a positive one through the use of humour (Tamminen & Crocker, 2013).

MANAGING EMOTIONS

Having reviewed a range of impacts that emotions may have on individuals at the mental and physical levels, and considering the devastating impact that these may have on performance, it is important to understand how these situations can be prevented or managed.

PRACTICE

Preparation for an event

Cognitive reappraisal

To understand how we can reappraise situations that are anxiety-inducing, it is useful to consider Reversal Theory (Apter, 1989) where our interpretation of the event is defined by the *hedonic tone*, as either pleasant or unpleasant, and our level of arousal, creating four different emotional states (Figure 6.12). Optimal performance occurs at the centre of the interaction, but reinterpretation of some of these states may reduce the negative impacts upon performance, as we will see.

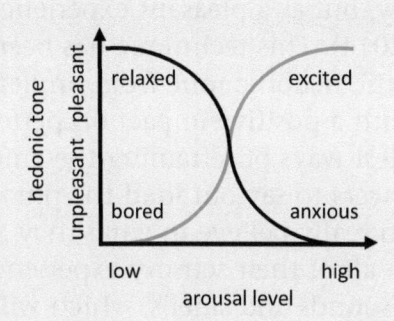

Figure 6.12
Reversal Theory

Source: Based on Apter (1989).

Reappraisal as calmness

One of the most natural responses to dealing with those who are experiencing anxiety is to try to calm them down. Although suggesting that they become relaxed may seem logical, there is evidence to suggest that suppression of anger (Szasz, Szentagotai, & Hofmann, 2011) and anxiety may be counterproductive, and in some cases can increase physiological and subjective experiences of anxiety (Hofmann, Heering, Sawyer, & Asnaani, 2009). The problem is that the request requires a change not only of the hedonic tone (from unpleasant to pleasant) but also to change the level of arousal (from low to high), therefore requiring a cognitive and somatic shift. Understanding this will help highlight why other approaches may be more effective in reducing anxiety.

Managing expectations

One way of managing the cognitive appraisal of the situation is by putting the performance in perspective, through *cognitive reappraisal*. This can be achieved by reviewing expectations, and not placing such an emphasis on the importance of the event (Klockare, Gustafsson, & Nordin-Bates, 2011).

This may be achieved through a conversation prior to performance examining what potential pitfalls may occur and reassessing the importance of them. Posing the question 'What's the worst that can happen?' allows a consideration of outcomes and consequences. Such a conversation initiated by the teacher or director may help dancers realise that the pressure they are feeling is self-inflicted. From this they may understand that perfection is not required, and that incidents occur to the very best dancers, what matters is that we get up and carry on.

Reappraisal as excitement through self-talk

Reframing anxiety as excitement requires the engagement with the sensations of high levels of arousal, but interpreting them not as threat-related anxiety, but as a pleasant experience, therefore *excitement* (Brooks, 2014). This technique has been shown to be effective in altering the hedonic tone from unpleasant threat-related to a pleasant state with a positive impact on performance.

One of the simplest ways of reframing the emotional experience is to ask anxious dancers to say out loud the phrase 'I am excited' while asking them to really believe in what they are saying. Ask them to engage with all of their sensory experiences, and try to enjoy all the sights, sounds and smells, which will help evoke excitement now and in future performances.

Pre-performance routines

One technique that is used by many dancers as a means of dealing with potential performance nerves is the adoption of pre-performance routines, which are the implementation of a set of thoughts or actions that are systematically applied prior to the event. There are various factors that make these routines effective. They help focus attention on the task at hand, distracting from negative or irrelevant thoughts and help concentrate on performance goals rather than the mechanics of the movements. With respect to memory, the routines may help trigger recall of the choreography and establish the correct level of arousal for the piece to be performed (Cotterill, 2010).

Many dancers' routines focus on the tools of the trade: shoes, costume and make-up, but there are also those that are linked more to personal superstition than practical preparation. Other routines may be quite protracted and specific routines are adhered to for hours before a performance, which may include elements of exercise, rehearsal, eating and practical aspects of preparation (Baselga, 2015). Although this may be positive in anxiety reduction, it is important to ensure that the dancer is not reliant on complex or protracted routines in case circumstances prevent them from being actioned prior to a performance. Equally, the loss of a lucky legwarmer should not be the cause of a crisis.

Therefore, the problem with recommending pre-performance routines is that they tend to be highly personal, and not necessarily grounded in logical explanation, but understanding the importance of such a routine can be helpful in allowing individuals their space and idiosyncrasies.

Anxiety reduction

For some, it might be the need to feel prepared for the event, so being early, or having the opportunity to examine the stage or performance area in advance might help remove anxiety linked to fear of the unknown.

Others feel prepared by adopting a ritual kit check, by getting out their shoes, costume or make-up in a certain order, by laying them out in a specific way, or putting them on in a particular order. This helps reduce stress by allowing the dancer to see that they have all that they need for the performance, and behaviourally the ritual becomes calming, giving the dancer a sense of control.

For others, it may be the need for isolation before a performance so they do not become affected by the nerves of others. This may be expressed by lack of social interaction, or finding a space which is out of the way, or metaphorically removing yourself from the situation by using earphones. Music can be used as a distraction, and tempo can be chosen to modify arousal levels.

Concentration

The ritual of applying make-up can help concentrate the mind, and gradually envelop the character. This may also help moderate the level of arousal as a steady hand is needed to apply make-up effectively.

Routines may not necessarily be the same for every performance. It may be that specific routines are adopted for different performance types. A performance-specific routine may help the dancer get into character, trigger the memory of the particular choreography or may help generate the level of arousal for the type of dance that they will be performing (Baselga, 2015).

Superstitions

Some dancers may adopt rituals which are less logical, and may be grounded in superstition. If wearing your lucky socks for warm-up or offering a prayer to Saint Vitus works, then this is all that matters.

Somatic anxiety relief

Relaxation

Somatic anxiety can have such detrimental impacts on dance performance, however, if tackled properly, it can improve the dancer's form. One way of combatting the physical tension experienced when stressed is to produce a state of being that is incompatible with muscle tension – that is *relaxation*. Based on a method conceived of by Jacobson in 1929, Progressive Muscle Relaxation (PMR) is a technique that teaches the individual to release tension from their muscles through a systematic and gradual process. The sensations they experience while learning the technique will help them identify their personal areas of tension, as well as be able to recognise these stress symptoms at other times, and correct them quickly.

Physical and mental recovery is essential to those who perform regularly. If dancers cannot relax sufficiently, issues linked to muscle tension and sleep deprivation may limit full recovery with subsequent performance decrements. PMR has been shown to be especially helpful for dancers with high trait anxiety who have problems falling asleep (McCloughan, Hanrahan, Anderson, & Halson, 2016).

Progressive Muscle Relaxation technique

PMR can be learnt in a matter of weeks, yet once learnt can be deployed whenever necessary. Here are some simple steps to get started (Davis, Robbins Eshelman, & McKay, 2008).

Getting ready

To start, sit or lie down somewhere comfortable without limbs being crossed and loosening restrictive clothing and shoes. Initially take a few deep breaths to bring the respiration rate down, and try to feel as relaxed as possible. Once this is achieved, active tensing can commence.

Muscle relaxation process

Working through each of these muscle groups, undertake each of the following processes: tense the muscles of the group, without causing pain, for up to 5 seconds. While this muscle group is tense, feel how far this tension carries throughout the rest of the body. Consider the sensations of this tension. Then relax this muscle group and feel the sensation of relaxation flood through this muscle group. Once this has been repeated several times, move on to the next muscle group.

Muscle groups

It is suggested to work through these groups in this order:

1. Fists, forearms and biceps
2. Head and neck
3. Face
4. Shoulders, back and stomach
5. Buttocks, legs and toes

Utilisation

Once this technique has been mastered, and the dancer has learnt what areas of the body they tend to carry tension in, it can be used in times of anxiety. In order to manage stressful situations, the dancer can mentally scan the body for muscle tension, and by contraction of the muscles in this area, muscle relaxation can be achieved.

PMR as a distraction

As a means of blocking out environmental stressors, music-induced PMR can be employed where the protocol of the PMR is learnt while listening to music chosen by the dancer (Kim, 2008). The music can be selected based not only on personal preferences, but consideration of the tempo. Selecting the right tempo can help regulate the level of arousal in order to avoid becoming too relaxed for the exertion of the performance. Through the use of headphones this technique can be used prior to auditions, examinations and performances, to reduce anxiety and block out external distractors.

Five-breath technique

The five-breath technique works well just before a performance as it is short, and works rapidly, especially if the techniques of Progressive Muscle Relaxation have been learnt previously (Karageorghis, 2007).

This can be done standing or sitting, inhaling through the nose slowly and deeply, and exhaling gently through the mouth.

- Breath one – exhale, relaxing the face and neck.
- Breath two – exhale, relaxing the shoulders and arms.
- Breath three – exhale, relaxing the chest, back and stomach.
- Breath four – exhale, relaxing the legs and feet.
- Breath five – exhale, relaxing the whole body.

Cognitive anxiety relief

Self-talk

As seen in Chapter 4, self-talk can aid the dancer in choreography recall and skill development, and Chapter 3 has demonstrated how it may be used to maintain motivation. Here the same technique can be used to deal with emotional focus, either before a performance, acting as a positive motivation to dissipate anxiety, or during the performance to distract attention from anxiety-inducing thoughts (Noh, Morris, & Andersen, 2007).

Devising words or phrases in advance has two advantages. First, the fact that the cues are pre-rehearsed means that the dancer understands that there is something simple that can be done to help manage the situation – to use their cue words. Second, the thought has gone into the choosing of the cues to add an interpretive element – that they have been given meaning (Hardy & Oliver, 2014). This will then be interpreted as a calming stimulus, which should lead to the learnt response of anxiety reduction.

Self-talk as a motivator

If combatting pre-performance nerves in the wings, repeating rehearsed positive phrases, internally or externally, can help direct the hedonic tone from anxiety to excitement. It may also be used in a group setting as a pre-performance mantra, helping to get everyone focused on the performance, and bonded as a group. It might be a simple message to self, saying 'calm' or it might be a 'we're going to nail this' mantra within the troupe.

Self-talk as distraction

Once performing, negative and anxiety-inducing thoughts sometimes creep into the mind. Pre-rehearsed, demonstrative cue words can be used to distract from any negative train of thought, and help focus attention back onto the task at hand, teaching the dancer to be in the moment. The types of phrase that might be useful are 'focus' within the moment, or 'move forward' after an event.

Self-talk to refocus

If frustration is getting the better of you in training, possibly by not being able to master a new step, it is easy to succumb to tears or anger, which will make the achievement all the less likely to occur in that session. Using refocusing cue phrases can help the dancer focus on positive aspects, and bring down levels of arousal that might be building from frustration. Again, these should be personalised so they have meaning to the individual, but may be longer and more instructive than those used in a performance. Suggested phrases may be, 'stop, breathe and focus' which addresses both cognitive and somatic elements of anxiety.

Imagery

As shown in Chapter 4, mental imagery can assist in dance skill development, and Chapter 3 has shown the impact that imagery can have on motivation. Imagery has also been used in managing anxiety in performance situations (Fish, Hall, & Cumming, 2004).

Pre-event preparation

Anxiety is often at its highest due to first night nerves. If the anxiety experienced is the fear of the unknown, by experiencing the unknown prior to the performance, much of this worry can be prevented or at least reduced.

Familiarity with the venue may help with anxiety reduction. If possible, organise quality dress and technical rehearsal time in the theatre with others posing as an audience. Take this opportunity to become aware of the environment, the smell, the sights and the sounds. If prior access is not available, video footage of the dressing rooms and backstage area leading to the wings and view from the stage can help dancers acclimatise to the venue before arrival. Recreating the image of the space where you will be performing the routine while undertaking breathing exercises can help reduce potential anxiety. This can be recreated in your mind at any point prior to the performance, and as frequently as necessary.

Imagery as a means of reducing anxiety

Performance anxiety can lead to a state of panic in the moment, and unless dancers have a tool to manage the situation, it may have debilitating effects on the performance. This can be managed by training yourself to create the correct level of pre-performance arousal.

Getting ready

Find a time and space where you feel comfortable and will not be disturbed. Loosen restrictive clothing and lie or sit in a relaxed position.

Close your eyes and concentrate on your breathing, trying to clear your mind of unnecessary thoughts.

Recreating the situation

Now imagine yourself arriving at the venue. Look at the building, imagining what amazing performances will be seen by the audiences coming to the performance. Now imagine entering the building, noticing the energy and buzz of the atmosphere as everyone is rushing around preparing for the performance.

Imagine being in the dressing room, it is busy with dancers chatting and laughing. You have your costume on and are touching up your make-up. Look at yourself in the mirror. You see your character staring back at you, lose yourself in the character.

The music comes to an end. Imagine taking your final position, letting the audience float back to their seats. Breathe out your character and breathe in yourself. Imagine the applause and embrace it. It's for you.

Dealing with the anxiety

Now focus on the inner sensations. First, what thoughts come into your head at this point? Are they intrusive or negative? Reject any such thoughts by the use of positive self-talk.

Now switch your focus to your body. Scan for areas of tension. Focus on your breathing, breathing is key to achieving the right level of arousal. Use deep breaths to gradually reduce your respiration and heart rate. Listen to the controlled and regular pattern of your heart and breathing. Concentrate on how this feels, concentrate on how you have rejected the worry and controlled your level of arousal. Remember these sensations, these will act as a template for the real performance.

Becoming aware of your breathing again, feel the sensations of appreciation and try to keep these feelings with you. Gradually bringing yourself back into the present, open your eyes.

Imagery as a motivator

In times of anxiety we may not feel like engaging with the task at hand. Being able to bring to mind the feelings and sensations of previous successful performances can help the dancer reinterpret the perceptions of anxiety as that of excitement, making potentially debilitating symptoms facilitative (Monsma & Overby, 2004).

Imagery sessions can be done after successful events, encouraging dancers to remember the experience in a multisensory manner. Ask them to mentally recreate the scene at the highest point of their success. This must include as much visual information, but must also include auditory information – the judge calling out their name or the applause of the audience. Try to include olfactory cues too – the smell of the dust on the stage or hairspray in the air. Now include emotional sensations, the pride and joy at having achieved this milestone. Once this image is easily visualised, it can be recalled at times of doubt to help recreate the feelings of prior success, converting anxiety to excitement.

Imagery to manage freezing

There is often the tendency to focus on the one error rather than the hundred perfect performances, therefore balance needs to be achieved. When a mistake has been made in a previous performance, there is the potential that the dancer will start to feel anxious as the same sequence is approaching in the next performance. To prevent the dancer freezing with fear, and becoming unable to remember the steps, the bad memory needs to be replaced with productive recall. Visualising previous correct performances acts as a mental template for future performances – thawing the negative image.

Imagery as a distractor

In a similar way to the use of cue words of phrases as a means of distracting from negative thoughts, the same can be achieved using imagery for those who are more visual learners. Creating a mental image of a cue that acts as a prevention for creeping negative thoughts can stop the negative thoughts taking hold, and help refocus on the needs of the task. Images are personal but those chosen may have metaphorical links to the action, therefore red traffic lights, stop signs or other images related to barriers to access are helpful. Previous consideration of the image and practice at creating it quickly in the mind ensure that a strategy is in place to help manage the intrusion of negative thoughts.

Group approaches

Interpersonal emotional regulation

Groups of dancers may have to spend much time working closely together, and moods or emotions can be quite infectious within a group setting, especially as they near the point of performance. Understanding the impact that our emotions may have on each other helps us to see the importance of controlling these to prevent emotional escalation.

Having plans in place when emotions may be running high can suppress escalation and get the group back on track, especially when things are not running smoothly. Techniques utilised are context-dependent, therefore having a range of methods agreed as a group will enhance the chance of early and effective intervention.

Pre-event distraction

The nearer we get to an event, the higher the emotions run, especially anxiety, therefore, it is important to have strategies in place to reduce its escalation. As cognitive anxiety increases the nearer we are to the event, increasing levels of worry, then it is important to reduce the potential risk of this taking hold. If everyone is involved in a mentally absorbing task, this may distract from the worry ahead. If the task is something that is being done as a group, then this will enhance cohesion as well as distract from anxiety.

Having a playlist of songs that the group like to sing to can be an excellent emotional outlet while travelling to events, although ensure that the songs are not those being performed to later, as this may serve to increase stress by reminding them of the event.

Busying the group with behind-the-scenes activities such as chaperone duty, costume change and make-up assistance for younger dancers should remove attention from the impending performance.

Another way that emotions can be combatted is through incompatible emotional states, therefore if positive emotions can be summoned, this will reverse a negative emotion. One way that this can be instigated is through the use of humour. Not only will this lead to a positive cognitive state, but the action of laughing may counteract the physiological state of anxiety, and will further bond the group.

Emotion reduction in training

In training or rehearsal, frustration can be managed by helping at a practical or technical level, by assisting the group member in the movement they are finding problematic. If group members show true empathy for the difficulty of the movement and then allow time for

MANAGING EMOTIONS

this component to be practised until the individual is happy with their level of competence, anxiety will dissipate the emotional outburst and lead to better depth of learning.

When learning new, and potentially quite complex choreography, be aware of the body language of each group member, looking for signs of frustration. If this is noted, taking a break, or introducing a more familiar piece of choreography may reduce frustration, and the resultant anger and upset,bringing the group together again.

Emotion suppression in performance

If the situation is a group performance, then negative emotional outbursts may be due to the concern of having let group members down. If this occurs within a performance, it is important to dissipate the belief quickly. This can be achieved by reassuring the dancer that the error does not matter, and to move on and focus on the future: *what's done is done*. Although this may seem problematic in the midst of a performance, the more cohesed the group are, the more the tiniest acknowledgement can be translated and acted upon. Reassurance may be offered through a wink or a subtle body contact. The higher the group cohesion, the less likely negative interactions will occur and impact on performance.

Group support

Sharing concerns with colleagues can help regulate emotions as their tempered responses act as calming role model. Even the process of verbalising your concerns can help reduce anxiety.

Key concepts glossary

Activation A process that prepares the body for action.

Anxiety An emotional response to a perceived stressor.

Arousal A state of alertness to meet the needs of a situation.

Cognitive anxiety An emotional response to a perceived stressor expressed through thought processes such as worry.

Eustress A state of pressure that is interpreted positively.

Interpersonal regulation The bonding between members of a group.

Somatic anxiety An emotional response to a perceived stressor expressed through thought bodily responses.

State anxiety An emotional response to stressors as they occur.

Stress A state of pressure that is interpreted negatively.

Trait anxiety An emotional response based on the dispositional drive to interpret events as a stressor.

References

Apter, M. J. (1989). *Reversal theory: Motivation, emotion and personality*. London: Routledge.

Baselga, M. A. (2015). An investigation of professional ballet dancers' pre-performance routines and superstitious behaviours. MPhil thesis, University of Birmingham.

Brooks, A. W. (2014). Get excited: Reappraising pre-performance anxiety as excitement. *Journal of Experimental Psychology: General, 143*(3), 1144–1158.

Cerin, E. (2003). Anxiety versus fundamental emotions as predictors of perceived functionality of pre-competitive emotional states, threat, and challenge in individual sports. *Journal of Applied Sport Psychology, 15*(3), 223–238. doi:10.1080/10413200305389.

Cotterill, S. (2010). Pre-performance routines in sport: Current understanding and future directions. *International Review of Sport and Exercise Psychology, 3*(2), 132–153. doi:10.1080/1750984X.2010.488269.

Davis, M., Robbins Eshelman, E., & Mckay, M. (2008). *progressive muscle relaxation: The relaxation and stress reduction workbook*. Oakland, CA: New Harbinger Essentials.

Duffy, E. (1962). *Activation and behavior*. New York: Wiley.

Easterbrook, J. A. (1959). The effect of emotion on cue utilization and the organization of behavior. *Psychological Review, 66*(3), 183–201. doi:10.1037/h0047707.

Fish, L., Hall, C., & Cumming, J. (2004). Investigating the use of imagery by elite ballet dancers. *Avante, 10*(3), 26–39.

Hardy, J., & Oliver, E. J. (2014). Self-talk, positive thinking and thought stopping. In R. C. Eklund & G. Tenenbaum (Eds.), *Encyclopedia of sport and exercise psychology*. Thousand Oaks, CA: SAGE Publications, Inc.

Hardy, L. (1999). Stress, anxiety and performance. *Journal of Science and Medicine in Sport, 2*(3), 227–233. doi:10.1016/S1440-2440(99)80175-3.

Hofmann, S. G., Heering, S., Sawyer, A. T., & Asnaani, A. (2009). How to handle anxiety: The effects of reappraisal, acceptance, and suppression strategies on anxious arousal. *Behaviour Research and Therapy, 47*(5), 389–394. doi:10.1016/j.brat.2009.02.010.

Jones, J. G., & Hardy, L. (1990). *Stress and performance in sport*. Chichester: John Wiley & Sons, Ltd.

Jones, M., Meijen, C., McCarthy, P. J., & Sheffield, D. (2009). A theory of challenge and threat states in athletes. *International Review of Sport and Exercise Psychology, 2*(2), 161–180. doi:10.1080/17509840902829331.

Karageorghis, C. (2007). Competition anxiety needn't get you down. *Peak Performance, 243*, 4–7.

Kim, Y. (2008). The effect of improvisation-assisted desensitization, and music-assisted progressive muscle relaxation and imagery on reducing pianists' music performance anxiety. *Journal of Music Therapy, 45*(2), 165–191.

Klockare, E., Gustafsson, H., & Nordin-Bates, S. M. (2011). An interpretative phenomenological analysis of how professional dance teachers implement psychological skills training in practice. *Research in Dance Education, 12*(3), 277–293. doi:10.1080/14647893.2011.614332.

Lovallo, W. R. (2016). *Stress & health: Biological and psychological interactions*. Los Angeles: SAGE.

Magill, R. A. (2001). *Motor learning: Concepts and applications*. Boston: McGraw-Hill.

Martens, R., Vealey, R. S., Burton, D., & Martens, R. (1990). *Competitive anxiety in sport*. Champaign, IL: Human Kinetics Books.

Martinent, G., & Ferrand, C. (2009). A naturalistic study of the directional interpretation process of discrete emotions during high-stakes table tennis matches. *Journal of Sport and Exercise Psychology, 31*(3), 318–336. doi:10.1123/jsep.31.3.318.

McCloughan, L. J., Hanrahan, S. J., Anderson, R., & Halson, S. R. (2016). Psychological recovery: Progressive muscle relaxation (PMR), anxiety, and sleep in dancers. *Performance Enhancement & Health, 4*(1–2), 12–17. doi:10.1016/j.peh.2015.11.002.

Monsma, E. V., & Overby, L. Y. (2004). The relationship between imagery and competitive anxiety in ballet auditions. *Journal of Dance Medicine & Science, 8*(1), 11–18.

Noh, Y.-E., Morris, T., & Andersen, M. B. (2007). Psychological intervention programs for reduction of injury in ballet dancers. *Research in Sports Medicine, 15*(1), 13–32. doi:10.1080/15438620600987064.

Oxendine, J. B. (1970). Emotional arousal and motor performance. *Quest, 13*(1), 23–32. doi:10.1080/00336297.1970.10519673.

Rojas, I.-G., Padgett, D. A., Sheridan, J. F., & Marucha, P. T. (2002). Stress-induced susceptibility to bacterial infection during cutaneous wound healing. *Brain, Behavior, and Immunity, 16*(1), 74–84. doi:10.1006/brbi.2000.0619.

Ruiz, M. C., & Hanin, Y. L. (2011). Perceived impact of anger on performance of skilled karate athletes. *Psychology of Sport and Exercise, 12*(3), 242–249. doi:10.1016/j.psychsport.2011.01.005.

Selye, H. (1976). *Stress in health and disease*. Boston: Butterworths.

Smith, S. M., & Vale, W. W. (2006). The role of the hypothalamic-pituitary-adrenal axis in neuroendocrine responses to stress. *Dialogues in Clinical Neuroscience, 8*(4), 383–395.

Spielberger, C. D. (1966). *Anxiety and behavior*. New York,: Academic Press.

Szasz, P. L., Szentagotai, A., & Hofmann, S. G. (2011). The effect of emotion regulation strategies on anger. *Behaviour Research and Therapy, 49*(2), 114–119. doi:10.1016/j.brat.2010.11.011.

Tamminen, K. A., & Crocker, P. R. E. (2013). 'I control my own emotions for the sake of the team': Emotional self-regulation and interpersonal emotion regulation among female high-performance curlers. *Psychology of Sport and Exercise, 14*, 737–737. doi:10.1016/j.psychsport.2013.05.002.

Thomson, P., & Jaque, S. V. (2016). Overexcitability: A psychological comparison between dancers, opera singers, and athletes. *Roeper Review, 38*(2), 84–92. doi:10.1080/02783193.2016.1150373.

Totterdell, P. (2000). Catching moods and hitting runs: Mood linkage and subjective performance in professional sport teams. *Journal of Applied Psychology, 85*, 848. doi:10.1037//0021-9010.85.6.848.

Uphill, M., Groom, R., & Jones, M. (2014). The influence of in-game emotions on basketball performance. *European Journal of Sport Science, 14*(1), 76–83. doi:10.1080/17461391.2012.729088.

Watson, C. L. (2015). *Human physiology*. Burlington, MA: Jones & Bartlett Learning.

Whitworth, J. A., Williamson, P. M., Mangos, G., & Kelly, J. J. (2005). Cardiovascular consequences of cortisol excess. *Vascular Health and Risk Management, 1*(4), 291–299.

Yerkes, R. M., & Dodson, J. D. (1908). The relation of strength of stimulus to rapidity of habit-formation. *Journal of Comparative Neurology and Psychology, 18*(5), 459–482.

Further reading

Cotterill, S. (2010). Pre-performance routines in sport: Current understanding and future directions. *International Review of Sport and Exercise Psychology, 3*(2), 132–153.

Hanton, S., Neil, R., & Mellalieu, S. D. (2008). Recent developments in competitive anxiety direction and competition stress research. *International Review of Sport and Exercise Psychology, 1*(1), 45–57.

Koole, S. L. (2009). The psychology of emotion regulation: An integrative review. *Cognition & Emotion, 23*(1), 4–41.

Index

Achievement Goal Theory 66–70
action tendencies 176
activation 164–166, **189**; cognitive 97, neural 97
advice, from role models 53; from significant others 53–54; from self 54–55; reflection on 146
aggression 21, 176, 178
anxiety 12, 32–33 **45**, 47, 62, 69 135, 164, 170–171 **189**; cognitive 171–173 **189**; cognitive reappraisal 179–180; distraction 94; emotional state of 47, 164; ethics, 12; flow state 96; imagery *174*, 186–187; impact on others 176–178; impact on performance 173–175; influences 132, 146; state 173 **189**; somatic 171–173, **189**; managing 80, 85, 105, 117, 147, *175*, 181–186, 188–189; measuring 14–16; perfectionism 44, **45**; safety needs 71; social physique 29–30, 44, **45**, 55; trait 173, **189**
arousal 164–166, 168, 170, **189**; cognitive reappraisal 179–180; imagery 104–105, *174*; regulation 181–183, 185–186; negative emotional states 178; positive emotional states 176; relationship with performance 171–175; reticular activating system 6; self-talk 108–109
association 96, 100, 119
attention 82, 92–97, *125*; anxiety 171; attention seeking 148; attentional field 173; automatic processing 102, 115, 119; concentration 95; distraction 94–95, 188; divided 95; focussing 181; impact of arousal *175*; managing performance 81, 118; selective 94–96; self-talk 120, 123, 184–185; personal 134
attitudes 9–10, 17; body image 35; communication 141; effort 67; group formation 135; leadership 137; measures of 15; motivation 64; negative emotional states 178; peer influence 37; self 30, 32, 41
autonomy 87; Basic Needs Theory 63–64, 69; burnout 75; career 74; goal setting 86; motivational climate 70; motivational hierarchy 60; self-talk 82

Basic Needs Theory *60*, 63–66; belongingness needs 71; burnout 75; goal setting 86; motivational climate 69, 70
biological psychology 4–7, **25**; evolutionary psychology 10; neuroscience 9
body image 30, 35–39, **95**; appearance comparison 37; disability 51; management 48; mirrors *39*; parental influence 37; peer influence 37; perfectionism **45**, 50; Social Comparison Theory 36
brain 4–8; energy 77; imagery 102–103, 112, 120; marking 118; methods of investigation 9; motor programs 122; skill acquisition 100; stress 168–169

burnout 74–75, **87**; energy maintenance 77; leadership 132; marking 97; motivational climate 69

Catastrophe Theory 172–173
choreography 91; anxiety 171, 174; feedback 46–48; imagery **93**, 104, 113–114, 119, 124; motivation 79; recall 117–119, 121, 181–182; self-talk 82
chunking 99, 115
cognitive appraisal 164, 170–171; positive emotional states 176
cognitive Evaluation Theory 61
cognitive psychology 7–9, **25**, information processing 92
cognitive reappraisal 179–180
cohesion 136–138, **159**; achievement goals 67; communication 141–142, 146–147, 149–150; group formation 135; leadership 132, 134; motivational climate 69; social 138; social bonding 21; task 138; team building 155–159; trust 154
communication 140–141, **159**; avoiding negative forms 146–148; biochemical 7; conflict management 150–151; Competence-Based Model of Interpersonal Conflict 143–146; group 156; interaction 149–150; motivation 134; non-verbal 22; social cohesion 157; teacher 141–142
compartmentalisation 33, 49–50
Competence-Based Model of Interpersonal Conflict 143–145
concentration 96, **124**; association 96; distraction 94; Flow State 96; maintaining 48, 120; self-talk 108; Theory of Attentional and Interpersonal Style 92–93
confidence 78; careers 74; collaborative goal setting 85–86; ego-orientation 67; esteem needs 73; imagery 105, 114, *174*; motivation 80–81; negative emotional states 178; perfectionism **45**; self-efficacy 33; self-talk 108–109; Transformational Leadership 134; teacher communication 141
conflict 143–146, **159**; Competence-Based Model of Interpersonal Conflict 143; group bonding 76; group formation 135; socio-cognitive 150; management 150–151; performance-oriented climate 69; teacher-dancer relationship 139
context-dependent memory 100
correlations 15–16, **25**

declarative store 99; skill acquisition 115
dissociation 95
distraction 94, **124**; anxiety reduction 181, 183; concentration 95; interpersonal emotional regulation 188; self-talk 185
distress 170–171
drives; biological drives 70; impression management 140; intrinsic motivation 61
Dual Concern Model 151–152

ego orientation 66, 67–68, **87**; motivational climate 68
emotional regulation 105, 178, interpersonal 188
emotions 164–191; attentional style 93; communication 22; distraction 94; imagery 80; leadership 134
encoding 96–97, **124**; Context-dependent Memory 100; Information Processing Model 92
entertainment 22
ethics 11–12, **25**
eustress *164*, 170–171, **189**
evolution 5; evolutionary explanations of dance 19–22; evolutionary psychology 10; stress 166, 169
expectations: anxiety 171; collaborative goal setting 86; group formation 135; impression management 41, 180; managing 150–151; roles 156; self-esteem 33; unrealistic 143
experiments 16, **25**

feedback 46–47, 132; climate selection 76; competence 64; Flow State 96;

goal identification 84; group bonding 76; instruction 149; leadership 131, 154; modelling 118; non-verbal communication 147; reinforcement 86–87
fitness 23; esteem 36
flow state **94**, 96; intrinsic motivation 61

genetics 5
goal setting 83–87; performance profiling 82
groups 134; cohesion 136–138, 149, 154, 155–158, **159**; conflict 143; formation 135–136; goal setting 85–86; team building 154

health 3, 169; perfectionism 44–45
Hierarchy of Needs 70–73

imagery 102–107, 116, 119–120, **124**; character 123; injury 121–122; kinaesthetic 117; mental 116–117; motivation 80–81; multisensory 113–114; performance 123–124; teaching 111–113
impression management 39–43, **55**; self-handicapping 34; storming 135
information processing 8–9, 92, **124**
injury 121; confidence 78; self-handicapping 43
instruction 149; leadership 131
interaction 138–139, 149–150; psychological perspectives 4
intervention studies 16; teambuilding 155
interviews 15, **25**

leadership 130, 153–154 **159**; cohesion 137; Multidimensional Model of 130–131; qualities 131–132, 152–153; Transformational 132–134

marking 97, 117–118; concentration 120
memory 98, 121, **125**; anxiety 174; brain structure 6; information processing 9, 92; long-term 99–100, 115; pre-performance routines 181; recall 100; working 98–99, 115, 116

mirrors: appearance comparison 38–39; body image 39; feedback 47–48; recall 119; social physique anxiety 43
motivation 75, 77–81, **87**; action tendencies 176; amotivation 63, 64; anxiety 184; burnout 75; climate 68–70, 76, **87**; cohesion 157; communication 142, 148; competence 64; emotion 178; extrinsic 62–63, **64**, **87**; goals 85–86; Hierarchy 60–61; imagery 104–105, 112; impression 40; interaction 139; intrinsic 61, **64**, **87**, 96; leadership 134, 152–153; perfectionism 44, **45**; performance profiling 82–83; self-efficacy 33; self-talk 82, 107–109, 120, 122
Multidimensional Anxiety Theory 171–172
Multidimensional Model of Leadership 130–132
music: anxiety 181, 183, 186; choice 156; imagery 81, 114; memory 100, 119, 121, 124

neurotransmission 7

observation 14–15, **25**, 103–104, 116, 118, 120; imagery 107

perfectionism 44–45, **55**; motivational climate 69
performance enhancement 122; imagery 123–124; emotion 176; task cohesion 156
performance profiling 82–83
perspectives in psychology 4–11
pre-performance routines 181–182
procedural store 98, 99–100, 115
psychological perspectives **4**

questionnaires 15

relaxation 184; Progressive Muscle 182–184

scientific method 5, 12–13
self-concept 30–32, 43–45, 49–50, 51–52, **55**; impression motivation 40–41; motivational climate 69

self-efficacy 33; Basic Needs Theory 63; cognitive appraisal 170; communication 141; feedback 46; goal setting 84–86; imagery 80
self-esteem 32–33, 36, **55**; appearance comparison 38; goal setting 84; impression motivation 40–41; intrinsic motivation 61; needs 73; perfectionism 45; self-handicapping 43; task orientation 67
self-handicapping 43, **55**
self-regulation 32, **55**; extrinsic motivation 63
self-talk 122–123, **125**; anxiety 180, 184–186; content 109; dimensions 107–109; motivation 82; skill acquisition 115, 120; structure 109–111
self-worth 32–33; perfectionism 44
sexual attraction 19–21
skill acquisition 100–102, 114–117, **125**; feedback 46; imagery 104, 113; self-handicapping 43
social bonding 21
social cognition 10
Social Comparison Theory 35–36
social engagement 22
social physique anxiety 43–44, **55**; perfectionism **45**
social psychology 9–11

stress 16–169, **189**; autocratic behaviour 132; burnout 75; Catastrophe Theory 172–173; cognitive appraisal 170–171; ethics 11–12; injury concerns 78, 121–122; reduction 175, 182–184; skill acquisition 102; symptoms 169–170

task orientation 66–68, **87**; group cohesion 137; leadership qualities 131
teacher-dancer relationship 138–139
team-building 155
temporal patterning 173
the 3+1Cs model 139–140
Theory of Attentional and Interpersonal Style 92–94
touring 158–159
Transformational Leadership 132–134, 153–154; cohesion 137
Tripartite Influence Model 36–39
Two-Component Model of Impression Management 39–43

well-being 3, 21–22; ethics 12; intrinsic motivation 61; motivational climate 70; perfectionism 44; self-concept 31–33